Empath and Psychic Abilities

A Survival Guide for Highly Sensitive People. Develop Intuition, Telepathy, and Clairvoyance. Healing with Guided Meditations to Open Your Third Eye and Expand Mind Power

Mediumship Lodge, Liam Chakra Varma, James Holland

Table of Contents

Introduction

Congratulations on purchasing *Empath and Psychic Abilities,* and thank you for doing so.

An empath is a person who can place themselves in other's shoes and understand everything from that person's perspective. They can feel that person's pain as if it was their own. In other words, if you are an empath, you can understand where that person or his/her feelings are coming from. Keep in mind that sympathy and empathy are two different things, even though people tend to get confused between the two. They are often used interchangeably even when their meanings are different. Sympathy is simply the other name of pity, but an empath walks that extra mile to understand why someone is behaving the way they are behaving, and they do everything they can to alleviate other people's pain.

But empaths need to nurture their quality in order to truly be able to use it to the best of their abilities. On top of that, if you are a psychic empath, it will be even harder for you to spend your day-to-day life because you can literally feel all the energies surrounding you. But in this book, we will learn how you can prevent yourself from getting overwhelmed by emotions and how to practice greater control over life, in general.

There are plenty of books on this subject on the market; thanks again for choosing this one! Every effort was made to ensure it is full of as much useful information as possible, please enjoy!

Chapter 1: Who Is a Psychic Empath?

Some people are blessed to have extrasensory perception, allowing them to see, feel, or hear information that is otherwise hidden and not perceivable to the normal human senses. These blessed people are often referred to as psychics, and in this modern era, psychics are devoted to helping other people.

What Is Psychic Power?

The word "power" can be referred to in regards to a number of aspects. For psychics, their psychic powers come from deep knowledge, learning, and understanding of their abilities. They utilize their extrasensory perception to harness the energy around them to perform "powerful acts" that help other people. Since all of 'us' humans are intelligent beings with a soul, we surely do have innate natural "psychic" powers, sometimes referred to as our sixth sense. However, only some are more sensitive and attuned to these abilities so that they can harness these abilities into "powers" after they have studied and practiced these abilities. However, this does not imply that psychics are able to get in tune with them as soon as they are born. If a person wants to harness and build this psychic energy, the individual must be spiritually and mentally connected to his or her inner and higher self. To be able to connect and respond to the different forces around them that are beyond the range of ordinary human perception, one needs to go through constant learning and training. With a sense of purpose, psychics choose to develop and harness these abilities so that they are able to help other people.

Certain planetary placements in birth charts, card spreads, or even casual conversations with regards to manifestations and such can reveal an individual's psychic abilities and perceptions to another psychic practitioner such as a tarot card reader, an astrologer, an occult practitioner, and so on. Although a lot of people might think how amazing it is to possess and be able to harness such a powerful ability, being a psychic person does not come easy, and many people have misconceptions about what this gift actually entails. Working with psychic skills requires a considerable amount of patience, self-love, and practice.

From an early age, a majority of us are warned by our elders to be cautious when it comes to the services of psychic practitioners as scams and, hence, we begin to perceive and associate psychic gifts and abilities, at large, as dubious and fraudulent. Some of the otherwordly or psychic experiences we come across as children are also, therefore, discredited, and even if we incline towards exploring divination practices in adulthood, we are still quick to raise an eyebrow and start to doubt when we hear the word "psychic." While there are many charlatans for sure who either exaggerate their skills or make them up entirely, these kinds of people are definitely not psychics, but they are con artists who use manipulation and fear tactics to prey on gullible and vulnerable targets. However, it is crucial to know that truly psychic people, on the other hand, are simply individuals who are able to see,

3

hear, feel, sense, taste, or have intuition beyond the boundaries of the physical world and ordinary human beings. As individuals start to expand their sensory spectrum and continue to explore this psychic realm more, it becomes abundantly clear that some senses become increasingly less common among psychic individuals. It is through this awareness that many psychic individuals become fully aware of their unique, inherent psychic abilities and powers.

Fundamentally, psychic skills or powers are defined by an innate ability to process sensory data, both tangible and intangible stimuli, on an extremely deep emotional, physical, or spiritual level. Obviously, this is rather a very broad definition of psychic power. Extrasensory gifts vary greatly in intensity and application; it is best and easier to imagine psychic skills on a spectrum.

Here is an example of a psychic spectrum:

To visualize a psychic spectrum, imagine four friends meeting for lunch. The first individual to arrive greets the host and takes her table, notices her table is missing a fork, sees that her glass is already filled with wine, and takes a sip out of it as she is feeling thirsty and waits for her friends. The second individual comes in, sees that the host is scrolling through his phone, and senses that he might be bored or under stress, and greets the host warmly. The host welcomes him, and he then joins his friend at the table. The third friend enters the restaurant, and as she is approaching the host, she is overwhelmed with stimuli.

She notices the restaurant's garish decor, the servers' swift movements, and a distinguishingly loud gentleman at the back who is dominating the conversation. She can feel that the energy that this particular person is radiating is arrogant and abrasive, and his company seems to be both uncomfortable and embarrassed. She then starts to wonder how his children will grow up to be like. Will they grow up adopting this behavior from their parent, or will they reject it and become soft and docile? Suddenly the third friend is snapped back into reality as the host greets her. Once she arrives at the table, she starts to discuss her observations with her other friends. Finally, the fourth friend arrives at the restaurant, and upon his arrival, he feels extremely overwhelmed by the lights, the sound, the movement, the smell, and the overall energy inside the place.

Within a few seconds, he becomes aware of the internal personal dynamics at each table, the complex relationships of the people there, the pungent smell of a certain dish that links back to his past memories, a few charred rafters on the ceiling. He starts to wonder if there had been a fire there recently that had caused the charred rafters. Suddenly, he senses extreme heaviness and knows that there had been something very bad in that restaurant. He becomes nervous and trying to shake off the feeling; he ignores the host and hurries over to his friends. However, this feeling persists throughout lunch even when he tries to ignore them, exhausting him.

Hence, we can see that the first two friends demonstrated a relatively standard range of sensitivity, while the latter two friends demonstrate more extreme extrasensory abilities. This is how the psychic spectrum operates as the power and the sensory abilities vary from one psychic individual to another.

What Does It Mean To Be Psychic?

The word "psychic" gets thrown around a lot and in meanings that are misunderstood and mistaken, but what does it actually mean? The word "psychic" comes from the Greek word "psykhikos" which means "of the soul." A psychic is a person who has a strong sensory perception that enables them to foresee things and connect to other energies and spirits. Their sixth sense or intuition enables them to experience unusual things, have visions of the future, or have strong telepathy experiences.

You will be surprised to learn that you can show signs of this gift and not even realize it, and that is because the signs, although almost bizarre, still often seem relatively meaningless to us. Here are some signs that might actually mean you are psychic:

1. *Frequent Deja Vu Experiences* - Although the cause of Deja Vu is widely researched and debated, and science does have a physiological reason, however, if you experience it very frequently, it is often cited as a sign that you have psychic abilities.

2. *Sensations Around Third Eye* - The Third Eye is the space between your eyebrows. If you feel any kind of sensation or pressure, it could be because your chakras are opening up, and you are beginning to pick up on psychic signals.

3. *Looking At The Clock At The Same Time* - It is known that spirits try to communicate with the living through signs, and repeating numbers are said to be such signs, for example, 1111 or 111. Numerology has a divine meaning for each number and if you happen to look at the clock at the same time very often, look up the meaning behind the number. These messages could be a sign of channeling psychic ability.

4. *Strong and Vivid Dreams* - Do you frequently have vivid dreams where you can even recall the most minute of details? Do you experience the same dreams? Do most of your dreams come true or have a meaning or message behind them? All of these are known to be signs of psychic abilities.

5. *Psychometric Experiences* - Psychometry enables you to sense the history of an object, place, or person by touching them. You would often find a psychic holding the hand of a person and experiencing his past.

What Are The Different Types Of Psychic Abilities?

Seeing into the future is a natural occurrence, and we all are psychics only varying in degree. Time is simultaneous, and there is no past or future to our eternal self, that is, our true nature. To the eternal self, there is only the eternal now; everything happens at once. The term psychic is generally used to describe a person with the ability to recognize things that are hidden from the five basic senses and are able to sense something through the use of extrasensory perception. Being a psychic is actually a generalized umbrella term that is used to describe different forms of psychic abilities. There are many types of psychic powers, and all of them have distinguished ways of sharing information and perceiving things. Everyone possesses varying degrees of psychic abilities, from a simple"gut instinct" through to foreseeing future events; here are some of the most common and talked about psychic abilities:

1. ***Clairvoyance*** - Also known as "clear seeing," it is an interior vision. Clairvoyant mediums have the ability to "see" things presented to them in the mind's eye or the Third eye. They see these visions as mental flashes, including pictures as people, scenes, places, objects, spirits, symbols, and colors. Clairvoyance is seeing beyond what the ordinary eyes see. It is also possible to receive many visual insights and see the auras of people, animals, and even plants using clairvoyance. Those with excellent clairvoyant senses are even known to see fairies, spirits, angels, and many other spiritual beings. Often a clairvoyant medium can see objects or symbols which may have a specific personal or universal meaning, as well as light anomalies such as flashing lights, orbs, and sparks. It is a psychic seeing, and it is essential to note that every clairvoyant medium has different depictions of what they see and how they see it. You can think of it as a sort of screen that pops up before them to provide

information and messages in the form of pictures, symbols, and so on. It may also show up as a visual of a person with distinct characteristics or a warning of a future scenario. They may see a person with their distinct visual characteristics or warn you of a scenario they see in your future.

2. ***Clairaudience*** - Also known as "clear hearing," clairaudience is the ability to hear messages from the spirit realm. In this type of psychic ability, messages are transmitted directly into the mind of the clairaudience medium. At times the medium may hear a non-descript voice call their name or a mix of voices as if they are listening to a radio. It is the ability to hear beyond the physical hearing of an ordinary individual. This is what is known as inner hearing. Those who are clairaudient mediums hear many different things such as bells, voices, music, and sounds. Sound is of extreme importance to the metaphysical and spiritual traditions throughout the entire world. Most of the time, before an important insight is received or as an opening to a spiritual experience occurs, a sound is heard through clairaudience. This sound may be a soft ring in the ear, a quiet whisper, or sometimes it may be much more intense. It is also known in some traditions that this sound is referred to as the bells of paradise or the trumpeting before the gates. The sounds heard through the clairaudience are often described as radio signals from varying levels of universal airwaves, including our own higher self. The voices that can be heard through clairaudience are often described as giving spiritual guidance or warning of impending danger.

3. ***Clairsentience*** - Also known as "sensing feelings," clairsentience is most commonly described as gut feeling or intuition. Clairsentient mediums have the ability to sense and feel emotions from the spiritual

realm, both positive and negative. These feelings are being transmitted from their guides and are very distinctly and clearly different from the medium's own feelings. The mediums can receive warnings or information this way as in feeling that something is not right or get an excited, elated feeling when something wonderful is about to happen. It can also be described as empathy with the ability to feel or sense information beyond the physical sense. This is a tactile psychic feeling. For instance, an example of clairsentience would be shaking hands with a person and almost instantly feeling comfort sparked by their touch as if you have known them all throughout your life. This is an example of clairsentience, also known as psychic sensory experiences. These vibrations and energies are meant to clue the medium into the particular feeling itself for gaining extraordinary information.

4. ***Clairalience*** - It is basically the sense of smell, only heightened and attuned to clairalience medium beyond the physical sense of smell. It is the ability to sense or smell a particular fragrance or odor that is being transmitted by the spirit. Each time, the other people around are not able to usually sense or smell the odor. It can be related to the spirit who is sending the message, such as smelling cigarettes or pipe tobacco for someone who smoked or the person's favorite perfume or fragrance.

5. ***Clairgustance*** - This type of psychic ability is linked to the sense of taste. The medium has the ability to taste the essences being transmitted b the spirit. A spirit can transfer a character or behavior influence to the mediums, and sometimes it comes to them in the form of a flavor. This is usually something that they really loved and enjoyed while they were in the body.

6. ***Clairtangency*** - Also known as psychometry, the mediums with this type of psychic ability are able to

receive a message by touching or holding an object in their hands. The object is usually personal and contains the vibration and energy of the owner in the composition or the material of the item. By doing this, they can tell the personality of the owner and perhaps see, hear, or feel situations that are going on around the person, past or present. Psychometry is the ability or art of deriving information about people or events associated with an object solely by touching or being near it. Objects belonging to a person are used to help induce psychic intuitions about them. This ability to touch an object, item, or person and receive information about them can be received in mind as pictures, a moving short film, or a sudden knowing of information.

7. ***Remote Viewing*** - Remote viewing is a form of clairvoyance and is known as the process of observing from a great distance. This psychic ability allows the remote viewer to see what is happening in another place describing details about the target that is inaccessible to the normal senses.

Psychics usually have one or more of these gifts, which can be used on their own or all together. Among these, the most commonly found ability among psychics is clairsentience. Having one to three psychic abilities in one person is usually common; however, having all the abilities is very rare.

Popular Myths Surrounding Psychics

1. ***Psychic Mediums are Scammers*** - One of the most popular myths that surround the whole concept of psychic abilities and mediums is that they scam people and use cold reading to con men and women. In almost every industry, it is usually common to find fraudulent people who treat others unfairly and take advantage of them; hence, similarly, these types of

people are also present in the psychic industry as any other industry. However, in this industry, con artists are generally pretty easy to spot. They make claims of having the ability to help you and make you money or save you from bad luck and bad finances. These scammers are usually not around for very long as they always end up with a bad reputation earned by their dubious and fraudulent activities and claims. Most true psychics are genuinely gifted, though in varying degrees, at what they do and will generally have the client's best interest in their mind. The psychic industry is greatly unpoliced, and if a person is clever and bold enough to engage in scams, they are able to trick those that are vulnerable. However, it is important to keep in mind that when choosing a psychic or a medium, always do your research and ask others for feedback and recommendations.

2. ***If Psychic People Were Real, It Would Be Easier to Find Missing People*** - Although these types of cases are scarce and do not happen very often, there have been several real-life cases wherein psychics or mediums have helped to solve murder cases. It is not as simple as it sounds to get involved in a murder or a missing person's case as a psychic or a medium. The medium may be able to connect with the spirit of the person in question, and they can be provided with various information such as impressions of the circumstances surrounding their deaths, including locations. However, there may often be dozens or even hundreds of different sites that may match the impressions that the medium was provided with. Much of the information that is received with regards to murder cases is usually very general and not specific enough to be of any real help in finding their bodies. Even when psychics do have a piece of specific information, it can be very difficult to find a connection that will lead to a breakthrough in the case. Although, with the right circumstances and a

good connection, psychics can be of valuable importance in the cases of finding missing persons, however, unfortunately, there are just too many factors that affect the information and how the mediums relate to it. Therefore, it is often not precise enough.

3. **Psychics Can Read Minds** - Psychics and mediums cannot and do not read other people's minds. They are definitely able to tune into your individual energy field that contains information about your life; however, they cannot just simply read your mind or know what you are thinking at any given time. Mediums and psychics receive information through their psychic senses about the person they are connecting with, and information comes through to them in bits and pieces. They may see images, hear brief sounds and noises, voices or words, get a glimpse of a particular smell or taste, and/or feel an energy shift in different parts of their bodies, indicating a message or information. This information can be about places, events, or people related to their past, present, or future.

4. **Psychics Research Their Audience** - another one of the most common myths that people believe is that psychics or mediums research everyone present in their audience before a show. However, this is very rare and even very difficult for a person to do so. Perhaps with some expertise and time, it would be possible to gather some background information on some people attending the show; however, that person is required to study the information and memorize it. The amount of time and effort required to do so is not simply worth it. It is much easier and logical for a psychic to tune into their abilities than it would be to do all that research and memorizing before each show.

5. ***Psychics Predict Future*** - Psychic and mediums do not actually predict the future. However, what they can do is that they tune into energies connected to the future events in people's lives using their psychic abilities to give insights into possible outcomes. Using tools such as tarot cards, palmistry, and astrology combined with information gathered with the help of psychic senses can often give insights into possible future events with some degree of accuracy. However, psychics are human, too, so they may misinterpret the meaning of the information they receive and can get wrong.

All of the above myths were debunked by Suzie Price, a renowned psychic who was awarded the "People's Choice Award" by the International Psychic Association in 2014.

What You Should Know About A Psychic Empath

While it is well known by now that everyone has some degree of psychic ability, it can take a number of different forms. For some people, psychic ability manifests itself as the ability to be what is known as an empath. Empathy is the ability to sense and feel what others are feeling without their telling us verbally. Someone who is a psychic empath often needs to learn basic shielding techniques; otherwise, they can find themselves feeling drained and exhausted after absorbing the energies of others. The psychic form of empathy should not be confused with the basic human form of empathy, and the basic difference is that the former can pick up non-visual, non-verbal cues that another individual is feeling pain, fear, or joy. Sometimes, this is a matter of detecting energy fields or auras; other times, it may simply be a "knowing" that the person is feeling a certain way, despite no obvious clue to that effect.

Most psychic empaths are effective listeners and tend to gravitate towards professions in which they can use this ability to help others such as, social work, counseling, Reiki, etc. Mostly, empaths train themselves to detect subtle changes in the energy vibrations of others. Others are often drawn to them as they feel comfortable and relaxed while speaking to them. Psychic empaths intensely feel the emotions of others, even more than their own. This can cause a bombardment of emotions that can overstimulate a psychic empath causing them to manifest anxiety or even erratic behaviors.

There are different types of psychic empaths, including physical, emotional, and intuitive empaths, to name a few. If you feel extreme empathy towards other people and want to know whether you are a psychic empath, here are a few signs that you might relate to:

- You often find yourself drowning in a crowd because you easily absorb all kinds of energy in the crowd, both positive and negative.

- Psychic empaths are drawn to nature more than ordinary individuals and love to spend time alone in nature than with someone by their side.

- Since it is quite challenging to be too close to another person and their emotion, psychic empaths isolate themselves very often and love being by themselves most of the time because this is where you find peace and healing.

- You find it very difficult to manage close contacts. Spending too much time with another person may cause you stress and can be challenging to maintain romantic relationships.

- Psychic empaths have a heightened sensation that makes them greatly affected by certain flavors or odors and loud noises, and strong touches.

- Psychic empaths find it very difficult not to care as you tend to feel as intensely as the other person is feeling. There may be instances where you bend over backward to help them ease their distress because their emotions consume you.

Being born a psychic empath is not something that we have under control - it is something that people are bestowed with. Once it is clear to you that you are a psychic empath, it is crucial that you start developing strategies and mechanisms that will help you cope with the gift that you have in your day-to-day life. It often tends to get quite stressful and draining. However, with proper understanding and learning, you can begin to harness the gift you are bestowed with to better others and yourself.

Chapter 2: How to Enhance Your Psychic Abilities?

Psychics, as some would already know and some would be surprised to believe, are simple everyday individuals like any one of us who, along with possessing regular abilities like all of us, have the added benefit of being able to see, hear, sense, taste, feel things in more details than us. They also have a very strong intuitive force to see beyond the boundaries of the physical world. What is the matter of concern is that it needs to be analyzed what knowledge and perceptions can be recognized as "normal" or regular by the world that we live in. The society that we live in will otherwise have us believe that everything is either black or white. Most of the time, the nuances of things get lost in understanding as the different shades of things fail to register to the common eye. But, it is through these very regular experiences that some of us might realize how the events or the sense perceptions that we are experiencing are very different from what others are experiencing. Along with that, certain things are only becoming known to us while others are remaining oblivious to them. These realizations make us aware that we might have some unique traits in us that others don't have and how this awareness of ours is helping us tap into our inner psychic abilities.

Psychic abilities in a person can be described as their inherent skills or ability to process the data that are sensory, both in their tangible and intangible form, and that is to say, to understand and analyze everything in a much more deep-rooted manner. It is where a person's emotional, physical, and spiritual plane gets heightened and much more receptive than what other people experience. But telling only this doesn't do it justice completely because the psychic spectrum is huge. So, all the other possibilities need to be kept in mind while talking about psychic abilities. There are many ways in which a person can understand and thereby enhance their psychic abilities. Psychic abilities can emerge most of the time during a person's childhood, in cases when such abilities are passed on to the particular individual from someone else in the family who has had a great impact on the child directly or indirectly. It might also be that a person develops these psychic abilities through the environmental influence around them.

While we are growing up, however, it is common for people to hear it from the elders to stop being so sensitive to everything and to see things for what they are. That things are not always such as we find them to be, and we should take things only for their face value. But the inherent psychic in the concerned person can't really be ignored like that. It is not so simple. The psychic abilities cannot get lost just because someone chooses to or is forced to ignore them for long. With some work, these abilities will get polished and will be reignited. So, let us look at us how one can enhance these abilities.

Meditation

For any person to enhance their psychic abilities, it is very important to have a calm mind and a relaxed body to tap into the inner psychic in someone. One of the very first and extremely essential requirements for a practicing psychic is to be in an environment that is not disturbing to the inner soul and outer body. An environment that is soothing to the mind so that there remain no distractions to derail the person's thoughts and concentration. For that, it is essential to practice meditation on a regular basis. It has to be made into a habit where a significant amount of time will be given behind meditating every day so that the inner core can be reached and its power can be tapped. This is important for any person who wants to enhance their psychic abilities to reach their core with a minimum effort. It is important to connect with one's soul to understand what's going on there and help you connect with the world and the universe.

It is essential to settle on a focus point and keep your concentration fix on it. Try using a candle and fix your eyes on the flame, for example. Try and stop other thoughts from clouding your inner vision. The next thing you need to do is calm your breathing and take regular, deep, and calm breaths so that your body is in a state of rest. You can also start with meditating while keeping your eyes open at the beginning before you get into the habit completely, by looking at trees or clouds floating by, for example. It is entirely on you to find out for yourself what works for you. As you slowly start getting into the habit of meditating, you can shift your procedure of close eye meditating. The more focus you have, the more you can actively and successfully unravel your feelings and look beyond the apparent. Meditating will help you become more aware of your surroundings. The next time you start getting intuitive, all your senses will become alert without misleading you or without you getting distracted. You will start getting familiar with your feelings and intuition.

Start taking Psychic Classes

Having psychic abilities only is not enough. Like every other trait or talent that a person might have, psychic abilities too need to be practiced, polished, and perfected over time. It takes a lot of diligence, determination, and patience to perfect anything and psychic abilities are no better. They need to be practiced regularly, and they need a professional training. Otherwise, it will only be on a surface level. Only with professional training will you get to know what and how you should do things so that you can use your talents to their full extent. Psychic classes come in the picture then. With regular and proper classes on how to train yourself to enhance your psychic abilities to the fullest, you will be able to take it at your own comfort and preferred pace. You can start practicing at home even to see how things are working for you.

Nowadays, there is also no dearth of online classes that will help you get in touch with professionals who will train you to enhance your psychic abilities. These online classes cover a range of different subjects and topics that are sure to satisfy your curiosity. That will help you find out what suits you and what you find yourself most interested in and then go on to study those subjects in further detail. Taking such classes will help you clear your doubts and come to terms with everything that you are going through. It will give you knowledge regarding things that you might otherwise have a problem talking to with others. It will give you clarity regarding how you want to deal with things and help you get a clear picture of how things should proceed. So, if you really want to tap into your inner spirit and enhance your psychic abilities, taking classes can be really helpful for you. Instead of fumbling in the dark regarding things you are not sure of, try and get help from professionals for better results.

Take Care of Yourself and Your Body

No matter what you do, what new ventures you take, you have to keep in mind that nothing will work out if you are not healthy, both physically and mentally. You have to take care of yourself and look after all your needs to see how much you can take, what works for you and what doesn't, what makes you happy and, what doesn't. Remember that only if you feel good from the outside and inside will anything that you do bring you success and will be enjoyable as a journey. The same goes for when you want to channelize your inner power and enhance your psychic abilities. Remember that enhancing your psychic abilities is as much psychological labor as a physical one. If you are doing it right, it will take you a ton of emotional and physical labor to actually bring all your core strength to their optimum power. And as a result, it is the most natural to overlook your own needs as your mind will tend to be always preoccupied with something or other. That is the reason, no matter what you are doing, you need to keep your health in mind that realize that you are as good as your health. Take care of yourself and what your body needs.

Eat correct food at the correct time. Do regular exercises, do things that you enjoy so that you are refreshed and relaxed. Don't ignore your medical conditions if you have any. Don't go out of your way to force yourself into doing things that you don't enjoy or which is uncomfortable for you. The better your physical and emotional ability is, the easier it will be for you to enhance your psychic abilities. Get rid of all the bad habits that you might be having, like smoking or drinking. Alcohol and tobacco are extremely bad for not only your health, but they cloud your judgment and distract you all the time. You need to have a balanced lifestyle with a proper sleep schedule for you to be at your best so as to concentrate fully on your inner abilities. You cannot expect to give your psychic practice your best shot unless you know that you are completely ready physically and emotionally. If you are well-rested, well-fed, relaxed, and in good health, then automatically, things you do will be much more productive and successful. You will have a much better chance of enhancing your psychic abilities that way.

Work With Your Spirit Guides

Each and every one of us has spirit guides who are always there present around us to help us. They are present to assist us in all of our needs. Be it with our choices or be it with our experiences. Our guides are ever-present to look out for us and to see that everything is alright. What we need to understand that they are just a thought away. It is completely on us to realize that and feel their presence. Whether we want to be aware of their presence or not is completely on us to decide, but their presence is something that we cannot ignore. What is essential then is to learn and know of ways in which we can connect with our Guides. We need to be aware of all such ways we can connect with them in a more conscious way so that they can help us by providing us with a more powerful and more effective tool to develop our inner abilities.

Getting connected with our spirit guides will help us break away from the barriers of distraction and come in control of our abilities completely. We just need to be more consistent and patient in all our efforts so that we can work with our guides more because the more we work with them, the easier the connection with them will become. The easier it will be to have communication with our guides, and that will ease all our work. It is up to us how much of such a connection we allow. The more such connections take place, the easier it will be to start believing your instincts and inner voice. The easier it will be to form insight and also trust yourself. With trust in yourself will come more confidence and self-belief. That will be like a guiding force to enhance the inner psychic in us. All we need to remember is that our guides are always present. You need to ask for their help. They will definitely work with you.

Build Trust

Always remember that a person's psychic abilities are bound to get increased and get enhanced if the person concerned trusts themselves and their intuition. Accepting one's thoughts and emotions for what they are and by not ignoring or neglecting one's gut feelings, one's psychic abilities are sure to get stronger, and that's what any practitioner should do. You need to strongly accept and rust what you are feeling, and you need to proclaim them boldly. This is not achieved in a single day. If you feel that you indeed have psychic abilities, you need to act upon them. You need to trust your instincts, and day after day, you need to build a strong communicable bridge that will help you communicate with yourself and come to terms with all that you are feeling will become much easier.

Always keep in mind that accepting your reality and trusting what you are feeling, that is, the information you have in you, is probably the most crucial and primary thing that anyone needs to do when starting out in this path of psychic practice. In order for your practice to become perfect and in order for you to attain the utmost level of efficiency and accuracy in your practice, you need to trust yourself. The more trust you have in yourself and your abilities, the easier it will be for you to practice with efficiency. Trusting becomes a huge source of enhancing your powers and giving yourself credit for who you actually are.

Some people who have psychic abilities and yet they don't trust themselves enough with it tend to have a lot of problem with themselves because if someone has psychic abilities, it is only natural for them to feel things in a deeper way or get intuitive knowledge about something that other people will not have. Now imagine the situation where among a group of people, you are the only one who has a different feeling or a different opinion or, for that matter, different knowledge about something. If you don't trust yourself enough, you will start getting the feeling that something is wrong with you or you are acting weirdly, which you are not. Only if you trust yourself enough will you understand what the actual scenario is.

Open Your Seven Chakra Centers

Suppose you are someone who takes their psychic abilities seriously. In that case, you need to think of a stable future where you can put your abilities to use, and that only be done if you are successful in developing a strong understanding of your spiritual core. That will help you get closure with your divine attributes and will help you further your practice. One way you can do this is to open up all the seven chakra centers in your body. If you can successfully tap into all the seven chakra centers' power, it will become all the easier to enhance your psychic abilities. Now, what are these chakra centers? So, basically, there are centers in your body, seven to be precise, where all your inner energies are focused. By getting in touch with these centers, all the energy that exists in your body will be yours to control and command. These are the places in your body that have the most reception of psychic intuition, and if you are in contact with these chakras inside you, your psychic abilities are bound to get enhanced.

There are many ways in which a person can receive psychic information, and opening up these chakras does exactly that. It eases up the process of receiving information and channeling the power of the inner core. It does take some practice while tapping into your chakras, but once you get them opened, things are going to be much more fluent. If you activate your chakras, your senses will be much more alert, and you will constantly be able to communicate with yourself and the outside universe. When all the seven chakras of your body are active and working, it will also help you open your third eye, which is what helps you see things that others can't. That is what makes you a psychic. The feeling that you get which makes you look at things differently is the power of your third eye. That power will get enhanced if you activate your chakra centers.

Practice Seeing Auras

Suppose you are someone who not only wants to enhance your psychic abilities, but you also want to do it specifically for the purpose of being in the healing profession, where you want to help others treat their medical conditions through your psychic abilities. In that case, you need to start practicing seeing your auras. Let me explain it in detail. An aura is basically like a very vibrant ray of color that is composed of a lot of energy and flows around a person or living things in general. It indicates the different moods that a living being possess, and our aura gives other people the first impression about us. Any person who is even a bit observant should be able to guess what kind of a personality we have given the attitude with which we start talking, and that gives away our aura. What needs to be understood here is that there are many psychic abilities that you need to be born with in order for you to practice and develop upon them. But unlike those abilities, seeing auras is not something that you need to be born with. This is a psychic ability that you can develop over time and keep practicing it in order to perfect it. All it takes is for you to have patience and dedication.

Some people get it easily, and after few days of practicing the art of seeing auras, they start seeing the different colors. While at the same time, others might take a bit longer to master the art of seeing the colors. The best way to see the auras or the different colors is to keep your chakra centers clean and open. The more you tap into your chakra centers and keep them activated, the more you keep them polished, the easier it will be for you to see the auras and sense the colors. That is the reason, the more accurate you are in understanding the aura that the other person is giving out, the easier it will be for you to deal with that person and tackle the situations that might arise.

Use Psychometry

To understand what psychometry is, it is basically the power that a person with psychic abilities possess where they can understand traits about a certain person or get useful information about that person by touching the possessions of that person. As a psychic, this is a very useful power to have, and in order to enhance their psychic abilities more, this power of psychometry needs to be practiced. With more practice, a person can tone this power into a powerful source of extracting information about others. After a point, he\she will be able to extend this to strangers as well, were given something in their possessions, getting to know things about them will become an easy task. However, when a person is just starting out, it is better to start off with the possessions of someone whom they are really close with so that understanding things becomes easier. The closer that person is to you, the more familiar you are with that person's belongings, the easier it will be for you to understand and get more information. Practicing psychometry is one of the most prominent ways of enhancing your psychic abilities.

As a practitioner, you need to sense any impression that you might feel of that concerned person whose objects you have taken. This will develop a kind of bridge between you and that concerned person, and this mode of communication is bound to strengthen your psychic powers. Unlike some other practices, psychometry is one that you as a practitioner can start working on very soon and can start developing upon from the very beginning. As a practitioner, you will be surprised to see how fast and how smoothly you can develop this skill as it usually comes very fast to people who have psychic powers.

Take Help of Other Useful Tools

Along with all the above-mentioned ways in which you can enhance your psychic abilities, there are some tools that can come in really handy while practicing psychic abilities. Tools such as tarot cards, for example, or pendulum are very easy to learn and very useful at the same time. All you need to do is learn about these tools in detail as to how they should be used, what angle they should be kept at, which hand you should keep them, and what your body language must be like while you are using them. Remember that these tools are basically the agents that will help you get in touch with your inner core of power and your higher self. They will help you get the necessary information that you need in your psychic practice, helping you get answers to questions that you had been seeking out.

Maintain a Journal

Let us understand this now that no matter what powers you might have, they won't ever add up to much unless you want them to. Your powers are as good as you are. They will be as strong as you want them to by working hard. So, if at all you are serious about enhancing and developing your psychic abilities, you will need to make many conscious decisions about them. You will need to keep track of all that you want to achieve through these powers, all the new things you want to learn, and all the new things you have to practice. It is not always possible to keep everything in mind, and things might get lost in the process. That is why you need to maintain a proper journal where you need to put in all the necessary things for your practice. Try writing down all the questions that you might be having at any given point so that you can go back to them when in need and you can find answers to them. You need to be diligent and systematic about the entire process so that no stone remains unturned and so that you might not regret it later. The key is to pay attention to proper attention to all your dreams and keep them right in front of you to constantly remind you of what they are and what you need to do about them.

Psychic abilities are certain powers that many people are gifted with. They are gifts of nature, and they can be enabled within a person by tapping into their chakra centers. Psychic abilities help a person see beyond what is the normal realm of existence that we are accustomed to. People with psychic abilities have the power to sense and see what others can't, and every person possesses some of these powers to a lesser or higher degree. What matters is then to tap into them, and if a person is interested enough, then to practice them and perfect them eventually.

All the points mentioned above will be helpful in enhancing the psychic abilities of a person, and if someone decides to pursue their powers seriously, these ways are sure to be helpful in their way. Psychic abilities are unique gifts of communication that a person is endowed with, and they should be wasted. Trusting oneself and diligently keep at practicing them is the key that can help a person polish their skills and excel in their practice. Keeping alert and activating one's chakra centers will definitely help a person understand everything that is going on, making the entire process easier for them.

Chapter 3: Communicating With Your Spirit Guides

Spirit guides are entities that are not human but which act as a protector, a guide, or an advisor for human beings. These entities have a strong rooting in different thought schools of Western spiritualism, and spirit guides have now become a much more commonly discussed topic in everyday lives, and people are gradually opening up to the idea of actively seeking out support from their spirit guides. This chapter is the perfect read for you if you are trying to learn more about this topic, as it will take you through the basics about the different kinds of spirit guides and the ways in which you can establish a connection with them and then strengthen it further.

Types of Spirit Guides

Spirit guides vary in what they stand for and how they are related to you. This means that some spirit guides have been with you for the entire duration of your life, while on the other hand, certain spirit guides have been with you from even before you were born, and certain other kinds only enter your life as and when you need their presence. Therefore, there can be different kinds of spirit guides, and each of them serves a different purpose in our lives, which is why there are also various ways to connect with each of them. Six different kinds of common spirit guides have been described below:

1. **Guardian Angels:** Perhaps the most commonly known spirit guides, guardian angels belong to you completely and exclusively (unlike other spirit guides who can at once cater to the needs of multiple people). Your guardian angel has devoted their entire life to helping you out solely, which means that you can turn to them at any moment for immediate and urgent

assistance. These angels help people from all religions, spiritual faiths, and beliefs, making them non-denominational in nature. Finally, unlike some other kinds of spirit guides, your guardian angel will love you unconditionally and forever

2. **Archangels:** Archangels are considered to be the leaders in the world of angels, and they usually possess a considerably large energy signature. When you invite an archangel into your life, you would- in all likelihood- feel a shift in the overall energy levels in the room. This is especially bound to happen if you are very sensitive to energy or are an empath. Different archangels come with their own distinct specialties; for example, the Archangel Raphael is best known for working on healing and can work with almost countless people at once, unlike other Archangels who have a limited pool of energy.

3. **Departed Loved Ones:** As their name suggests, these spirit guides are deceased family members or other loved ones who choose to actively extend your support even after them having passed away, and their help is extended in the most real and practical ways- since they were once very much a part of your everyday life- which might include nurturing a certain troubled relationship which you are a part of or sending suitable job opportunities your way. However, your spirit guide does not necessarily have to be a person with whom you were very close during their lifespan. Even loved ones whom you did not know very well personally but were attached to in any form can be very helpful spirit guides. This also extends to the idea that any human who was once living and with whom you can identify some sort of common ground can become your spirit guide. For example, suppose you are a singer. In that case, the chances are that you can have a spirit guide by your side which was once a singer or performer and now

just wants to help you with figuring out the artistic aspects of your life, and this can happen despite you not having known the person very well.

4. **Spirit Animals:** Your spirit animal is most likely to be a pet from your past who was really close to you and had passed away, after which they have become a part of your larger squad of spiritual guidance. Besides that, spirit animals could also be an animal which has the potential to teach you something. An example of this would be how wolves can teach you the significance of meeting your survival needs on your own or how a peacock has the capability to make you realize how to confidently own your own qualities. You can meet your spirit animal for the first time in many ways- you could chance upon them in a dream, randomly through some merchandise, or even in your backyard.

5. **Helper Angels:** These angels are the spirit guides which perhaps have the least personal attachment to you. They act as 'freelance' spirit guides, which implies that they are simply looking for humans to connect with and help out in specific situations during which they seek some kind of support and guidance. This help can range anywhere from finding a suitable office space to finding friends during a difficult phase in their lives.

6. **Ascended Masters:** Ascended masters refer to spirit guides who were actually once human beings and lived their personal journeys of great spiritual development and influence. Some examples of this would include deceased personalities such as Mother Mary or Buddha, both of whom- among many others- were humans at one point in time but are now occupying a special place in the world of spirits and can act as spiritual teachers or guides to human beings. A common idea about ascended masters is that all of them are actually partners, and they work

together regardless of the religion, faith, or culture they belonged to when they were alive and were on the earth.

Effective Ways to **Communicate with Spirit Guides**

Our spirit guides often communicate with us by sending different signs our way. These signs are also known as synchronicities- which has been defined by the famous psychiatrist Carl Jung as "a meaningful coincidence." An example of this would be that perhaps you need to improve the relationship you share with your parents and that is something which has been on your mind for some time, and out of the blue, you notice a book on your friend's shelf the very next day which addresses communication issues between parents and their children. This can very well be a 'meaningful coincidence' that has been sent your way by your spirit guide, who has been aware of the issues which have been bothering you and wants to give you a nod in the right direction.

Spirit guides can also communicate with you by using number sequences, musical messages, or even dreams. You might come across a possible solution to a problem that you have been tackling with, in your dream, and work on that to fix your real-life problem, or you might find out that the song that you find inspiring or uplifting just happens to be playing on the radio after you have had a long, tiring day. Another way in which they communicate with you is by sending helpful opportunities and people your way. This is when you chance upon an opportunity which will only work out if you actively act upon it, and not otherwise, but the way in which you find it can be absolutely random and unprecedented (examples of this could be impulsively purchasing a ticket to a workshop which goes on to change your life, or asking an intriguing new person out for lunch, and so on). These are ways in which your spirit guide is communicating with you, not just about the problems you are facing but also letting you know that they are aware of your hardships and are willing to lend a helping hand when you need one.

Listed below are 12 effective ways which could help you communicate with your spirit guides –

Try to be present in your daily life

Often, when you are too busy and caught up with your daily lives, it becomes hard for you to be mindful of everything else that is taking place around you. This also makes it difficult for you to rightly spot the spiritual wisdom and guidance that your guides send your way regularly. Therefore, the first step to communicate with your spirit guides would include you to be more aware and live in the moment so that you can recognize the messages they have already been sending.

Example: You can try making some open space in your daily schedule, or you can remove some responsibilities from your routine if that is feasible for you. Doing this will make sure that you would not be running around as much as you usually do, and you can use that time up to be more present in your surroundings and notice small messages from your spirit guides. You can also use the time to get into the practice of meditation and other relaxation techniques, which might help you clear your mind out and make more space to welcome the help that is trying to find you.

Build yourself a sacred space

Another thing you can do- which goes hand-in-hand with the previous prompt- is to create a quiet, sacred space for yourself that will help you connect with your inner spirituality, in turn helping you communicate better with your spirit guides. The realm of the earth is pretty heavy, and it is not the most comfortable place for spirits to exist in, which is why making this space would not benefit just you but your guides as well, at the same time. In this sacred space, you can try and raise the intensity of your own spiritual energy, which will actually help your spirit guides meet you halfway on your journey of spiritual development and guidance.

Maintain a special spirit guide journal

Journaling is always a good solution to keep track of important things in your life, and if you are just beginning to connect with your spirit guides, maintaining a special journal specifically dedicated to this can be really helpful. This journal can be a safe space for you to write down the signs that you are receiving from your guides, and putting all of them in one place over a period of time can also help you identify patterns and trends among these signs. Besides doing this, you can also use your journal to write down your requests for help and guidance from your guides and let them assess your needs.

Example: To kickstart your spirit guides journal, write a letter to your guides at the start of the next week to express how grateful you feel for all the help you have received from them for navigating the tough situations in your life. This will also get you into the habit of communicating with your guides through writing, which is a practice you will need to be closely in touch with once you start updating your journal. After you write this letter down, also note down very briefly the areas for which you seek assistance from your guides during the week. Spend the week jotting down any synchronicities you might notice specifically pertaining to those areas.

Keep an eye out for signs from your spirit guides

You will slowly start to recognize more signs sent by your spirit guides as you increase the time and effort you put into looking for these signs. However, while being open-minded and receptive, also make sure that you are not forcing anything upon yourself in the process and are not mistaking occurrences that are not signs of being otherwise. Also, the more you start picking up on the signs, your spirit guides will understand that you are becoming more mindful and aware about the channels of communication between the both of you, and they would then be more likely to send even more signs along your way.

Example: Remind yourself about how your guide is sending you messages while you are in the middle of daily, mundane tasks- such as washing your hair or catching the bus to work. Especially if you are going through a hard and indecisive time in your life, you can expect the situation to be navigated by the signs and guidance which are being sent to you by your spirit guides.

Get to identify and know your spirit guides

It might help the process of communication if you become more accustomed to your guides in a way in which they start feeling close and more familiar with you. One of the first and most useful steps of establishing this connection is by giving your spirit guide a name that you can use to identify them easily. The name you select for them can be anything you feel comfortable with- it can be a name which you have always felt a certain fondness for, or it can also be the name of a character from your favorite novel, and so on. Giving your spirit guide a name is important because, in a way, this makes them appear more real, which will also motivate you to try and communicate with them regularly. Once you start communicating more closely and more frequently with them, you might even be able to learn more about their personalities and the ways in which they function over time.

Example: Try to find a name for any one of your spirit guides. You can do this through simply your intuition or through using particular synchronicity, or else, you can also just be creative and come up with a name you feel some positive attachment towards.

Allow your spirit guides to join you

Many spirit guides will not interfere with you if you are not personally welcoming them into your lives. You can practice this exercise to put into place an invitation which would make your guides feel more welcome and will help them reach out to you better –

a) Relax and try to clear your mind. You can do that by meditating or by taking some deep breaths. Next, try to create a clear space in your mind into which you will invite your guide to enter.

b) You can call out to your guide and let them know that you have created a safe space for them to enter. Once you have done that, you need to check for any signs which might indicate that your guide is now present with you. You do not have to force anything. Just try to be as open-minded about possibilities as you could be at that moment and let things happen to you organically.

c) Try to merge all your energies into one channel, and when you feel ready, you can call out to your guide and let them know that you are ready for their assistance and support. You can also try to let them know what is wrong in your life at the moment and what sort of help might help you take care of those situations.

d) As you sit there, in your sacred space, with your guide, trying to sense the thoughts that are being projected into your mind, let yourself be free of all inhibitions and allow your guide to let you know of any thoughts or feelings they want to you transmit.

e) Once you feel that you cannot continue this and the time has come when you need to stop the session, thank your guide and let them know their support has been well-received on your part. Take some deep, relaxing breaths to center yourself back into your body. Next, become aware of your body- starting with your toes, and go all the way upwards to your head. Inhale and exhale while being mindful of the recent spiritual exchange and the ways in which it can change your life.

Work on improving your intuition

Helping build a better sense of intuition can help you communicate with your spirit guides better, as it will also make sure that you are being more receptive to the signs they are sending out for you. Intuition is something we all have, and we all can also improve it through study and regular practice. There are four major types of intuitive pathways that you can try and develop further. These paths include (a) clairaudience, or hearing voices, (b) clairvoyance, or seeing visuals, (c) clairsentience, or identifying feelings, and (d) claircognizance, or knowing things. By sharpening these four 'clair'-s, you can be in better touch with your guides. You can also try and figure out which of the four intuitive feelings you are the strongest at and then work towards sharpening that specifically instead of trying to build all four of them up, as being considerably strong in any of them would naturally give you a headstart into things.

Example: You can practice your intuition to make smaller decisions in your life that would not impact you negatively in the larger scheme of things. Such decisions can include picking a place for lunch or choosing an outfit for a casual day. By starting with smaller, more trivial decisions, you are already actively working on improving your intuition skills so that, in time, they can be utilized to make greater decisions in your life.

Send your guides a message through your thoughts

This might sound like the quickest and the easiest way to connect with your spirit guides, and it might look very simplistic, but more often than not- this actually works. There are multiple ways of doing this. You can send your guides a more formal prayer to seek their blessings; on the other hand, you can also simply communicate your needs and your gratitude towards them in merely a couple of sentences in your thoughts. This tip can be especially useful for times when you perhaps do not have your spirit guide's journal handy or need a quick breather in between a hectic day.

Example: Once you are done with reading this chapter, communicate your thoughts with your guides and inform them about one thing which you have been worried about over the past few days. However, do not leave it only up to them to fix; try and talk to a friend or a loved one about it as well, and you would soon receive the help that you need- through advice, synchronicities, or maybe both of those at once.

Explore different tools for divination

There are numerous divination tools that have helped humans establish contact with the world of spirits for centuries now. To better communicate with your guides, you can turn to one (or more) of such tools as well. Some of the most commonly accessible divination tools include tarot cards, oracle cards, runes, etc. You can check out and indulge in various of these methods to figure out which one works the best for you and then divert your focus to that exclusively.

Example: Before getting to work with your tool of choice, hold your cards (or other similar items) in your hand and close your eyes for a minute. Then, take a few deep breaths, center yourself, and then move on to asking your spirit guides to send you a healing message through this method of divination.

Surrender something over to your guides

When you feel stuck, helpless, or frustrated about a particular situation or get the feeling that you are losing control, you can attempt to surrender the concern completely over to your spirit guides. This might help you out in different ways, but most importantly, it will at least be effective in giving yourself a break, which will help you regain composure. You can utilize this break to explore fresh, new insights about things. At the same time, your guides would also enjoy more freedom to do their thing to help you out without your interference of any sort in the process.

Example: Even if only temporarily, practice energetically venting out an issue to your spirit guide. Do this, and simultaneously let your mind enjoy some quiet instead of constantly being engaged in strategizing. To do this, you can also use affirmations such as *I am handing this issue over to my guides because I trust their sense of guidance.*

Develop short and long term spiritual practices

Building and nurturing certain spiritual practices will help you be more in sync with your spiritual side, which will help facilitate better communication with your guides. Spiritual practices can be daily, weekly, or even monthly. Some of these can include drawing one oracle card every morning to get some inspiration, signing up for a yoga class that takes place every week, or turning up for monthly spiritual gatherings. These activities will help you develop a deeper level of intimacy with your spirit guides, besides aiding the journey of you discovering your spirituality.

Example: You can start with trying to develop a new practice in the coming weeks, such as a new moon or a full moon ritual, which will help you create the mindset of building regular spiritual practices in your life. Other than that, you can also try listing down the different spiritual beliefs which act as important guiding principles for you. These will also help you understand your spiritual side better.

Make efforts to learn more about spirit guides

Last but not least, being more involved in how spirituality manifests and functions can help you form a better chain of communication with your guides. Researching on spirit guides in your leisure time is bound to strengthen the connection that you are trying to build with them. You can also reach out to experts on this matter to know more and read or gain more information on spirit guides that empower and heal, as that would further reinforce the faith you place in your guides. You can gain knowledge by reading and through more interactive methods such as attending an online course or a workshop on this, or even by just striking up a conversation with like-minded people.

Feeling Disconnected from Your Spirit Guides

Even after you have practiced and aced most of the steps listed in the previous section, it might still be the case that you are experiencing some difficulties connecting with your spirit guide after a rough patch and are feeling a sense of disconnect in general. This might be because you are going through a particularly difficult patch in your life or are facing some major changes and transformations which have shifted your routine lifestyle. However, there is nothing to worry about, even if you are feeling this way! You need to remember that- even during the lowest points of your life- your spirit guides will not leave your side and will not take their support away from you. They would always be working for you relentlessly behind the scenes, even during the phases when you are not completely able to sense them or their presence.

This disconnect also often comes up during the hardest times in your life- which are also the times when your spirit guides want to help you out the most, which should assure you that in spite of any apparent lack of communication, your guides are still working in your favor. Even during these times, your spirit guides really do want to share a closer relationship with you, which would be materialized once you try and open yourself up to communicate more mindfully with them. Once you try to be more aware of what is going on around you, you would actually be surprised to see how many signs your guides have been sending you all this while, signs which you have missed out on due to being engrossed and overwhelmed with everything else that has been going on in your life. These signs serve as the invitation from your spirit guides for you to start identifying the subtle ways in which the communication is already happening between you and your various spirit guides.

Chapter 4: Gemstones for Psychic Abilities

Psychic abilities can be greatly enhanced by the use of different kinds of gemstones as they help a person get in touch with their inner spirit and tap into the core of power and energy that resides in them. Gemstones can be of great help as they help a person to open their third eye and see into their inner walls of wisdom, and these stones can increase a person's intuition which is a must for a person who is practicing psychic powers. The powers of the person are sure to get stronger if the correct stones are put to use. There are a host of various gemstones that are used for different purposes, and proper knowledge about them is a must. This chapter shall deal with some basic gemstones that are useful to a psychic.

What are Gemstones?

A piece of rock or mineral will be called a gemstone when it has been cut with precision and polished properly, and it has been used as a piece to enhance and decorate a piece of jewelry or has been used as a form of any other accessory. Gemstones are usually made from minerals, but they could also be made from other materials like lapis lazuli or, say, amber. It depends on their hardness, which can be measured in the Moh scale of hardness as to what extent they can be used. If they are not hard enough, they will be brittle and won't be able to be used in jewelry. If one is to know in detail about a particular gemstone and examine its quality, then the four Cs need to be thoroughly examined, and they are Colour, Clarity, Cut, and Carat. Buying a gemstone is not easy as people can be easily duped into believing it is of good quality when it is not. So, a thorough prior knowledge is important.

Best Gemstones for Enhancing Psychic Abilities

Psychic abilities can be greatly enhanced by the use of different gemstones as they each have a unique quality about themselves. Whatever "hunches" one might get or "visions" one might see through their individual psychic abilities can be enhanced through gemstones. That is why gemstones are very popular among psychic and shamas and turret readers. Let us see a few of these gemstones and their uses.

Alexandrite

This stone falls under the family of chrysoberyl family of stones and is a very rare stone indeed. On the Moh's scale, it sits at 8.5, which basically means it is one of the hardest stones on earth. Don't mistake them for being a member of the emerald or morganite family, though.

This stone is well sought after because it helps bring happiness in a person's life, and not only that, it helps a person tap into their inner strengths and find for themselves their own source of happiness without having to depend on anyone. What it also does is to facilitate the awareness of beauty in others and oneself, which invariably helps a person become happier than what they were used to being. After using this stone, a person is bound to become more appreciative of things that they have, thereby giving them more reasons to celebrate life.

Alexandrite provides a person with hope by helping the concerned person to become more aware of everything that is happening around them and helps them identify more possibilities around them, and as a result of this, naturally, a person can make use of things around them and grab more opportunities to become happy. This gemstone is usually marked as the birthstone for those who are born in the month of June but then again, as they are really rare, it becomes a task getting hold of them. They are costly so if your jeweler offers them at a lower price, make sure you find out whether it is real or not.

Amethyst

This is one of the most popular gemstones of all time, be it for using them in jewelry or for enhancing psychic abilities. They are actively used for crystal healing. There are usually two kinds of amethyst, black amethyst, which means that it has an inclusion of hematite, and thus it appears to be deep dark in color mixed with the original deep purple. And the other is Moroccan amethyst which is deep purple in color, and it usually contains chevrons and a crackle-look to it and also violet fire. It has a seven on the Moh scale of hardness.

This stone has a lot of benefits and thus is so popular. It tends to start vibrating with a high frequency while at the same time creating a bubble of protection of positive energy and power to protect a person from negative energies. For the person who wears it, they are sure to awaken to a higher degree of consciousness which is sure to help them enhance their intuition. Amethyst helps in cleaning the aura of a person, and at the same time, it helps a person remain clearheaded even in times of difficulties and confusion. amethyst helps a person remain in control and become the best version of oneself and as a result that is sure to help a person in all sectors of their lives, be it in the family or a job or wherever. It will help you become a person who can make more responsible decisions in life and thus take the best advantage of any given situation.

Apatite

It is not a very known gemstone, but it has significant uses. However, it needs to be kept in mind that they are very brittle in nature and thus have to be handled with care. It sits on number 5 on the Moh scale of hardness, and apatites can be found in yellow, green, violets, browns, and also blues.

And they have a unique and beautiful hexagonal shape. If one has to look for a perfect apatite for themselves, they need to keep in mind that the intenser the color, the better the quality of the stone. So, do not settle for a lighter-colored apatite.

As far as enhancing your psychic abilities are concerned, and the uses of apatite are concerned, they are very helpful in reducing anger levels in a person and also help them keep their stress levels in check. Apatites help a person enhance their creativity levels and caters to being a positive force behind pumping up a person's imagination. Intuition, which is one of the most important things necessary for enhancing a person's psychic abilities, is something that apatite helps enhance in a person. One can go for apatite bracelets or, for that matter, apatite necklaces or rings. Keeping this stone near you will help you relax a lot, and your judgments will not get clouded, which will help you get a clear vision of what's happening. The green-colored apatite will also help you to soothe your nervous system while at the same time helping you to maintain your inner balance.

Azurite

Azurite is a very soft gemstone sitting on a 3.5-4 on the Moh scale of hardness. They are usually found alongside malachite and also in places with copper deposits as azurites are byproducts of copper. It is interesting to know that azurites are not only used as gemstones for both jewelry purposes and to enhance psychic abilities, but they are also used as dyes for their beautiful colors as they come in beautiful shades of green and a mixture of blue and green, making a lovely combination.

This gemstone helps a person stimulate their third-eye chakra, which is extremely helpful in enhancing one's psychic abilities. What happens as a result of that is the inner vision of the concerned person and their dreams get enhanced. Azurite is sure to help a person learn new concepts by making them more receptive to changes and new things. It helps increase a person's insight because the mind becomes calmer, the understanding level of a person gets enhanced. This helps a person make more productive connections with people, which will invariably open new gates for the person concerned, helping them more opportunities on their way. Azurite is indeed very helpful for people whose work needs them to take firm decisions based on their intuitions and also for students as they are in the age of grasping new things and concepts and also on the verge of meeting new people and they need to get hold of more and more productive opportunities. It has its own healing purposes and is very famous among spiritual practitioners.

Blue Calcite

This is the gemstone that will help you explore your unconscious in great detail and in deeper intensity. Blue calcite will help a person to unblock all their creative resources and source of inspiration while at the same time, this stone will help a person to dissolve any limiting believes that they might be having regarding anything. Blue calcite helps a person to strengthen their positive outlook, which invariably acts as a source of power and strength for the concerned person to try and succeed in new things.

Wearing blue calcite will help a person to broaden their horizon of dreaming and exploring life, and a person will become open to changes in life and new possibilities. What is also very interesting to know is that blue calcite helps a person from all sectors of life that does not only do it help a person become emotionally and mentally strong by taking away the extra baggage of worries and anxiety that we tend to carry all the time, it also helps a person remain physically healthy. Blue calcite is a very good choice to get one's psychic abilities enhanced. If one combines blue calcite with a blue opal or blue chalcedony, it will tend to have an increasing effect on helping a person get rid of the creative blocks from their path. How it does this is by stimulating the third eye vision, which helps in further dismantling the negative beliefs in a person's mind.

Dumortierite

Dumortierite is basically an aluminum boro-silicide mineral and has a beautiful dark blue or indigo color. It is also possible to find this gemstone in other colors such as violet, blue-green or red-brown. These stones tend to get crystallized and can be found in metamorphic rocks.

This gorgeous, blue in color, gemstone of indigo color is one that greatly enhances a person's psychic and as well as their mental abilities. Dumortierite helps a person become more insightful and increases a person's understanding abilities. This gemstone helps you gain more insight into any given situation as it will surely help you look at a situation more clearly and with greater practicality.

All your mental and psychic abilities get a channel through which one can guide their spiritual energy. Tarot readers, as well as psychic practitioners, prefer this gemstone as this helps a person give focus on one's self-awareness. One of the most potent abilities of this stone is to strengthen a person's mental discipline, which helps a person look at things differently with much more patience and with deep understanding. At times if a person feels emotionally stuck to a certain thing, this gemstone can help take the person out of that situation by helping to find clarity. New pathways are sure to be opened in front of a person who is using this gemstone as divine guidance is sure to come. One might easily wear this stone in their rings, bracelets, necklaces, or pendants as they are beautiful to look at while at the same time having the above-mentioned uses.

Iolite

Iolite is a beautiful gemstone of violet color and is also known as cordierite, and it is a silicate of magnesium and that of aluminum. We usually find this stone in places like Madagascar, Sri Lanka, India, Brazil, etc. An Iolite is sure to enhance a person's ability to meditate for a long time with full concentration as it helps a person become calm and composed. It helps a person to remain in more control of their thoughts and subsequent actions as well.

This gemstone helps facilitate a person's inner vision strongly, including a person's shamanic abilities. Iolite, as a gemstone, helps create a strong bond between the rational mind and the non-rational energies in a person. It is sure to enhance the powers and strengths of a person's inner soul and spiritual core. It helps a person in reaching the depths of their heart and helps them become more comfortable and confident about their intuitions. If used properly, an Iolite can help a person study their unconscious in detail, thereby creating an understanding in the person of the past and the present. It will invariably be helpful in resolving issues that had remain pending so far, helping a person to bring forth their innate creativity and potentiality. This gemstone can be easily worn through bracelets, earrings, or necklaces. Pendants, rings, or even raw stones can be used.

Kyanite

Kyanite is a kind of aluminum silicate mineral, and that is the reason it is usually blue in color, but at the same time, they could be found in other colors as well, like white or black, green, grey, orange, and sometimes even pink. If it is sold in its raw form, it can easily break off into splinters, and that is why it is good to be very careful while you are handling them if you don't know how to or you are not a professional. One might use this stone in necklaces, in rings, in pendants, or bracelets. Raw kyanite can be kept with oneself, but that is not an easy thing to do.

As mentioned earlier, kyanites have different colors, and they tend to have different properties about themselves. For example, suppose the gemstone is of blue color. In that case, that kyanite helps a person enhance their communication powers and will also help the person transfer energy mind-to-mind, that is, between the conscious mind and the unconscious of the dream world. It will help the person break away from the chain of complex twisted dreams, making them more lucid and less complicated. This happens as the mind feels less pressure due to the effect of the stone. The bridge between the physical and the astral body becomes stronger, making the person more in control of himself and his subconscious thoughts. The kyanite will help the concerned person communicate easily with the disparate parts of the self and between the disparate parts of different people.

Labradorite

If one is familiar with the entire practice of tarot card reading, then they will know that this gemstone is a must for any such practice. Every good tarot reader needs good labradorite for themselves to help them in practice. Labradorite helps a person enhance their multi-layers of awareness of the reality around us, and that is why with shamans, this gem is a must and with those who work with the Akashic records. This gem helps a person keep their aura very strong and protected as they help to block any intruders. The concerned person will also be helped by being able to remember their experience while they were traveling through the other realms or when they recall their past life memories.

To enhance one's psychic powers, one needs to use their spiritual energies to a great extent. They need to make use of their telepathy skills, their clairvoyance abilities. At the same time, they need to use their divination powers and astral projection while all along maintain communication with their spirit entities. So, one needs to be emotionally, physically, and mentally strong and confident to go ahead with their practice for all these things. Labradorite helps a person get clarity on all these things and a mastery over them over time.

Lapis Lazuli

Lapis Lazuli is usually blue as it is mainly made up of calcite and lazurite. History tells that this stone was extremely famous in ancient Egypt among the then emperors as it is known to bestow people with wisdom. Beautiful to look at, they are either blue or indigo in color.

The name itself means a deep sense of self-knowledge and self-awareness. This stone has a storehouse of royal energy in it, which invariably helps a person to tap into their core, and that helps a person to uncover and also get access to their innermost noble nature of divine energy and power.

Lapis lazuli is very helpful in activating psychic powers and intuitive abilities. This stone tends to bridge the gap between a person and his spiritual awareness so that it becomes easier to become aware of them and give and receive guidance for the same. The power that this stone gives helps a person to discern the truth, and at the same time, it helps a person discover their truest selves. A person can use this gemstone in bracelets, necklaces, pendants, or even earrings. They can also be worn as rings or as a string of beads. Raw Lapis Lazuli can also be kept with oneself.

Magnesite

It is a very soft magnesium carbonate mineral, and that is why it is usually white in color but could also be yellow at times or even brown or grey. It can be mistaken for another gemstone known as turquoise though they are not related at all. This gemstone can be used in various industrial processes as well.

It's a stone that helps balance a person's emotional turmoil by making one receptive to changes and different kinds of situations in life. It helps a person control what's happening in their lives so that they could be well prepared for any changes that might occur. Magnesite helps enhance a person's higher consciousness whereby they can easily discern their inner core truth and their heart's desires. This gemstone also helps a person to deeply experience spiritual communication and transcendence as well. The chakra centers are always alert with the help of this stone which further enhances the awakening of the third eye.

This helps the person to get in touch with all the spiritual realms. A person's psychic awareness is sure to get enhanced as clearer messages will be available to them with the help of this gemstone. Once again, this stone can be used as necklaces, rings, bracelets, pendants, or as earrings. It can as well be kept with a person in its raw form.

Mookaite Jasper

This stone has a very distinct reddish-purple, yellow and brown coloring at times known as mook jasper or the ozokerite. As it is mostly found in Australia, it is at times known as the Australian jasper as well. It is a rock that is usually formed from sediments that are rich in Silicate, and that is what makes an opaque chalcedony, which is a subclass of quartz. This gemstone is also a form of radiolarite.

As this stone is a vibrant mixture of many colors, as a result of that, it gets connected to our root chakra (red and brown mookaite), to our solar plexus (yellow mookaite), and our third eye (purple mookaite). That is the reason psychics find it very interesting to work with this stone, as it always garners a unique response. This helps a person to remain young at heart as it helps change our perspectives towards things, and also it helps shape our mentality in a positive direction. Mookaite helps us connect our inner spiritual strength with that of the earth and aligns our spiritual energy with that of our ancestors who have walked this earth before us. This has an intense effect on our emotional terrain, helping us understand and transform our emotional patterns and behaviors in a way that has been passed down to us by our ancestors. This understanding has great healing powers and is extremely beneficial for a person.

Moonstone

It is a feldspar mineral gemstone, and it is pale and iridescent. It looks really similar to some opals, but they are chemically very different. Moonstone is usually milky-white, and the iridescence is usually gray, blue, or peach in tone. One might use this stone in bracelets, or rings, or necklaces and earrings. White moonstone jewelry is very popular as they are beautiful to look at. Raw moonstone could also be carried with oneself.

Moonstone is filled with a sort of feminine power and mystery, and it helps a person enhance their journey inwards by finding looking for and finding truths that might be hidden in our unconscious and also in our past lives. Intuition, which is one of the primary necessities of a psychic, gets enhanced by a moonstone, and it also encourages our level of patience and trust in our divine timing. If one is familiar with the practice of tarot reading, then it is a known fact that the priestess card has to always correspond with the moonstone. Moonstone helps a person stimulate the brain's thinking process, which allows the concerned person to take confident leaps in their insight without having to wait for a long time. So, a moonstone is a must if a person wants to connect themselves with their femininity, be it whether male or female.

Pietersite

This gemstone is a form of quartz that comes in a host of different shades like mottled brown, blue, gold, and grey. It contains the tiger eye, which gives it the chatoyancy effect. However, this gemstone is only found in China and Namibia. It could be worn in bracelets, necklaces, pendants, rings, earrings, as well as raw stones, can be carried.

This stone is extremely helpful for people who feel that they are stuck in the world of their inner thoughts and feel a bit shook up with the problems they are facing. This gemstone helps people calm down their anxieties and get a sense of purpose to decide the correct direction for themselves. If at any point you feel blocked, or lost, or uncertain, this stone is sure to help you out of it as it will help you get your spiritual core get aligned with your intentions and desires. Pietersite can help you bring a kind of spiritual catharsis in a person as it will help clear all the stagnant energies and help you recognize your true intentions. This stone helps build a connection between the third chakra and the sixth chakra, which enhances a person's willpower and intuition. Psychic practices involve astral travel, which helps a person stay centered and connected with one's spiritual core. Pietersite enhances a person's intuition and also helps spark flashes of insight which will help the person get a much clearer picture of everything around the person.

When you consider gemstones, there are endless possibilities, which is why proper knowledge needs to be acquired about them to choose the correct one for yourself. Make sure you purchase them from a trusted and authentic source so that you won't be deceived and will be given one of proper quality. Keeping the correct stones with yourself invariably helps you enhance your psychic abilities to a great extent and help you in your practice. It will help you explore all your possibilities to their fullest level, and with time, you will become like a trusted companion who will almost stay with you at all points in life, helping you choose what is right for you and encouraging you to be your best self. I hope this chapter has been helpful for you to know in a bit more detail about some of the above-mentioned gemstones. If you are someone who already practices their psychic abilities or is interested in it, getting proper gemstones can be really helpful as they will give you a push in the right direction, helping you know things in greater detail.

Chapter 5: A Complete Guide to Psychometry

A very important part of enhancing your psychic abilities is learning psychometry, and we are going to discuss all aspects of it in this chapter. In brief, psychometry is the art through which a person can automatically understand or 'read' an object's history by simply touching it. They either touch it to their forehead or hold it in their hand. Any kind of touch gives them impressions about the object. These impressions can be in the form of sounds, smells, images, emotions, or even tastes.

What is Psychometry?

Psychometry is a special ability through which people can practice seeing things that are not usually seeable in the real world. It is often referred to as the psychic way of seeing. Different people see in different ways. Some people use the surface of the water, black glass, or a crystal ball – everyone has their own ways. The main characteristic feature of psychometry is that people can practice this extraordinary talent through touch.

A person who has psychometric talents is often referred to as the psychometrist. Let me give you an example of how it's done. Suppose you give them an antique watch, and they hold it in their hands. They can tell you all about that watch and who owned it with their power of touch. They might even be able to tell you about the different experiences the person had when they had that watch in their possession. You will be surprised to know about the different things the psychic can tell you – they can give you a hint of what the person who possessed the object was like, what they did in their lifetime, or even how they died. But among all of these things, the most important thing that the psychic can tell you is how that particular person was feeling at a certain point of time in their life. It is said that an object can very strongly store a person's emotions in them, and thus, even psychometrics can sense it very easily.

You must keep in mind that a psychometric might not be able to display the same level of seeing/reading with all types of objects. The accuracy of their psychic abilities differs from one object to the other. Most people get confused about the basic idea of psychometry – it is not focused on the future but on your present and past. That is how it differs from a typical crystal ball reading.

The concept of psychometry and the term itself was coined by Joseph Rhodes Buchanan, an American physiologist and physician. He explained psychometry with the example of geologists. Just like geologists study the past from the fossils, psychometry is related to 'mental fossils.' An object gives off a certain energy, which is then used to study the science and history of the human mind.

Essentially, psychometrists are of the belief that each and everything on this planet has a soul, including objects. They acquire a memory based on how a person is interacting with them. A person can figure out the history of that object or its owner if they are sensitive enough to feel the energy emanating from these objects.

A Brief History of Psychometry

In the year 1842, Joseph R. Buchanan was the person who coined the term 'psychometry.' The word is derived from two Greek words – psyche and metron. Here, psyche means 'soul,' and metron means 'measure.' Out of all the experiments conducted with psychometry, Buchanan was one of the first to do so, and he was an American physiology professor. He kept different types of drugs in glass vials.

After that, he asked his students to hold the vials and identify what kinds of drugs have been kept there through the power of touch. It was more than chance that they succeeded, and the results of this experiment were published in his book – Journal of Man. To put it in a brief sentence, Buchanan explained this phenomenon, saying that all objects have the ability to retain a memory because they have a 'soul.'

After that, William F. Denton started his own experiments in psychometry after being inspired by the works of Buchanan. Denton was an American geology professor, and his aim was to make sure whether the concept of psychometry works on the geology specimens he works with. He then invited his sister, Ann Denton, to help him out in his experiments in the year 1854. He took a piece of cloth and used it to wrap around all the geological specimens he wanted to test. This ensured that Ann couldn't see what the specimens were. Ann took the package and touched it to her forehead. She received very clear mental images, and with their help, she was able to describe all the specimens correctly.

Then came Gustav Pagenstecher, who carried out work on psychometry from 1919 to 1922. He was a psychical researcher and a doctor of German origin. In between these years, he discovered that one of his patients possessed psychometric abilities. The name of the patient was Maria Reyes de Zierold. Maria could prominently talk about the past of an object and its present by simply holding it, during which she also entered a trance-like state. She could state the experience of the object in this world and go on describing smells, sounds, sights, and several other feelings. So, based on this observation, Pagenstecher had formed a theory that every object has certain vibrations condensed into it, and if a person can tune into those vibrations, they can learn about the experience of that object.

How to Know If You Have Psychometric Abilities?

With all this talk about psychometry, I'm sure you are very excited to know whether you have psychometric abilities or not. Well, in general, it has been noticed that most psychometric readers are empaths. The tendency is even more strengthened if you have the skill of clairsentience to a reasonable level.

But, for a better idea, if you want to know whether you have psychometric skills or not, here are some signs that you should look out for –

- You feel a strong vibe from antique stores, or they simply make you feel weird.

- When there are too many objects in a space, you feel uncomfortable because many objects mean too much energy.

- You only use new furniture. Used furniture makes you feel uncomfortable.

- You cannot wear used jewelry or someone else's clothes.

- If you have picked up any used object, you have this impulse at the back of your mind to immediately wash your hands.

- You feel overwhelmed while visiting pawn shops.

So, have you been experiencing any of the signs mentioned above or anything similar to that? If yes, then there is a high chance that you will excel at the psychometric skill. All of these signs show that a person is ready to read the energy in an object and even explain what the object has gone through.

In fact, psychometric skills can even help you figure out why you hate certain objects in your life, like, your uncle's couch.

3 Kinds of Psychometry

Now, let us have a look at the three kinds of psychometry that is there –

Object Psychometry. It is the type of psychometry that most people know about and is the most popular out of all three. Like I mentioned before, there is a certain amount of energy present in all objects of earth. The owner who had that object with him/her leaves behind a unique imprint on the object.

People who practice object psychometry work towards establishing a solid rapport with the item/object they are working with. They also work on building a close relationship with the energies that have been imprinted inside the object. There are three different ways in which you can read the imprints in any object –

- By holding the object in your hands

- By placing the object against your face or forehead

- By placing the object against your solar plexus

When you place the object in either of the above-mentioned ways or make contact with it, you will get an idea about the history of the object or its owner through the impressions.

Location Psychometry. This type of psychometry is very similar to what we commonly refer to as déjà vu. In short, even when you haven't been to a place, and you get this sensation that you have been there, it is referred to as déjà vu. It also has similarities with different forms of diving and dowsing, for example, finding out the feasibility of mining in a place by attuning to one of the ore samples.

Some traces are left by incidents in the location they happened. This is even truer for strong and emotional events. These locations get imprinted with the energy of that event. And thus, you can read these imprints.

Person Psychometry. This type of psychometry relies on the idea that there is an energy field surrounding everyone on earth. Almost all people implement this psychometry method. Have you ever encountered a situation where you were able to assess a person's mood without even speaking with them? I'm sure you have. Then, there is another very common example – every time you meet someone new, you are either repelled by them or attracted to them. This is also because of person psychometry. There is no complete explanation of how these impressions work, but every person will vouch for the fact that they have a strong effect.

How Does It Work?

Out of all the explanations, researchers have paid extra careful attention to the vibration theory proposed by Pagenstecher. Psychics have always claimed that the vibrations from an object are conveyed to them, and these vibrations are imbibed in that object through actions and emotions that were accumulated in the past.

Keep in mind that the concept of messages being conveyed through vibrations is not your regular New Age talk. There is a substantial scientific basis too. Michael Talbot wrote a book called *The Holographic Universe,* and in this book, the author has stated that the past is never really lost. In fact, some form of human perception always keeps the past alive. Talbot used the scientific knowledge that vibrations are exuded by all forms of matter on earth at a subatomic level. Using this information, he stated that "reality and consciousness are present in a type of hologram where a record of past, present, and future exists.' It is the power of this record that psychometrics can use to their advantage.

If you consider the literal meaning of the term 'psychometry,' it comes down to measuring a soul since 'metry' means measuring something, and 'psych' refers to the soul.

So, people who have the special gifts of psychometry and have mastered the art implement their extrasensory talent to study the objects and understand the energy that is coming out of them. It can even be described as an energy signature. Every object tries to tell its own story through its energy signature. As you all know, most people who have psychometric abilities are also empaths by nature – this means they can guide others by understanding their emotions and energy.

I have heard from most people that the easiest reading experience they had was with metal objects, but if you practice enough and master the art, you can read just about any object with equal expertise. In fact, if a person is very sensitive to energy, they can even pick up signals if a person's photograph is shown to them. This is also the basis of online psychometric readings where the reader cannot meet the person face-to-face.

Practicing Psychometry

Have you ever been to a second-hand store or an antique shop and got a weird feeling? Or, did you ever feel a bad vibe from a piece of rental furniture for absolutely no reason at all? If this has happened to you, then there is a high chance that you have the ability to perform psychometric readings because you are very sensitive to the energy around you.

All those weird sensations or feelings that you experienced are because of the energy that is given off from the things around you. It can be quite overwhelming for sensitive people to be around shared objects or older items usually found in hotels or flea markets because they have more energy stored in them because of the multiple owners they have encountered in their lifetime. All of these different people have imbued the objects with their own energy, and so when you come in contact with them, you might be sensing and picking up some conflicting auras and energy.

No matter what, you should always keep in mind that psychometry is not exactly backed up by science. People use their individual talents of intuition and other gifts to sense and understand the energies coming out of objects. Every person's method is different from that of the other. For example, some might be picking up an emotion while others might rely on some vision or a particular smell.

If you want to practice psychometry yourself, here are some steps that you should follow –

- **Select a space where you can think without any disturbance.** Thinking with clarity is always the first step. Choose an environment that helps you concentrate on thinking. For example, you can close the shades, play some music you like, or light a candle.

- **Relax.** The importance of relaxation in the process of psychometry has been confirmed by several famous psychics around the world. They claim that it helps you enter a sort of trance state and achieve a much higher level of consciousness. So, it will, in turn, help you form a stronger connection with the object that you are trying to analyze with your psychometric abilities.

- **Touch the object or hold it in your hands.** Pick up the object in your hands or touch it. Another thing that you can do is ask someone else to place the object in your hands.

- **Explore your feelings or sensations.** Start feeling the energy that the object is emanating. Allow yourself to pick up on the energy. Whatever you start feeling or thinking comes from your intuition and is usually correct. In fact, at times, you might also find yourself experiencing intense emotions and visualize complete images in your mind.

- **Say what you are thinking.** Sometimes people assume that what they are thinking is meaningless or trivial and so they don't say anything. But you shouldn't do that because you never know what might be significant for the object you are reading.

Using Psychometry

Scrying and psychometry have some noticeable similarities between them, but at the same time, there are some differences as well. When you psychometrize an object, you delve into the astral vibrations that it is emanating. You first hold it in your hands and keep cradling it while you sense the vibrations. After that, you can pass it from one hand to the other and then even turn it around in your palms. Your awareness of the object and its energy will keep increasing the more you increase your contact with it.

When you finally enter this state of tranquility and ultimate relaxation, you let go of your analytical thinking and allow your reflective capabilities to start acting. This gives your consciousness a free pass to receive the sensations from the astral vibrations of the object. This type of reading is purely instinctual in nature.

After a while, when you are further into this relaxed state, you will feel an increase in the flow of the energy, and this increase will allow you to receive the signals in a passive manner. It's like you keep listening as the object keeps talking. The psychic material starts forging its own course, and you enter a state where you are 'dreaming awake.' The stages keep unfolding in a progressive way. In fact, some people compare this process of psychometry with that of the water lilies and how they grow. The concept goes something like this – the lake with its placid and serene water resembles your mind, and the water lilies represent the material bound by psychometry. Here, the lilies blossom from the depths of the lake into consciousness, just like your mind.

Similar to scrying, there are various forms in which the object can present itself to you – it can be feelings, ideas, or mental imagery. But whatever it is that is coming to your consciousness – you should say it out loud and verbalize it. So, even if you are alone and practicing psychometry, this is a good way of doing it. The vibrations are interpreted by when your mind delves deeper into your unconscious mind. The predictions are even truer when they arise from the depth of your consciousness.

Your proficiency in predicting the astral vibrations will keep on increasing as you make further progress into the art of psychometry. With time, you, too, will improve.

How to Do a Reading?

Just like any other skill, the more you practice, the better you will become at giving readings. With practice, it will become easier too. Psychometry can be mastered by anyone as long as you can display the right amount of empathy.

So, while performing a psychometric reading, here are some of the basic steps that you need to follow –

- The first step is to wash your hands with water. Then, dry them completely. This step ensures that all the residual energy in your hands is washed off, but you don't need to be hospital sterile for this. Once the existing energy is washed off, it will no longer interfere with your readings.

- Now, create some warm-up energy by rubbing your hands together. This energy is created through friction.

- The next step is to check and understand whether some energy has been created or not. For this, start by placing your palms in a way that they are facing each other. Now, start pulling them apart. Remember that you have to pull them apart by approximately a quarter of an inch. Do you feel any energy or some weird sensation between your palms? If you do, then energy is present, and you are all set to do a reading! But if not, then it means that you have to rub your hands a bit more, and energy will be created.

- Now, take the item you want to read in your hands. It is always advisable that you begin your reading with something that is more of the personal kind and is a small object. For example, a piece of jewelry that holds sentimental value is a good place to start. For beginners, it makes it easier to go past the initial exercise. Another thing to keep in mind is that it would work well for you if the person whose belonging you are using is not someone you know closely; for example, you can ask one of your family friends to lend you a family heirloom jewelry for a couple of days.

- The next step is probably the most important one – you need to relax! Take whatever measures you need to for this – you can even choose to close your eyes.

- Now, open your mind and allow thoughts to come in. Allow the feelings, emotions, images, and memories to come into your mind because these are being sent by the energy that is stored in the object. So, what are you sensing – taste, smell, see, or hear?

I am listing some very important questions that you can use during psychometric readings –

- Who does the object belong to?

- Can you sense the personality of the owner after holding the object?

- What are the experiences or memories that the owner had while they had the object with themselves?

- Has the owner passed away, or is he/she still alive?

In the beginning, when you try to perform such readings, the first thing that you will sense is emotions because that is the strongest energy that is there. Three of the most common and powerful emotions that people feel in a psychometric reading are love, fear, and hate. These are often the strongest vibes that come off an object.

Another important factor to keep in mind during your psychometric readings is that you don't necessarily require an object that was physically used or worn by someone. The more you practice and become an expert, you will find yourself performing readings even from things like graves, homes, and photographs. The best way to take the next step and improve your reading is to find a photograph of a family member who passed away, and then you can try to connect with the spirit by performing a reading.

Pointers to Keep in Mind

By now, you probably have a pretty good idea about psychometry, and in this section, we are going to wrap it up by going over some of the pointers that you need to remember.

1. When you are just a beginner, it is best that you practice psychometry on your own without anyone else present in the room. This will prevent any distractions from coming in your way. During these sessions, you must have a tape recorder in place that will help you for later references as you can listen to whatever you said during that session. There's another advantage of recording the reading – this will ensure that you don't have to remember every tiny detail regarding the object.

2. To gain more experience in psychometric readings, you should try to use different types of objects that will give off a distinct astral vibration. This will provide you with the opportunity of realizing what different things feel like. A good rule of thumb would be to select objects based on different occasions that might have some contrasted distinguishing features as well as some common traits. This will, in turn, give you the confidence and ability to understand different vibrations in each case. For example, you can start with an old and used novel and then also try to psychometrically analyze a used prayer book. Next, you can take a newly-tumbled gemstone or a piece of used jewelry. Take your time throughout this process. There is no need to rush from one object to the other. This is a part of your self-training, and when you do it with care, it can be very self-rewarding, at the same time, fascinating. Once you have practiced enough and feel confident, you can move on to perform psychometric readings for family members or people you know.

3. You might find groups where people practice psychometry. Here, the benefit is that you get objects with a verified history that you can analyze. On a

typical psychometry session, people in the group might bring objects from their own family that you can read. But whoever brings an object should always do so after wrapping it carefully in a piece of clear polythene or paper (not with anything printed on it). The wrapping should be opened only by the psychometrist before reading the object. At the last part of the meeting, verification of the psychometrist's reading is done to check how accurate the psychometrist was.

Tips for Beginners

Now, in the last section of this chapter, I have some tips for my readers who are new to psychometry. I sincerely hope these tips help you out –

- **If your readings are a bit muddled or inaccurate in the beginning, don't feel discouraged by it.** Just like most other things in life, it takes time to get better at psychometric readings. The more you practice, the better you will become. Remember that even the most renowned psychometrists of the world don't always produce 100% accurate readings. Their accuracy rate is usually something between 80-90%. The remaining 10-20% of the time, they are off.

- **Don't judge the impressions right away.** Whether you are practicing with an object from a friend or providing a serious psychometric reading, this is true for all instances. Sometimes, the sensations of images that you are receiving might be confusing and make no sense to you, but after further analysis, it is often discovered that those nonsensical impressions are of importance to the owner of the object. There will be some very detailed impressions, and there will be utterly vague ones – don't be so quick to judge.

- **Psychometry is rooted in truth, even according to science.** Several experts believe that psychometry is more about natural human ability, so anyone who wishes to perform it can do it. All you need is to hone your skills and practice as much as you can. The energy from the past, also referred to as vibrations, is present in all objects around you, especially those with some significant meaning or emotional value. If you pay attention and try to read these vibrations, your mind will tell you what they are trying to say. Once again, it's all about how well you hone your skills.

So, wrapping up, here are some of the things that we learned in this chapter –

- Psychometry is defined as the process through which you bring emotional impressions or any other type of knowledge into your consciousness after your unconscious mind has picked up on the energy vibrations from the object concerned and its astral substance. The object itself produced some vibrations. But other than that, the human beings who were in possession of these objects leave behind their emotional imprints on them, and these emotions are always the easiest for your unconscious mind to 'pick up.'

- In general, when a psychometrist tries to read an object, the first thing they can sense is the most recent impressions that have been left on that object and not the earlier ones. But if an earlier impression is very powerful, then it can come to you once rather than a later one that is comparatively weaker—another thing

67

to keep in mind that repetition can often intensify impressions of the past.

- In order to analyze an object through psychometry, you have to touch it or hold it in your hands. At that moment, all the outer levels of your psyche that are more analytical in nature need to be stilled. You simply have to sit and listen while you allow the object to talk. You are said to be in a state of 'dreaming awake' when you are psychometrically analyzing something.

- Whatever you feel during the analysis, you need to speak it out loud. It is also advised that during your practice sessions, you should keep a recorder to record what you are saying. This will keep all your utterances recorded, and so, you don't need to try hard to remember what had come to you before.

- Until and unless you are fully confident, it's better not to go into group psychometry. In the initial days, it is better to practice alone.

- For practicing more psychometry, make it a habit to collect items – both old and new – because each of those items will have a different influence, and the more you practice, the more you will be able to distinguish between them.

- All the objects that you have collected with the intent of psychometrically analyzing them should be stored extremely carefully. You need to keep them wrapped in a clean piece of cloth or paper without anything printed on them. You can wrap it only before you want to examine them. This should be made into a custom.

- When you are in a group psychometry session, if there are things that you want to discuss, reserve them for the end.

- Lastly, don't forget to meditate. Such good practices in daily life will only improve your psychic ability, and all the levels of your psyche will remain in proper harmony with each other.

Chapter 6: Importance of Spiritual Quotient

In previous times, people used to consider only a person's IQ as a valid mode of intelligence that could be acknowledged and respected at the end of the day. But fortunately, time and people changed for the better over time, and it was during the 1990s that people started grasping the concept of emotional quotient or emotional intelligence. It became common knowledge over time that how people deal and conduct their emotional intelligence could be as important and at times more so than their intelligence quotient. Some more years passed, and the concept of measuring one's intelligence in ways not prescribed by society started becoming more acceptable to people, and it was during the 2000s that people came face to face with the concept of spiritual quotient and its different facets.

The question that arises then is what exactly this spiritual quotient is. What is required is to understand it completely and how someone can truly exercise it in their day-to-day lives. Another set of questions that emerge naturally out of this is that if a spiritual quotient is really a form of intelligence, then, like other forms of intelligence, can it be used to fight problems like terrorism or psychological problems, say insensitivity?

How Did This Term Originate?

Danah Zohar and Ian Marshall can be attributed to coining these terms "Spiritual Quotient" or "Spiritual Intelligence," which are based on their path-breaking book which is called "SQ: Connecting with Our Spiritual Intelligence." Danah and Ian, while describing Spiritual Quotient, tells us that it is the most fundamental of all our intelligence, and it is our spiritual quotient that helps us develop the inner capacities in us of value, meaning, and that of vision—allowing us to strive hard and giving us the passion and courage to dream. Our values always play a role in any action that we take, and that is perhaps the reason our spiritual quotient helps us to explore the beliefs and values in us so that we can live up to our full potential and our lives can become much more satisfying and worthy.

Aspects of Spirituality

1. **Responsibility** – It is very important for every one of us to have some purpose in life because, let's face it, we are not going to be around forever. That is why it becomes imperative to use every moment that we have at our disposal in ways that could be helpful for us and meaningful for everyone around us. We need to realize that we have come here on earth with certain responsibilities towards ourselves and others and need to accept and respect those responsibilities.

2. **Humility** – It is very important for everyone to realize that we are just one among the 7 billion people who inhabit the earth. While it is important to know one's worth, it is also important to maintain a certain level of humility at all points because only if we can give other people their due respect will we be able to give ourselves the respect that we deserve.

3. **Happiness** – We need to find out for ourselves what exactly happiness means to us. It is a concept that has no fixed definition. It depends from person to person, and it is upon us to find out all its connotations and work hard towards actualizing that in our lives.

Difference Between EQ, IQ, and SQ

1. **IQ – Intelligence Quotient** basically refers to the attempts that we make to measure human intelligence. Every human being has their respective cognitive strengths as well as weaknesses, but psychologists have found out that there is one common component among us all known as the general intelligence or G. this can be beautifully defined in the words of Robert Feldman, "the capacity to understand the world, think rationally and use resources effectively when faced with challenges."

2. **EQ – Emotional Quotient** can be defined as the ways that we choose for ourselves to manage all our emotions in a positive manner so that no matter what situations we might face in life, we should be well equipped emotionally to deal with them. In the mid-1990s, Daniel Goleman came up with this, and it has been revealed through proper studies that those people with a higher EQ find it easier to deal with any kind of situation than those whose score is less. People with a higher emotional quotient understand their own emotions better and thereby can deal with their own psychological situations maturely. Things like managing stress and dealing with conditions like depression can get a lot easier if the concerned person's EQ is high.

3. **SQ – Spiritual Quotient** is something that we need to go beyond our cognitive and emotional skills if needed to be understood. It is that understanding present deep within us that makes us realize that we are, after all, mortals, and so, we need to do our best to make our existence worthy by offering something fruitful and helpful that could be helpful for others. It paves the way for acceptance of one's weaknesses as well as achievements and to live a life of humility and respect. It also helps give things and people their necessary importance and balance work, personal life, and inner growth.

12 Principles of Spiritual Intelligence

Each of us has been endowed with these three above-mentioned kinds of intelligence, and it depends on us as to how we use them to our advantage while dealing with any kind of situation in life. Some of us have been equipped with more of one of these, but they are all present in us. They can be fostered in us individually as per need. And as per as spiritual quotient is considered, there are twelve principles that can be looked at in order to foster it properly. Let us look at them in detail.

Both physically and mentally, we all are consciously an adaptive system, so we hope to build flexible collaborations that will have dialogues with the environment around us. The principles that will be discussed now are great modes of such collaboration that will be underpinned by values, vision, meaning, and purpose.

- **Self-Awareness** – It has to be kept in mind that that spiritual self-awareness is different from the otherwise self-awareness that we know, which is basically having an idea about one's own thoughts and feelings at a given point in time. Spiritual self-awareness is being aware of what an individual feels, what an individual loves and cares for genuinely, and what they live for in life. Spiritual self-awareness also encompasses those things that an individual feels so connected with that they can even die for. Being spiritually self-aware is to remain true to oneself and others around. Only if we are remaining true to what we live for will we be able to communicate honestly with our deeper self. When that communication becomes strong, our communication with the outer world becomes strong as well.

- **Spontaneity** – It is not only enough to do whatever you feel at that point in time. It is equally important to do that work with self-discipline, self-control, and practice. Being spiritually spontaneous implies that we will be emotionally capable enough not to let our emotional baggage be a burden. Be it our childhood problems or some prejudices that we might be having, or be it even certain assumptions. We should be capable enough to regard things and situations for what they are and be responsive accordingly. Most importantly, we should be able to take proper responsibility for all that we do.

- **Being Vision and Value-Led** – It becomes essential to lead a life that has its values set based on a positive vision. Every work that we do, every action that we take should have a purpose to it. A purpose that makes it worthy of being done or thought of. Our life should also be like that, a life that is worthy and has the vision to strive for. We should have certain reasons for whatever we do. Be it education or job. It shouldn't be restricted to completing that one exam or reaching that one profit margin. We need to constantly ask ourselves questions like "what is the purpose that I want to achieve with my education?" or "what help will it be to the world if I reach this profit margin?" only when we are led in life by a vision, will our lives have any value.

- **Holism** – If we take quantum physics into consideration, holism could be defined as a system so integrated that each part needs to be defined with respect to the other parts. If we put this definition into a real-life perspective, we will find out that each and every one of us is defined in terms of others. That we are existing is bound to be related with others that we are in direct contact with. For example, if we take a speaker who is giving a speech to a large audience. At that point in time, the existence of that speaker is true only because there is an audience listening to him at that point. The relevance of the audience is also true because the speaker exists. This was a simple way of getting a broader picture of what Holism is. The faster we realize this, the better for us because only then will we be able to work in harmony as a whole.

- **Compassion** – Spiritual compassion will help you feel what the other person is feeling and act accordingly. It is not only enough to recognize or just to accept what the other person is going through. Only when you make an effort to actually feel what the other person is going through will it become easier for everyone to lead a much happier life or, for that matter, a much more respectable life. Compassion makes you and others become human beings who lends a hand to those in need, and it is always a joy to be around such people, to know that there are people who, instead of trying to judge you or take advantage of your situation, is willing to help you and support you mentally.

- **Celebration of Diversity** - It is extremely important to respect differences and celebrate the diversity around, because everyone and everything matters, even at times when things are always not in line with what we feel. Celebrating diversity is important because that teaches us what actually matters and that this world and our society have a lot more to offer than what we might think. Let us think this through for a moment. Most of us have had the opportunity to grow up in an educational environment where we had classmates from all sectors of society, from different classes of economy, catering to different religious beliefs. This is one of the most necessary things that every child should experience, as this will teach a child from the very beginning that nothing matters other than one's own deeds and values. Where they come from should be the least of our concerns because what matters is where we are going. This feeling is intimately related to compassion.

It is really a beautiful emotion to be able to celebrate the differences in people so that as a society, we can rejoice in every aspect of human life that we have. So that instead of focusing on things that are problematic, we can rejoice in things that are beautiful and that will bring joy in everyone's lives. As human beings, it is our responsibility to accept the fact that not everything will be the way we want to, and at the same time, it is necessary to understand that others' opinions are not wrong. Getting to know new things will invariably broaden our horizons and open our minds to a bigger and better world.

- **Field Independence** – Field Independence is actually a very simple thing if you understand it properly. It basically means having the courage to stand up for one's beliefs and focus on what you actually want rather than getting scared or persuaded into what others are trying to believe. It is basically to have the courage to stand in front of a host of people and say what you have to, not lose your ground and not let anyone force you into believing something else that you otherwise wouldn't have. It also means to not be unaware of what others have to say, listen to them properly, consider their points carefully, and not get easily swayed away. It is a stable balance between not disregarding others and, at the same time, not giving in easily.

- **Humility** – Humility is like being on the other side of the spectrum from field independence. It is to understand that no matter what happens, you have got to keep your head about things and not sit on your high horse all the time. As important it is to stand your ground about the views that you have of things, it is important to not disregard others and accept the faults you have any. If you feel like you are lacking somewhere and have committed any mistakes, then it is best for you as well as for others with whom you are interacting. If you accept those mistakes and instead of wasting time, work hard on correcting yourself and the situation. In life, there will come many people who will know more than you. It is only natural to feel intimidated by them. But let that situation turn into an unpleasant one. Use it to your advantage to learn and better yourself.

- **Tendency to Ask Fundamental "Why?" Questions** – Anyone who is aware of how this world works knows this basic thing that none of us are born with all the knowledge, and none of us can ever match up to the limits of knowledge that is available to us. So, if we think that what we know is enough, then we are wrong. There is always something more than what meets the eye. If we are to truly enlarge our horizon, we simply have to get into the habit of asking such "why?" questions. "Why is it that I have to be a part of this?", "Why is this thing done this way and not the other way round?". At an initial stage, it might feel a bit silly to ask these questions, but, in the long run, we will be in a position of advantage as we will slowly become more insightful. This habit of asking questions and not taking things for granted or at their face value is sure to make us into more inquisitive individuals who are emotionally more prepared to grasp things than others who are not so flexible in their approach.

- **Ability to Reframe** – It is essential to have the sensibility to look at what you have done objectively and, if need be, to change things when the time is right. Mind you. It is not easy to do this because not everyone has the courage to reframe. But, for those who know, understands how essential it is to detach yourself from your work for some point and look at it from a neutral point of view so that you can see for yourself what mistakes you have made and what are the things that need to be changed. You have to make this into a habit to take some time off at regular intervals and look back at what you have done so far. It is bound to be beneficial for everyone if this process is to be followed. This makes you always keep your feet on the ground and become aware of your mistakes. At the same time, it helps you always be prepared for changes. It keeps you updated with recent trends and makes your work much more relatable and contemporary.

- **Positive Use of Adversity** – At every point in time, life teaches us something new. It gives us reasons to go ahead and improve ourselves. It also teaches us that we are, after all, only humans, and it is alright to make mistakes. What life also teaches us is that the problems we face can all be used in a positive way if we have such a mindset. All the adversities that we face teach us many important things, and all we need to do is keep a close eye on them. Firstly, we need to analyze why did we face that adversity in the first place. I am sure that we will find some definite reason for that. We need to avoid those the next time. Secondly, we need to do a thorough search of what exactly did this teach us and make sure we use that detail to our advantage the next time.

- **Sense of Vocation** – The sense of vocation as a principle helps in summing up our spiritual intelligence with our spiritual capital. At present, it usually refers to practices such as medicine, law, and teaching. If a business becomes a vocational practice, it will invariably cater to a larger audience, and it will start having a nobler purpose, helping a larger community of people. The word vocation comes from the Latin word "vocare," which translates to "to be called." Initially, it referred to the practice of a priest calling out to God. It got its new connotations recently. As it has the capacity to reach out to a larger audience, it is sure to be of great help to many. So, if your spiritual quotient has the sense of vocation embedded in it, you are sure to become a source of aid for people around you.

Importance of SQ

Spiritual Quotient helps a person enhance their insight and their creative abilities. What is interesting to know is that, unlike Intelligence Quotient or Emotional Quotient, Spiritual Quotient helps a person deal with modern problems like inconsiderateness or even terrorism. Already emerging as the next huge thing for scientific consideration, Spiritual Quotient helps us deal with problems like lack of humanness which directly relates to a person's psyche like human awareness and human consciousness.

The spiritual quotient has the capability to recognize intelligence and senses that are beyond the five senses that we have. The universal power responsible for governing everything that happens within and without us, and this power is omnipresent. We are required to surrender to this power with all our awareness. Our spiritual quotient helps us understand all these things in greater detail so that we can get in touch with the core of strength that resides within us. That, in turn, helps us to balance the powerhouse without us, ensuring that there is a sense of harmony in the world and in our environment. It becomes easier to deal with the ups and downs and live a happier life.

Even the corporate world, which is devoid of emotions and feelings per se, has a lot of use of this spiritual quotient because no matter how professional that work sector is, it ultimately deals with human beings. It is not humanly possible to treat them like robots, with emotions and feelings, and then to expect them to garner good results. For any person to give their best in their work and at the same time for any workspace to have positive energy, it is important for everyone around and involved to have a healthy and spiritually progressive environment.

Using Spiritual Intelligence to Change Human Behaviour

Only when people treat each other as fellow human beings and start acting that way they should will we be able to make a world that is worthy, and all this is possible if we put our spiritual quotient to use. We might often come across people who are unreasonable, who are illogical, and often self-centered. We might be kind, but then it is possible for us to be taken advantage of by people who are shrewd. It might be the case that we successfully make only a few genuine friends in life. But that doesn't mean we will stop. It means that we try to work harder each day so that we and our future generations have a reason to live happily. No matter how much IQ or EQ we have, at the end of the day, if we don't have enough spiritual quotient, then nothing will eventually matter. We simply have to continue doing good. We have to continue being the best version of ourselves and help others to be the same so that the world becomes a better place to live in. It might so be that we will be called naïve, but that doesn't matter. The quality of life matters and that can only be made better with how deep our spiritual quotient is, and to what extent we are applying it.

Chapter 7: How to Recognize If You Are An Empath?

As social beings who are dependent on social interactions and emotional connections among us, we all experience and possess the feeling of empathy towards others, only varying in degree from people to people. We may relate to it as kindness, and almost all of us strive to become a person who is kind, who cares about and considers the feelings of other people. Empathy is, as defined by Webster's New World Dictionary, "a feeling, emotional or intellectual identification with another." The ability to understand the experiences and feelings of others outside of an individual's own perspective is known as empathy.

For example, say that your friend is going through a loss in the family. In such a scenario, it is empathy that allows you to understand the pain that your friend is going through and the emotions that she is dealing with, even if the situation and the circumstances are completely different from where you stand and what you are feeling. However, that is not all. As an empath, you take all of this a little further. An empath actually senses and feels these emotions that the other person is feeling as though it is their very own. If we explain in simpler words, it can be said that as an empath, someone else's pain or happiness or anger becomes your own pain, happiness, and anger. Empaths are hypersensitive people who are able to understand, feel, tune in to, and resonate with the feelings of others around them. This can happen voluntarily, but sometimes, this becomes the case even involuntarily.

What is a Psychic Empath?

While all of us strive and work towards becoming a better version of ourselves filled with kindness and understanding of those around us, some people are born with abilities beyond normal, ordinary kindness that we know of. Such people have the ability to connect and resonate with the emotions and feelings of other people on a very deep and powerful level that is beyond normal capabilities. Do you often feel an instant connection with the feelings and emotions of other people around you, like your friends and family, even when you are in a very different emotional state altogether? Let's dive into what psychic empathy truly is, how it works, and what it means. This will help you recognize and understand your own nature and abilities.

Empathy, as discussed earlier, is the ability to identify, understand, and feel sympathy towards the feelings of other people. The term psychic empath is derived from empathy itself and is used quite frequently to refer to a psychic individual who is intensely sensitive and receptive to other people's feelings, emotions, and energies that they experience all these emotions as though it is their own. The term psychic empath is becoming more and more popular and common in the psychic and the paranormal realms. This is because psychic empaths have the ability to probe deeply into the soul of another person and help them to identify and experience the feelings and emotions that may have been blocked. They display profound sensitivity to the emotional states of both themselves as well as others. Having said that, sometimes, it is even possible that the emotional states of others may overpower their own emotions as they are barely able to distinguish their own feelings from someone else's. There is always a probability that the empaths themselves are not aware of their abilities and may just refer to it as being super sensitive around others.

There is a distinct difference between what empathy is and what psychic empathy is, and it is very important not to get these two confused. Empathy is a human emotion that exists in all of us in varying degrees, and we all are able to connect and sympathize with people and their feelings. Psychic empaths, on the other hand, have an extrasensory perception that is above normal human empathy. Psychic empaths can easily detect and identify the feelings and emotions of people around them, and they can pick these up on non-visual, non-verbal cues. They just know what people are going through and the emotions they are feeling regardless of the fact whether that person is letting out his/her feelings at all or not. Therefore, they feel the moods, intentions, and motives of other people unconsciously. Some psychic empaths can even feel the emotional impact that is radiated by people, animals, and even plants in the surrounding environment and even the universe. While everybody who has healthy emotional states is able to feel empathy, psychic empaths have the ability to experience the emotions of others directly.

In addition to that, a psychic empath also differs distinctly from a traditional psychic as the former does not have the ability to sense, see, hear, or read into the spiritual realm or get glimpses of the future possibilities; rather, they are able to read and identify emotions. They have the ability to instantly enter into another person's aura. They can connect with the feelings and emotions the other person is feeling deeply and can understand their life experiences almost instantly and very intimately. However, similar to other psychic abilities, an individual may be born with it, and this ability is often known to be multi-generational. But, it is believed that a person might be able to obtain this ability after a near-death experience. This is not a confirmed statement open to debate, but this is widely believed.

Types of Empaths

Some psychic empaths have the ability to sense the emotions and how others are feeling by tapping into their aura or energetic vibrations, while others, on the other hand, are able to use a unique ability known as Claircognition to simply "know" the emotions and the underlying feelings of a person without having any obvious verbal, vision, or any type of clue. If you feel like you can instantly connect with someone's feelings on a personal and deep level and even feel very overwhelmed when you are in a crowd full of people due to their emotions draining your energy, you might be a psychic empath yourself. From empaths who are physical to emotional empaths, from earth empaths to animal empaths, there are several types of empaths present. These differences come forward due to the different types of ways through which they obtain information. Each one of these empaths has distinct abilities. Here are the main and most common types of psychic empaths that may help you recognize which one is you:

Emotional empath

As depicted by the name, these types of psychic empaths experience the emotions of others. It does not matter whether or not the people in question are related to these empaths or not. They may feel the sorrow of a fellow passenger who has just lost his pet, or the excitement of someone on the street who has just passed the interview, or the joy of the family that is expecting. These emotions do not necessarily have to be exhibited to be felt by the emotional empath; they just feel these emotions even if they are well hidden inside by these people.

However, as shown in the example above, this ability has both pros and cons as the empath may suffer the pain of someone who is suffering while they can also rejoice in the joy of someone else. This type of empath may feel emotionally drained by the negative and narcissistic emotions that they may feel as the day goes on. For example, the emotions of people who suffer from low self-esteem and always find themselves in crisis mode, seeking constant validation and reassurance can negatively impact the emotional well-being of the empath as well.

Physical empath

Physical empaths have the ability to experience the physical ailments of those around them. They respond to the physical symptoms and actions of people around them. Therefore, when someone is laughing or crying and expressing their emotions physically, the physical empath is most likely to mirror these actions regardless of whether you are experiencing these emotions yourself. Likewise, if you are around people who are suffering from illness or having some kind of body ache, you might experience similar discomfort as them. This ability has a lot of negative impacts on the well-being of the empath as it is obviously not delightful to experience the physical pain of someone. Hospitals prove to be a dreadful place to these empaths, as this generally happens when they are in the vicinity of injured people. However, in some cases, this can occur even across the further distance between the empath and the sufferer.

Due to all these negative impacts and effects, it becomes very important for the empath to train and concentrate on coping mechanisms. This is a major problem surrounding the physical empaths as they unconsciously manifest the physical symptoms of others onto themselves; therefore, it is important and helpful that they are surrounded with healthy and happy people most of the time so that these negative effects are set off. Another very important strategy that might help you if you identify yourself with one of these types of empaths is that you should set healthy boundaries with people and learn that it is okay to say "no" to spending time with people who will add to your stress levels.

Claircognizant empath

These types of empaths have the ability to identify and understand the true nature of any given situation or thing. They are able to instantly recognize when someone is lying or is misleading, and similarly, they always just know the ruth without any logical base. Not only that, they have the ability to know what is to be done and what is important in any situation. Due to this profound ability, the claircognizant empaths are the ideal people to turn to whenever faced with a crisis. The hallmark characteristic of this psychic ability is the empathetic ability to feel relaxed and at peace even when they face a crisis situation.

Psychometric empath

Psychometric empaths have the ability to receive impressions and even decode them, receive information, and on the whole, energy from physical and inanimate objects and even places. Some examples of these are jewelry, homes, pictures, piece of clothing, and so on. The information that they perceive and receive can be in the form of emotions, images, sounds, tastes, etc. A psychometric empath has the ability to know about the history of the object and receive information about an object by simply touching the object. After they have made physical contact with the object, they are able to get information about the owner of the object, the owner's life, the past of the object, and even the experiences that the owner had during the time he had been using or wearing that particular object.

Earth empath

Earth empaths are empaths who are in tune with nature and the environment. They possess the ability to feel and connect with the world and the universe as a whole. For instance, a forest fire can cause them to feel pain, and further, they are even able to sense earthquakes and severe storms even before it happens. These can come as physical symptoms. These symptoms and the sensations they feel before a natural calamity depends on the empath themselves and the disaster that is making its way. As an outcome of feeling and resonating with the earth, they feel calm, relaxed, and in peace after the disaster has passed. Earth empaths rejoice in being outdoors amongst nature, and they thrive when they experience the miracles of nature and are among the natural energy sources. Earth empaths get energized when they see a beautiful sunrise, waterfalls, and other natural beauties. However, the negative impacts of pollution and environmental toxins can cause detrimental effects to them that are heightened than other normal human beings.

Telepathic empath

Telepathy, as most of us know, is a communication type that operates from mind to mind. The information is sent from the mind of a sender to another person who is the receiver without any verbal communication whatsoever. Telepathic empaths, therefore, as the name suggests, have the ability to read the thoughts of others accurately. They can tell what others around them think, including people, animals, even plants and trees.

Intuitive empath

Similar to emotional empaths, intuitive empaths also connect to the feelings and emotions of the people around them. However, there is more to that in these types of empaths as not only do they pick up on the emotions of others, but they also have the ability to see what truly lies underneath the feelings and emotions on the surface. They go beyond these emotions to see what lies underneath. They sense what is being hidden, unspoken, and not expressed. Most of the time, this type of empath also has the ability to understand whether a person is being truthful or is lying. Intuitive empaths are hence, good judges of character who can find out when someone is not being honest and can therefore find out the reality and truth in every situation.

Medium empath

Also known as mediumship, these types of empaths are quite different from the rest as their ability differs and helps them to sense, i.e., hear, feel, etc., the presence and the energies of the spirits of even the deceased individuals. They are even able to consult spirits or other supernatural beings. They can see the past, present, and even future events of someone else. They can do so as they receive this information by tuning in to the energy that is surrounding the person in question. While it sure sounds fascinating and maybe a very useful ability, being a medium empath is not easy at all. They are known to be very sensitive to the environment and are often prone to contacting allergies without any known reason and/or show physical symptoms that are inexplicable.

Another drawback that is believed to be associate with medium empaths is that they may not always be able to work to their optimum level as the energies and the field they work in are very sensitive. To further elaborate, no matter how much they are willing to try and help you, sometimes they may not be able to do so for everyone, sometimes they may not be able to solve their own problems. It is a very important step for psychic empaths to learn to differentiate and shield themselves from others' feelings as a means to avoid the bombardment of information all the time upon themselves. If you relate to this type of psychic empathy, it is important that you learn to differentiate between your own feelings, emotions, and senses than that of the others. With enough practice and patience, a psychic empath should be able to tap into their abilities when in need and then switch it to the background when they are getting on with other things in life. However, because it is such a sensitive ability and, as mentioned earlier, it is not at all easy for medium empaths, sometimes, even with these shielding techniques, they need considerable time alone to shake off the emotions and keep themselves emotionally balanced.

Dream empath

To normal humans, dreams can be very difficult to make sense of, but empaths of this type are very gifted when it comes to unraveling the mysteries of the subconscious mind.

Dream empaths are able to remember their dreams vividly and in detail without even missing the most minute detail. They do not forget their dreams as soon as they wake up, as many normal humans do. Therefore, as they remember these details, they acquire knowledge and understanding about the situations that are going on in their lives and the solution as to what should be done. These dreams give them wisdom. Not only do they have the ability to bring clarity and solution to their own lives, but they also help other people to decipher the meaning behind their dreams and how it may apply to real-life situations helping them find clarity. Dream empaths can go beyond physical reality and are able to dream of the intuitive information from the universe while they sleep.

Precognitive empath

These types of empaths are blessed with the ability to strongly feel an event or circumstance that is bound to happen. Often, they receive premonitions as to what is going to happen that may manifest as dreams, or even sensations, both emotional and physical, and visions. They have the ability to sense or receive some form of warning before something dreadful takes place. Precognitive empaths often feel the feeling of incomprehensible doom. Developing and coping up with this ability might take some time and patience. However, it makes a huge difference and helps if an empath is able to use this ability to make the right decisions and avoid potential threats.

Geomantic empath

Geomantic empaths are very well accustomed to the environment and even the energies of the world. They have the ability to identify and read signals from the energy transmission of the air, water, soil, even rocks. The skills they possess come in very handy when detecting bad weather conditions, underground water, or any possible natural disaster. A very good example of such empaths would be animals. Animals are aware of the natural calamities before they happen, and therefore they know when to hide in times of tsunami, flood, etc.

Plant empath

Just as emotional empaths and physical empaths are able to connect to other people and their feelings, plant or flora empaths are known to form similar connections with plants. They are always in tune with the flora around them, such as the trees, flowers, etc. They are said to even be able to communicate with the plants, can hear their thoughts, and understand them. Therefore, they always know just what a plant needs to be healthy. Not only that, as they are one with the flora around them, they have the ability of healing and herbalism. Not only do they communicate with plants, but this spiritual connection can also be carried to form human connections as well.

Animal empath

Also known as the fauna empaths, they have the ability to connect with animals similar to flora empaths. They connect to their energy and can sense whether the animal is happy, sad, in pain, or is suffering. They can hear and understand the thoughts of animals and can even make their own thoughts understood.

However, sometimes an animal empaths ability to connect and sense the animals' energy is only connected to one species of animals, for reasons unknown. It can be a terrible experience for animal empaths to be in or around places like a zoo where the animals are captivated and sometimes even abused. They cannot tolerate any violence or cruelty to animals and are very sensitive about it.

Are You a Psychic Empath?

Do you exhibit strong empathetic tendencies? Do you feel the emotions that are oddly not even connected to your own life? Were you able to relate to any of the extraordinary abilities of psychic empaths that we discussed above? If yes, chances are you might actually be one. To make sure whether or not you are one, you must make sure that you try to separate your thoughts, emotions, and feelings from those which you perceive from others. By doing do you will able to differentiate your feelings. That way, you will be in a better position to make sure whether or not you are functioning on individual capacity or from information, emotions, and feelings that you have been perceiving. Here are a few questions that you might want to ask yourself:

a) Do you gain the knowledge and understanding about other people without being said anything, on a deeper and more accurate level, to be just a coincidence?

b) Do you experience Deja Vu on a regular basis?

c) Do you find yourself avoiding and neglecting your own feelings while you practice emotional labor on behalf of others?

d) Do you find yourself reacting more strongly than anyone else in the room when it comes to emotional situations and topics?

Most psychic empaths do not realize their abilities and their full extent. Sometimes, they do not even realize they are psychic. Psychic empaths have shared that most of them grew up differently, feeling weird and like they did not fit in with people around them. The heightened sensitivity that they experience may have led to intense interactions with other people. If you are still not sure but feel like you have a very high degree of empathy than others, below are some common signs you might be a psychic empath.

Signs You Might Be A Psychic Empath

It is important to note that all of the following signs may not be relatable to all empaths as we all know by now empaths differ and have different abilities. However, here are some most common signs that affirm you as an empath:

- Avoiding intense situations that may result in a conflict

- Extreme shyness, nervousness, anxiety in places and situations that are crowded

- Always sought out by people for help or to listen to their problems whenever they are in trouble as they are good listeners and great counselors

- Can tell if someone is lying or not being honest

- Avoiding public places and social encounters pretty often

- Getting attached to animals and/or children easily

- Sensitive to criticism and getting hurt easily

- Feeling a sense of responsibility towards other people and helping people in pain and suffering – empaths sense emotions very quickly and deeply

- Getting attached with characters from movies, novels, etc., emotionally and being able to relate to their emotions as though they are real

- Loving the beautiful harmony music offers. Tendency to drift away while listening to music because it means the opposite of chaos.

- Self-isolating oneself because it is difficult to be close to others, and you need time to heal and separate yourself from the emotions of the people around you

- Your gut feelings and hunches are never wrong.

Once you have confirmed that you are a psychic empath, it becomes very important that you practice some coping strategies and learn to protect yourself and your feelings, as sometimes the pieces of information and feelings that you perceive become so much that it overloads and it will be very difficult to handle. It is important that you do not lose your true feelings and emotions in the sea of emotions that come towards you. However, with practice and patience, psychic empathy is a gift that will help you help others.

How To Deal With Being A Psychic Empath?

Being a psychic empath and having to deal with others' emotions, whether positive or negative, is very difficult. Some empaths even go to extreme lengths to numb the emotions they are perceiving. Therefore, it is crucial to have constructive ways and coping mechanisms to deal with the gift.

- Whenever you are around unpleasant and negative people and sensations, *visualize a shield* that is fluid to separate yourself from them and their emotions.

- Practice meditation and yoga regularly to cleanse your thoughts, feelings, and emotions and release stress.

- Eat nutritious meals as empaths are sensitive people and are affected by the food they put into their bodies. If you eat unhealthy things, you may feel terrible. Eat well to be physically and mentally strong.

- Give yourself a lot of alone time and in that time, allow yourself to recharge, do things that you love and enjoy, and heal away from the interference of others.

- Focus on the positive and absorb as much positive energy as you can. Make a list of all the good things you have done with the gift given to you to look at when you feel overwhelmed or go out into nature and absorb nature's positive energy and channel the negative energy.

As you have seen, being empathetic is what makes you human but not a psychic empath. A psychic empath feels these feelings beyond normal perception, and there are several different empaths. If you have made sure that you are an empath, consider talking to other empaths and be patient and practice your abilities. This gift provides you with wonderful opportunities to help others, but make sure to understand your limitations and take care of yourself.

Chapter 8: Understanding Your Energy As An Empath

If you often feel like you are strongly impacted by the energy emitted by people and spaces, then there are high chances that you might be an *empath*. An empath would also feel drained, exhausted, and burnt out if they do not get adequate time in between social gatherings and events because that way, they would be denied any time to recharge themselves. Empaths are also often moved by things like films, novels, or music – all of which makes them experience emotions far more deeply than an average person would. Due to a high perceptive intuition and feelings, empaths are more prone to feeling emotions in their own body with a higher intensity – both about themselves and other people. Being an empath is quite common. But if you are an empath, you also need to understand how your thought processes are wired so that you are equipped to take proper care of your mind and body while also channeling your empath energy in a better, more meaningful way. In this chapter, we will quickly go through different ways in which you can better understand empath sensitivity and empath energy and the fatigue that can arise from being an empath, and various ways in which they can be tackled.

How are Empaths More Sensitive than Others

Here are the ways in which empaths are considered to be more sensitive than other people around them.

They have a hyper-perceptive emotional system: Most empaths have quite a highly perceptive emotional system, which impacts how they pick up on external energy and react to them. This means that they are more attentive to what is happening around them when compared to other people, which is why they feel drained if they do not give themselves enough time in between different social scenarios and interactions. Empaths need to regularly recharge themselves as they are not just receptive to what people around them are feeling or doing but also to the collective energy of places altogether, increasing the emotional load they have to deal with. This is mostly a reason why normal tasks, like attending a Zoom call or doing grocery might turn out to be more taxing for empaths, as they need to not just act on how they are feeling during the activity but also need to be mindful about the energies given out by other places and people.

Their physical body and energy are also more sensitive: Besides having a highly sensitive emotional system, they are also physically more sensitive to external energy- both individual and collective. This also means that they would feel external sensations- such as those from caffeine, alcohol, or other substances- a lot more strongly than the people around them. They can also be more sensitive to physical sensations such as a change in temperature or any sort of loud noise, or any other disturbing sensation in their surroundings.

Since each empath is different when it comes to how they respond to external energy, it is natural that they also have different thresholds for physical stimuli, and this threshold keeps changing depending upon the circumstances that they are put in. prolonged exposure to any kind of physical stimuli can also sometimes numb an empath to how they react to the stimuli. For example, if they find themselves really bothered by how noisy their workspace is, they might eventually get used to it and stop feeling as disturbed as they do in about six months.

They need to actively learn and practice how to tune others out: Since an empath is naturally more wired to what other people are feeling, it might come in handy for them to learn how to tune others off sometimes and be mindful about it as well. For a lot of other people, blocking someone off from your mind might not feel like a very difficult task and would not even take a lot of conscious efforts, but for empaths, it is an important process of self-care and self-recharge to tune others out after a point and tune back into their feelings once the empaths feel more in control of the situation and more capable of dealing with the emotional overload. While connecting with others at ease is a greatly beneficial quality, it can also get really overwhelming if there are no restraints put upon it, as everyone- including empaths- comes with only limited pools of energy at the end of the day.

They appear to be naturally more kind and compassionate than others: As the name itself suggests, an empath is someone who can feel other people's happiness or discomfort as if they were their own feelings. This naturally makes them kinder, more caring, and more compassionate people, as they have an increased ability to place themselves in others' shoes and understand what someone else is going through without necessarily having gone through the same.

Since empaths feel a lot and are not always able to control how much they should feel for others, if they do not properly connect with their energy, it might become difficult for them to prevent burnout. Therefore, it is important for empaths to show compassion to themselves as well. Sometimes, they need to put themselves and their needs before others. This is because if they get too caught up in the emotional experiences of others, they would not be able to devote a lot of time or effort to control their own emotions. This might leave them feeling bitter and frustrated at times.

In order to avoid these negative feelings of burnout, empaths must develop effective strategies to process their own emotions and prioritize them over other's feelings at all times. Keeping themselves emotionally grounded can also help them in establishing boundaries about emotions so that their own emotional burdens do not spill into others' feelings, and vice versa, and they can deal with all the feelings in their own space and time.

Their energy is easily affected by physical spaces: If you are someone who is usually morse 'picky' about places, then you might actually be an empath and are only drawn towards places whose energy matches with that of yours. A lot of empaths usually prefer clean, organized, and tidy spaces. This is because their physical surroundings have a great impact on them and their energy. An empath can simply walk into a room and feel a sense of energy – positive or negative – which greatly affects how they interact in and to that situation.

If you are an empath, it might be a good idea to inform your friends, partners, or roommates how you like your spaces to be maintained and how sensitive you are to changes in these spaces so that they can be aware of the relationship between your empath energy and your physical environment, and can help you out with how you try to manage this relationship. Other than physical spaces, empaths can also be sensitive to the energy of different kinds of virtual and digital spaces.

They are easily receptive to collective energy: Since empaths are highly perceptive, they are more open and sensitive to collective energy. This collective energy could mean anything, spanning from a park to a town or even a culture. The empath could be receptive to the collective energy in many ways- they can be exposed to the energy both indirectly (by reading on the news about an event that has happened somewhere far away) or directly (by coming in physical contact with space; for example, by taking a walk or shopping at a crowded market).

To keep a check on how they are being exposed to this energy and how they can react to it, it might help empaths to work on developing certain daily, weekly, and monthly grounding practices and then build a routine around all of those. These practices- such as meditating every morning, meeting your loved ones for dinner every month without fail, or listening to a particular podcast or reading a book- will help an empath feel stable and will foster a sense of regularity and routine in their lives, so that their energy stays under control and does not deflect due to the impact a strong sense of collective energy might have on them.

Other than that, empaths can also channel their sensitivity to collective energy to bring about a positive, impactful change. A lot of empaths are inspired by this sensitivity to become activists and other kinds of changemakers. On the other hand, empaths can also actively seek the type of energy they want to feel and use that to make themselves feel more at peace or more lively, depending on their mood.

They find themselves to be the strongest in the clairsentient pathway: Since an empath is naturally very intuitive due to their heightened sensitivity, clairsentience is the psychic pathway that becomes their strongest suit. This pathway focuses strongly on emotions, energies, feeling different physical sensations, and this is how the empaths are most likely to channel their energy in a productive way.

However, this might not be the only pathway they are adept at, as some empaths also tend to have great expertise in accessing clairvoyance and/or clairaudience- through which they can either see intuitive guidance in the form of images in their mind or can hear gentle, intuitive guidance. With more practice and a conscious attempt to hone their empath energy better, empaths can significantly get better at and more in control of their clairsentience over time.

Understanding Empath Energy

Generally, people think of *energy* as something which needs to be gained and preserved- in one form or the other. However, there is more to the term 'energy' when it comes to empaths than what it means to someone who is not an empath, who might think that energy is simply something that we spend and restore periodically.

Empaths are affected by both seen and unseen, identified and unidentified, sources and forms of energy. While most people can only see energetic bodies, empaths can *feel* them and connect better, as they are fundamentally energetic beings. Empaths recognize not just exchanges between people but also the flow of energy, which exists beyond simple social interactions, and are invisible to most other people.

An empath can also use the term *energy* to describe how another person feels to them, as they can often sense the 'vibe' a person gives off since empaths have a very strong sense of intuition. Although most people can only connect with each other on a physical- and sometimes emotional-level, an empath goes well beyond that and connects with them metaphysically since they are able to sense the energy people bring with themselves into any setting.

Understanding Empath Fatigue

Being an empath is not always very easy. Understanding how to properly channel your empath energy takes time, practice, and a lot of self-reflection. It is an exhausting task, and it often leads to a condition known as 'empath fatigue,' which tires an empath out and drains them of their potential to pick up on energies as usual. Here are a few things which empaths need to keep in mind in order to be better in touch with their energy, especially when they feel like they are nearing a stage of long-drawn exhaustion or fatigue –

1. **A deep sense of purpose:** We are often expected to have very superficial things that drive our sense of purpose, but as an empath, it might often feel very draining to have to live up to very broad, almost unrealistic expectations such as "taking care of

everyone" or "healing everyone around you." If you are an empath, you will have to understand that there is only so much you can do, and you will need to cleanse yourself of any conditioning which leads you to think that you can achieve the literal impossible so that you can identify a deeper sense of purpose in life.

2. **A clear distinction between empower and enable:** Much of the caregiving work we are taught to take up is focused on enabling and not empowering (the person who is receiving the care). However, as an empath, if you do not equip yourself to use your energy in a way that empowers other people, then the same people would come back to you again and again for help as they would not know how to deal with their issues on their own. This is why it is crucial that empaths take an approach focused on empowering (which involves taking care of oneself and learning to heal on one's own) others when they take care of them and provide them with any sort of guidance.

3. **Focus on separation and not oneness:** The focus during any spiritual exchange is often placed on the idea of 'oneness.' However, if you are an empath, the chances are high that this aspect is something you already have covered due to the energy you constantly experience and channel. Therefore, what you should turn your attention towards instead is the idea of 'separation.' Empaths need to focus on how to identify and maintain the distinction between their own energy and the energy they receive from other people, and then, they also need to separate which concerns need them to intervene and which do not, so that they are better in charge of where they are investing their efforts.

4. **Seeking help:** Empaths are often reluctant to seek help from others as they feel that it is always this responsibility to care for everyone, even themselves. This feeling of excessive self-reliance can often drive

empaths to a stage of fatigue as they are allowing themselves to only give- help and kindness and support- into the world without actively seeking any of it back. In order to strike a better balance between what empaths can do for others and for themselves, they need to open up to the possibility of baring their souls to another person and accepting help from them as well.

Tips to Overcome Empath Fatigue

Now that we have some idea about empath fatigue, let us look at a few things empaths can actively practice to avoid empath fatigue or to heal from it:

Get to know yourself

This might sound like a very obvious thing, but a lot of empath fatigue could be avoided if people were simply more aware of how empaths functioned or channeled their empath energy, as this would allow them to preserve their energy without facing a point of exhaustion. A lot of frustration and loss of energy can also be caused by failed attempts at trying to understand who we are. For example, many times, it is assumed that empaths are automatically introverts, so they are suggested to take more breaks and periods of alone time to re-energize. However, without first understanding how you function in particular, if you give in to such generalized pieces of advice, it might do you more harm than good. A lot of your attempts at dealing with empath fatigue would also become counterproductive at the same time.

Also, if you are aware of how your empath intuition works, you can use some of it to develop the best ways to deal with fatigue and exhaustion in the ways that might work the best for you. There are a lot of pieces of advice out there to deal with- although some of it needs you to keep a relatively open mind if it does not work for you, then there is no point in going at it expecting different outcomes later. If you have a gut feeling like something might not be a good fit for you, it is the best idea to move on to the next available option. How to deal with empath fatigue, therefore, is a calculated balance of understanding yourself and what works for you and trying out new tips and tricks.

Invest in self-care

Self-care is a necessity in today's world, which is becoming more chaotic and exhausting by the day. For empaths, self-care becomes even more important as they are constantly being drained of their energy by their conscious and subconscious social interactions. Also, due to high sensitivity to external energies, it might be extra hard for empaths to take time off to tend to solely themselves.

Most of the time, what happens with empaths is that they are too busy catering to other people and their needs, and in this process, they forget to take enough care of themselves. This is something that needs to change first and foremost so that excessive empath fatigue can be avoided. Empaths need to acknowledge that nobody can pour from an empty cup. If they push themselves to the point of fatigue that they cannot recover from, that would be harmful to themselves and all the other people they are so used to lending a helping hand and caring for. This is where self-care comes in handy. Thinking of self-care might immediately make us picture spa days and bubble baths, but that does not have to be the case always. In fact, self-care can be anything that feels beneficial and a little indulgent to you, even if it does not fit the bills for others.

Self-care for empaths might mean taking their time out to go for a walk or finish a book or a movie they had meant to catch up on for a long time. The only thing that is important here is making sure that whatever self-care activity is being chosen involves the empath and only the empath. It ensures that they have no choice but to dedicate their undivided time and attention to themselves and get more in touch with their feelings.

Learn to create boundaries

One of the biggest mistakes empaths sometimes make is to allow toxic people around them unnecessarily drain a lot of their energy which could be utilized someplace else. A lot of people take empath energy for granted and do not reciprocate in any possible way to the assistance and support they are receiving from empaths, and these are exactly the kind of people who empaths need to cut off from their lives- or at least maintain a healthy distance from- so that they are not constantly experiencing fatigue from only giving and not receiving anything.

Many a time, people with such draining behavior might realize their mistake and might even actively try to change their pattern of interaction, in which case the empaths can make an intuitive decision on how to further their exchanges. But some people, even after having pointed out their problematic patterns, will continue to take empaths for granted and will shrug off any accountability that might be expected from them. Such people are often tagged as 'energy vampires' as they suck off energy constantly without any return, and one of the most effective steps to deal with empath fatigue is severing ties with such people. This act also counts as self-care because this requires the empath to confront toxic people and prioritize their own selves before the needs of others. Although this might be somewhat hard and confrontational, the effects of this would be long-term and would ensure a lot of additional peace and comfort for the empaths.

Identify your triggers

As an empath, it is essential for you to know what exactly your triggers are. Since there can be many different kinds of empaths, the triggers for all would be very different from each other, and the way in which these triggers need to be dealt with would also be different. Since no one size fits everyone, empaths need to work on themselves and identify what kind of an empath they are, what triggers them (and how), and how they could possibly deal with these triggers.

Some empaths could be 'physical empaths.' For them, the physical needs of others would take precedence over other requirements. This implies that they might be quite triggered if they are exposed to physical pain and hardships, especially when they are nearing exhaustion. On the other hand, plant empaths are more likely to feel very deeply connected to nature and everything related to it, and for them, a common trigger could be being cooped up in a built environment for too long a period of time. A walk in nature can help them cope with longer periods in an urban, indoor setup.

Identifying what your exact triggers are might be very challenging at times, as they are very emotionally loaded signs which you need to identify rationally. In order to do this, you can try and turn your natural empath intuition inwards, which will help you pay close attention to your inner workings and how they are affected by things that are happening around you, which might give you some sense of the triggers you could be exposing yourself to, even unknowingly.

What goes in also goes out

This is another more commonsensical advice, but this strongly holds true for empaths- good things come out only when good things are going in. In terms of dietary needs, empaths tend to be a lot more sensitive when it comes to certain stimulants, such as sugar, caffeine, and alcohol. This is because many empaths are already highly aware and somewhat tightly-wound people who, when exposed to external stimulants, might be driven towards an uncomfortable sensory overdrive.

Often, when exhausted, it might be an easy and convenient idea to turn towards sugary snacks and other junk food to momentarily relieve you of the fatigue you are feeling. However, this has a lot of adverse consequences if continued over a prolonged period of time. This holds true because the exhaustion an empath faces is different from normal tiredness and cannot be easily cured by a sugar rush or anything similar. It does not stem from just a bad night's sleep. Instead, it comes from the empath depleting their inner energy. Until and unless certain inwards functionings are addressed, this fatigue would not be cured in any way, and short-term measures might prove even more harmful for the empath as they might give rise to unhealthy coping mechanisms.

This does not, of course, mean that an empath has to completely cut down on any forms of sugar or caffeine, etc. They just need to make small, mindful changes to their normal diet and especially to the resorts they turn to when they are having a bad day so that they do not take the aid of external stimulants to address fatigue caused by inner energy.

Stay close to the water

A lot of empaths tend to connect strongly with water and the energy it represents. A lot of empaths are not very aware of the calming and relaxing effect exposure to water bodies can have on them. Water acts as a significant source of healing and peace for empaths, and this water could mean many things. Empaths can seek this healing effect by going on a swim, soaking in the tub, spending a weekend at the beach, or even looking at pictures of waves crashing or other similar sights. All of this helps recharge the empath's sense of energy and revitalizes their inner capacity to connect with things and the people around them. A quick vacation that helps you get more in touch with nature - water, especially - might be a great help for empaths who feel drained for a long time and do not have enough time to invest in long-term self-care habits and rituals at the moment.

Being an empath is no easy feat, but if you are conscious about how you function and how you are affected by certain triggers are energies, you can achieve a lot through the gift you live with as an empath. Self-preservation for an empath also has to do a lot with the idea of empath fatigue, and this chapter is aimed at helping empaths to not only understand what their fatigue means or has to do with but also lists down various ways in which the fatigue can be kept at bay, which would certainly help empaths better help themselves as well as the ones around them.

Chapter 9: Everything You Need to Know About Psychic Protection

Do you sometimes feel that something is invading your energy? Such an experience can be uncomfortable, intrusive, and sometimes even frightening. It is in these instances that you need psychic protection. In this chapter, we will go over everything that you need to learn about the art of psychic protection in a step-by-step manner.

Psychic protection often revolves around setting up mirrors or shields that will send the negative energy right back at the perpetrator. There are other methods as well that involves the usage of light of different frequencies, and most importantly, white light that not only protects but also purifies. And there are others who prefer relying on angels and guides who can provide them protection during a psychic attack. But in this chapter, I will show you how you don't need any of these things but protect your psyche through some other methods like strengthening your auric boundaries and setting your chakras right.

When you are under a psychic attack, it means that a certain part of your energy field was open to infiltration. You need to close this energy door or raise the drawbridge so that you can protect yourself from the attack.

An interesting fact that is noticed by experts is that when someone has strong energy boundaries, they usually don't require any psychic protection in the first place. I am not saying that they do not face any challenges or their life is just perfect. It's not that, but at the same time, they are not victims of psychic attacks.

This shows that the need for protection doesn't arise if you are able to contain your energy. This ensures that your energy is not available and individuated for a psychic attack.

And in this way, you are able to break out of the cycle of victim and perpetrator.

But how can this energy containment be made successful? One of the ways is by setting your chakras right. You can also take part in grounding and centering practices to strengthen your energy boundaries. Read on to learn more about these techniques.

Centering and Grounding Exercises

Whether you want to manage your stress levels or protect yourself from psychic invasion, centering and grounding exercises can be really helpful. In fact, whenever we refer to any energetic or spiritual practice, these two things go hand-in-hand. Once you practice these exercises, you will feel the flow of energy through every part of your body, and you will also gain better control of this energy. Ultimately, these exercises help bring a sense of stillness or peace from within. Another importance of these exercises is that they make you aware of your physical, emotional, and psychic boundaries so that you can easily build your energy shields and effectively engage in psychic protection.

If you follow my advice, I'd recommend that you perform these exercises every day –good practice would be to do it for 15 minutes right after you wake up and another 15 minutes before you retire for the day and go to bed. There are plenty of ways in which you can practice centering and grounding, but for a beginner, the best way to go about it would be to practice breathing exercises.

What is Grounding?

With the hectic schedules that we all have, it's very easy to get caught up in all the things that you have on your to-do list for the day. And then there are the uncertainties of the future. All of these thoughts often pull a person far away from their present life. That is where grounding comes in.

Through the process of grounding, you can pull yourself back to reality and help yourself connect with the present. It will instantly remind you of the importance of being in the present moment so that you are always aware of the happenings around you and stay conscious. On days when you feel exceptionally detached from everything that is going on at present, grounding exercises can really shift your focus and bring you back to the here and now. It also teaches you to be mindful.

How to Ground Yourself?

The grounding exercise is pretty easy, and you will get better at it with practice. Start by choosing a place to sit down where you will be free of any distractions. Then, close your eyes. Start taking deep breaths. When you are breathing in and out, focus on your breathing and be mindful and aware of every inhale and exhale that you do.

After a while, you will feel ready and then start visualizing the energy from your body gathering at the center and going down into the ground. You can do this by imagining a network of roots growing from your body and that go further deep into the ground, and they carry the energy with them. The more these roots grow, the more you will feel heavy because they are pulling you into the ground. If it feels overwhelming, you can simultaneously visualize your spirit being pulled more and more towards your body. After a while, you will feel completely relaxed because now, your spirit and body are one. The next step you need to take is centering.

What is Centering?

Now that you have a basic idea of what grounding is, let us have a look at the next concept, that is, centering. For that, imagine this situation –

You follow your daily schedule and go to work, and the entire day, you are trying your best to keep your boss happy and maximize client satisfaction. You interact with so many people during your shift, and during the entire time, you put on your happy face. But there are many instances where you have a grumpy client/customer to deal with, and they have a very unpleasant behavior. By the time your day ends, you feel tired and exhausted not only physically but also mentally, and all you want to do is sit in front of the TV or watch some Netflix with your favorite snacks.

Does this sound something like your daily routine? It does to me! And this is also why it is important for every single person to practice centering.

Energy is a universal thing – everything that you see on earth has energy present in it. As you traverse life, you give away some of your energy and keep collecting some energy from others. This exchange of energy should not be left unmonitored. You need to keep track of it somehow; otherwise, soon, you will find yourself feeling overwhelmed due to the negativity of others, and this will start hampering your own soul.

When you practice centering, you bring back the energy that you had initially passed on to others. At the same time, you also shed away the energy that you had collected from people you met. The beneficial nature of this process is that it helps you restore the balance of energy in your body so that you can function more smoothly and effectively without feeling weighed down by something.

How to Center Yourself?

The first thing that you need to know before you center yourself is where your energy center is. There is a breathing exercise that you need to do, and before I explain the steps, there's something else that I need to tell you. When you perform the centering exercise, your aim would be to imagine the energy gathering inside your body in the form of a golden ball. Centering is usually about your naval area. That is why when you breathe in, it is advised that you do it through your diaphragm. But if you do not yet trust yourself regarding such clear visualization, you need not worry – you can simply imagine the energy flowing to any area it wishes to flow to. Developing or unlocking your psychic abilities has often been related to the power of visualization and so never put a barrier to your imaginations. When you make the best use of your imagination and wield it purposefully, you acknowledge the presence of energy inside you and eventually learn to silence the inner critic to make the best use of your psychic abilities.

So, start by closing your eyes and take deep breaths. You have to put your visualization to use when you are breathing in – imagine all the energy that you have given out into the world and imagine it coming back to you. As the energy comes back and fills you up, it will make your soul feel complete, and you get a feeling of fullness from within.

Consequently, when you exhale, you need to imagine that you are throwing away all the energy that you had absorbed from others. Imagine this excess rubble inside of you and then simply blow it away. This process will ensure that all of the negative energy blocking your energy flow is now sent away, and your body is neutralized. You feel free and lighter than before.

If you are facing trouble doing, here's an example of a visualization that you can do while performing the breathing exercises. Imagine your energy center and compare it with that of an empty cup. Imagine that the cup is surrounded by a lot of litter. Whenever you inhale, imagine the litter going farther away and your cup being filled with clean water. The water signifies your own energy and the litter – others' energy that you don't want. Or, you can also imagine a garden. With every inhale, visualize new flowers blooming in it, and with every exhale, imagine the weeds being uprooted.

Creating a Psychic Shield

If you feel like the negative energy of others always influences you, you need to know how to create a psychic shield. In this section, we are going to study the process of shielding in great detail.

What is Shielding?

What do you do when you go outside the house in winter? You protect yourself with warm clothes, right? Otherwise, you are going to fall sick from the cold. Shielding is something very similar to this example – it is an act of protecting yourself from unwanted energy around you. It gives you protection from draining away all your energy and also shields you from energy attacks. When you consciously construct this energy shield, you learn to send away all those energies that you know are not for your greater welfare and are only going to cause harm. So, no matter how many negative people you are surrounded with, their negativity will no longer have the same impact on you as it did before. The chaos that is present in your daily schedule is no longer going to stress you out or cause burnout because you'll know how to protect yourself from the negativity around you.

In the beginning, shielding might come off as a difficult procedure but don't let this intimidate you. With practice and time, you are soon going to master it like a pro. And you'll realize what a profound impact it can have on your spiritual and emotional health.

How to Perform Shielding?

It's important to center yourself before you practice shielding, but it's okay if you haven't. You simply need to relax and calm your mind down by taking a few deep breaths. This will give you better clarity and slowly bring about a sense of relaxation.

The first step is to close your eyes. Make sure you are in a place where you are away from all types of distractions. Take a moment and sit in silence. Slowly, you will feel a surge of energy inside you. But if you don't, you need to put all your focus on your energy center. Now, slowly and steadily feel the energy inside of you – it is pulsating – visualize it. When you feel that you are brimming with energy, start taking a few deep breaths.

When you inhale, you need to imagine that the air is filling you up and, at the same time, immersing you in positive energy. Keep repeating this until you feel positive and sense the positive energy inside you.

After that, you now need to focus this positive energy on the action. Keep taking those deep breaths, but when you exhale, you now need to imagine that the center of energy in your body is opening up. After a while, you will be able to feel when the energy center has been opened completely. At that moment, you need to visualize that the energy from your energy center has now started expanding. Remember that the energy that is now expanding is the same energy that will be later on used to form the shield, and you have to do that through visualization itself.

For a beginner, when you are shielding for the first couple of times, spend some time knowing the energy – this will ensure that the shield you build is very strong. Learn to identify different characteristics of your energy –

- What is the color of the energy?

114

- What is your energy made of? Is it liquid? Is it light? Or, is it something else entirely?

- Is it cold, or does it feel hot?

- How is your energy field moving around?

The effectiveness of your shield completely depends upon your ability to visualize. Now, the next step is to imagine your energy surrounding you fully. A very important step in creating a successful shield is focusing on the intent behind it. Your shield is going to block only those energies that are not meant for your well-being and will allow only those energies that mean you good. This intent is very important because that is what builds the foundation of the shield. Remember that it is okay if this part takes some extra amount of time because you don't want to mess it up, right? All the time needed here will ultimately be worth it, so stay strong and wait patiently for the shield to form.

Types of Shields

Now, there are different types of shields that can be formed, and we are going to discuss them further in this section.

Bubble Shields. Let's start with the most basic shield of all. These are also some of the easiest shields to make for beginners. It acts as a delicate net and filters energy exactly the way you want it to. Empaths can maintain this shield in their day-to-day life. But you must keep in mind that these shields will not be effective against telepathy.

Now, how are you going to construct this bubble shield? You have to utilize your grounding energy in the process. Take in the amount of energy you need and then visualize it forming a bubble around you. You have to imagine that the bubble is encompassing you completely. The shield should also be imagined as something bouncy – an idea in your mind that if someone throws something at the shield, it will bounce off. If you want the process to be a bit different and creative, you can even visualize the shield to be of a specific color. However, if you want to protect yourself from serious attacks, this is not the shield for that purpose.

Mirror Shields. As you can probably guess from the name, unlike the bubble shields, mirror shields are much harder, and if there is any incoming attack towards you, these shields will reflect and deflect it. During the creation of this shield, it is advised that you imagine the exterior surface of it as something mirror-like and diamond-hard. This shield cannot be manipulated easily and is, thus, much stronger than bubble shields.

So, if you want to create a mirror shield around you, you have to imagine the energy getting inside you and then slowly shape that energy into a shield. After it has attained the spherical shape, you can then put all your focus on creating its surface. Imagine it to be reflective and hard as a diamond. But remember that just like diamonds, if these shields are struck with a certain force and at the right place, they can be broken.

Elemental Shields. The main purpose of these shields is layering, and they are extremely powerful at it. Mirror shields are primarily static, but that is not the case with elemental shields. This is the reason behind them being so strong and flexible. These shields, as the name suggests, draw energy from a certain element, and if you are successful in creating them the right way, they partake of the power and essence of that particular element. But it is crucial that you remind yourself of that particular element's boundaries while forming the shield. The sub-types of elemental shields are as follows –

- *Wind Shields* – We have all seen how powerful tornados or cyclones can be, and that is the power that you are going to be harnessing in these shields. If your shield is good, then it should be made up of at least two layers where each layer will be moving in different directions.

- *Fire Shields* – Here, you have to visualize the flames encompassing you. This shield is pretty straightforward and easy to maintain for psychic empaths. But if too much energy is thrown at it at the same time, then there is a chance for it to become overloaded. Another advantage of this shield is that it allows others to feel comfortable around you because of the warmth it exudes.

- *Water Shields* – These are exceptionally strong and impressive because you are drawing on the power of floods and tidal waves. This is also a dynamic shield like the previous two elemental shields. The person casting it will feel a cleansing feeling and a sense of cool. But if the person doesn't like water in general or does not have an affinity towards it, the water shield can make him/her feel nauseous.

- *Ice Shields* – Ice shield is not meant for everyone. It has this nature of sucking out the warmth from all types of energy. Anything that comes in contact with it will freeze.

- *Earth Shields* – Here, the energy is drawn from earth, specifically a sandstorm. And so, this shield is highly corrosive in nature. You can imagine building this shield by visualizing a brick by brick construction. But a drawback is that it is not easy to maintain because it's a heavy shield.

I hope this chapter has helped you understand the processes of psychic protection. If you are new to this, start with the easier procedures and then move your way up the ladder.

Chapter 10: How to Deal With Spiritual Hypersensitivity?

A highly sensitive person or HSP is a term that is usually used to denote someone who the people of society think has a very deep central nervous system sensitivity towards social, physical and, emotional stimuli. Some people might also refer to this as SPS that is having sensory processing sensitivity. It is a general thing for people to judge others who are very sensitive, calling them "too sensitive" as people think it's a negative trait for which a person can be judged. But, on the contrary, being sensitive has its own challenges, and at the same time, it has its own strengths as well.

Who is a Highly Sensitive Person?

To make it clear in the very beginning, being sensitive is not a disease or a problem, nor is it something to be ashamed of. It is not something for which a person needs diagnosis or medication. It is just a personal way of being and feeling and reacting to a particular situation. Coming to the question of how to understand whether someone is hypersensitive or not, is it the case that people usually come to you and say that you "think too much" or "feel too much"? Has it been that people tell you not to react too much or behave a certain way because they think you are feeling a lot and "reacting unnecessarily" while all the while you feel that they are insensitive? This means that you are a hypersensitive person. If you have seen this happening with someone, then in all probability, they too are hypersensitive. Just to clear it out once more, this is not a problem that you or someone you know might be having. It is just that it has increased responsiveness towards all kinds of situations, be it positive or negative.

As we know, an over-sensitive or hypersensitive person is someone who has a depth in processing all the things around them. They have a very sensitive brain with a more active insula, which is that part that deals with our perceptions and feelings. Such people have the habit of analyzing every situation in great detail before taking any action or engaging with someone. As a result of this, they might have a slower pace in their work as they tend to accumulate information about people and about things before acting on it. In addition, hypersensitive people always notice the subtle details in their environment that other people might miss easily. So, they are much more emotionally impacted by their surroundings and by their social stimulations. This can result in a situation of them getting exhausted physically and more so emotionally by this high level of input of information.

We could categorize hypersensitivity to different traits such as:

- **Being Deeply Affected by Beauty** – This could be in any form of beauty, be it through nature or art, or even through the human spirit. You could be deeply moved when you see beauty in things and people. It usually gives you a lot of joy, which you might not be able to express all the time properly through words.

- **Feeling the Need for Downtime** – It might so be the case that after a stressful day, you desperately need to isolate yourself in the corner of your room because you feel that all the emotions that you had to go through or experience are becoming too much to take, and you need to let off some steam.

- **Feeling the Need to Avoid Violence** – Violence is something that we all need to avoid, but in your case, it even extends to watching violent movies or TV shows as it becomes really difficult for you to even tolerate that even though the screen or in a fictional world. Whenever you see violence in any form, be it even through books, you tend to separate yourself from that.

- **You Have a Rich Yet Complex Inner Persona** – You have come to realize about yourself that you have a very deep inner self with a complex persona because all your thoughts are very deep. And because you tend to think about everything in a lot of details than others around you. You have the tendency to feel everything in more detail and think about things from perspectives that are not similar to others.

- **Feeling Overwhelmed by Sensory Stimuli** – Things like very bright lights or a very crowded place or maybe something like uncomfortable clothing tends to make you really uncomfortable and ill at ease. You might not be able to understand why and most of the time, you might not be able to put the finger on it because you might not know yourself why it is and what the reason is, but nonetheless, these things tend to put you ill at ease.

Common Challenges Faced by Hyper Sensitive People

For those who are hypersensitive, they tend to remain exhausted due to them being overstimulated all the time, and as a result of that, they have to face a lot of challenges in life that become unavoidable. On top of that, these challenges tend to have a firm grip on the concerned person, given that they spend plenty of downtimes and they have access to regulation tools. Let us take a quick look at what these challenges might be.

Getting Overwhelmed Easily

Getting overwhelmed is something that every hypersensitive person feels almost all the time. But, unfortunately, it doesn't end in that. This leads to a lot of side-effects like being anxious all the time, having digestive issues, and the chances are that they can become chronic, being physically and emotionally exhausted all the time as processing everything becomes too difficult after a point, having poor concentration, because the things that are already present on your mind are taking up all the space, having a very low immune function, etc. as you are too overwhelmed all the time, it could so be that even happy situations or pleasant experiences can become very stressful for you to handle such as getting a place for yourself that you have always wanted, but not being completely happy or relieved, thinking of all the situations attached to it. Or, while transitioning into a new relationship, the effects and memories of the past relationship seem too burdensome to get rid of.

Being Anxious and Depressed

People who are hypersensitive are usually very anxious as they tend to think about every little thing in great detail, and they always feel that something might go wrong. This feeling constantly keeps them engaged that what if something goes wrong because it is yet again a tendency of such people to get deeply affected with any situation if that doesn't turn out to be the way they want. What happens as a result is that a person who is hypersensitive can suffer from conditions of depression. This could also be when a person has suffered from a lack of meaningful relationships in their lives or when a person has failed to create any meaningful attachment with their family and friends during their childhood. The lack of trusted people who are a source of comfort and strength can be of great help to a person as such people will always help you in times of need, giving you a helping hand as well as being a place where you can turn to if things go wrong. The lack of such people will always make you anxious as you will feel that you are all alone with no one to turn to. This, in turn, increases hypersensitivity.

Emotional Intensity

It is a common thing with people who are hypersensitive to get more affected emotionally in situations of both happy and sad times. As discussed earlier, they tend to feel everything in greater intensity, and as a result, they can't take any situation lightly, and they react in a subsequent manner. It might be the case that people around them don't feel all they are feeling, and a clash of interests might arise. Some might feel that the concerned person is being weird as they are reacting in a way that is not needed. However, that is not the case with a hypersensitive person. They genuinely believe in whatever they are feeling, and thus, their reaction and their feelings to them are completely justified.

Being Shy and Socially Anxious

Hypersensitive people or HSP mostly prefer meaningful conversations, and they prefer developing strong and deep bonds with people. They always prefer having a one-to-one conversation with people rather than mixing in a crowd. People who have hypersensitivity, with a lesser number of people that they have to deal with, feel that their emotions are more in control. They feel that if they have the situation slightly less complicated and more in their hand, it will be easier to deal with them and the people. The moment the situation changes and they have to deal with a lot of people – their anxiety gets triggered as they start feeling that they won't be able to handle the given situation or their feelings. That is why they feel that instead of making useless conversations that don't have any serenity to them, it is better to not engage in such events and with such people they haven't known for some time.

Having Difficulty with Boundaries and Feeling Guilty

As people with hypersensitivity tend to think and feel about every situation in much greater detail, they often have a lot of difficulties setting boundaries for themselves. Setting boundaries is a very important thing for all of us. that helps us remain more in control, and that also helps other people know what their limitations are. It helps maintain a professional relationship with people and also is a great way of dealing with all kinds of situations. But, if one is to not set proper boundaries, the chances are that people might come and easily take advantage of such people. That is what happens with hypersensitive people quite a lot. Thinking that the other person might feel bad or will be hurt, they tend to be unable to say a "no" on their face, and even if they do say a "no," they tend to be heavily guilt-ridden after that. This tendency of not saying a "no" renders them unable to set proper boundaries, and as a result, they can often be taken advantage of or even be cheated.s

Struggling with Transitioning and Making Decisions

Hypersensitive people struggle a lot transitioning from one thing to another. They often get stuck with the current thing they are doing and have their emotions invested in. they tend to neglect to get involved with new people or new things as all their thoughts are always on a deeper intensity. So, they can take a lot of time deciding something and coming to a conclusion. They are thus, not very good at making quick decisions.

Having Low Self-Esteem

Hypersensitive people often feel that they are misunderstood because people around them don't usually feel things in the intensity that they do, and they tend to have a slightly different perspective on life. As they don't often find people who think and act like them, many-a-times they believe that their actions and words are making other people misunderstand them. They seldom get the reactions they expect or are comfortable with, and hence they feel that something is wrong with them and others don't like their company or the way they behave. This constant feeling of being judged and being misunderstood is bound to negatively impact a person that happens in the form of having low self-esteem. Hypersensitive people tend to doubt themselves a lot and are often not as confident as they should be as they constantly have this thought of being misunderstood, which sometimes they are, but at other times, they are not.

Common Myths About Hyper Sensitive People

It is true that hypersensitive people are complex and sometimes difficult to understand, but that can be solved. All it takes is a bit of patience and understanding on everyone's part for better communication. Yet, there are many myths that are concerning such people which should be avoided. Let us look at some of those myths that you and I should avoid if we encounter someone who is hypersensitive.

- **Sensitive People are Weaker than Others –** This is probably one of the most basic and, unfortunately, common myths that people have in their minds towards sensitive people. People, unfortunately, take sensitivity as a sign of weakness. Society thinks that it is smart and cool to keep one's thoughts and feelings to themselves so that no one else can know what the person is feeling. The society also thinks that until and unless a thing or a person is bothering me directly, I shouldn't spare a thought for that thing. As this is not the case with hypersensitive people, and they tend to think in deeper respects about everything, and also they tend to get affected by those, people take that honest mode of self-expression as a means of weakness. But that is definitely not the case. If you think it through properly, you can take advantage of you being a hypersensitive person. Being sensitive can be extremely helpful in any kind of situation as that helps a person to analyze situations better and take necessary actions.

- **Men are Less Likely to be Hypersensitive than Women** – This has been an age-old notion among people that women are more hypersensitive than men in general. But that is completely a myth and is wrong in most cases. Being sensitive has got nothing to do with a person's gender. A person can be sensitive or not, and that depends upon a person's environment, how they look at life and how they experience the world. This also has a sociological connotation attached to it, given that we live in a patriarchal society, and we always expect men to be tough and practical and always on their toes. We, as a society, don't allow men to be how they want to be. So, we take it for granted that they cannot be sensitive as that is not "man"y" enough. On the other hand, we see women as beings who are always hysterical and who are easy to be swept off by things that happen around them. This is, once again, a baseless myth as a society cannot prescribe how a person will be or will behave. It completely falls under the discretion of the concerned person.

- **Hypersensitive People Cannot Handle Stress** – People tend to believe that hypersensitive people are very ill-equipped at handling situations of stress as that might become overwhelming for them. Given that hypersensitive people feel about things on a deeper level, it is true that they might take a bit more time to deal with something and wrap up that situation. It might so be that they need some alone-time after a certain event to regain their composure and get a grip of all their emotions. But that is a way of their being, and never for once does it tell anything about their capacity to handle stressful situations. It definitely doesn't give people the right to judge someone based on these conditions. Sensitive people think about any situation in greater detail, and so, in all probability, they are better equipped at handling stress as they will know exactly how they are feeling and will be able to understand how the other person is feeling. This will automatically make them more eligible to deal with the situation, given that they can provide more help and emotional support.

- **Hypersensitive People have Always been Sensitive** – While it is true that for a person to become hypersensitive at a point in their lives, they have got to be a certain level of more sensitive than others previously, it also doesn't mean that all hypersensitive persons have been like that for all their lives. It is a myth because circumstances and the environment have a lot of impact on a person's psyche. It might so be the case that a person has never been very sensitive previously, but certain events made them become one, and that has slowly contributed them into becoming a hypersensitive person at present. So, there is no need to restrict a possibility of a person becoming hypersensitive in recent times irrespective of them not being so earlier.

- **Hypersensitive People have an Issue of Over-Reacting** – This is once again a very common assumption that people generally make about hypersensitive people in general but, once again, it is a myth and has no base to it. Reacting to a situation has got nothing to do with being sensitive or not. A person can well be wholly insensitive but still respond to a situation in extraordinary ways. While at the same time, a person can be very sensitive and still not react in any way as they tend to keep things inside them, thinking about the situation in great detail within themselves. While simultaneously, it might so be that a person who is not sensitive doesn't feel any situation with any detail and so they prefer not reacting to anything and a sensitive person, owing to their feeling and experiencing everything in details finds it natural to react to things. Basically, it all depends on a person's nature regarding what they decide to do and how they decide to behave. Whether a person chooses to act out is solely dependent on their emotional terrain. So, being sensitive has got nothing to do with being reactive or not. Hypersensitive people are more receptive by nature, and so they can, by nature, pick up a person's emotions easily, which helps them to react a certain way.

Small Steps That You Can Take in Everyday Life

All things considered, being highly sensitive and being aware of one's own and other's emotions all the time can really be a difficult task and can indeed become a stressful situation for the concerned person. Let us then see some of the ways that we can practice on a daily basis to reduce stress and lead a happy life.

- **Keep Boundaries** – Setting up boundaries means setting them as far as your personal and professional relationships are concerned. It is very healthy to set boundaries that make people realize their limits and the extent of rights that they have over a person. It helps both the concerned person understand in the very beginning as to how much they can say and what actions they can do. It doesn't leave room for any miscommunication or misunderstandings and thereby lessens many problems that could have otherwise happened. It will help both parties to get their work done on time without unnecessary problems.

- **Practicing Mindfulness and Meditation** – Practicing mindfulness and meditating is very closely related to the earlier point of maintaining boundaries. That is because meditating and mindfulness help a person to create a firm but flexible boundary around them. These exercises help a person to remain firm in their own beliefs yet be open to the world outside.

- **Make a Relaxing Zone for Yourself** – Life can become very overwhelming at times, given that you have to take in a lot and deal with many things. That is why it is very important to find things that give you peace and relaxes your stressed mind. Take out time to do things that help you breathe better. No matter what work you have, make sure you give yourself proper time and do things just for yourself without being accountable to others all the time.

- **Find What Triggers You** – Hypersensitive people have certain specific things that can trigger them, making them more vulnerable than they otherwise are. If you can find out for yourself what those things are for you, you can easily start taking precautions accordingly so that next time a situation occurs, you know what to do so that the situation doesn't worsen. It will help you and others around you to remain more in control.

- **Take Care of Yourself** – If you are a hypersensitive person, the chances are that you are always more concerned about others around you, and in that process, you tend to neglect yourself. But you need to take care of yourself first and foremost so that your physical and mental health is well taken care of.

Coping With Hypersensitivity at Work

1. **Recognize Your Thoughts** – What this will help you do is keep you prepared for all kinds of situations. When you learn to recognize your thoughts, you will be priorly aware of what makes you stressed and what makes you relaxed. You will understand what kind of things bother you and what don't. It will invariably

help you create a kind of schedule for yourself based on which you will be able to navigate your work.

2. **Find Yourself an Outlet** – You need to do this for yourself if you are to have a successful work-life, whether you are sensitive or not. Each of us is bound to feel overwhelmed at times, which can hamper our work hugely. If you are hypersensitive, the chances are that you are more burdened with emotions, thoughts, and feelings. That is why you need to find out an outlet for yourself. It could be anything that helps you reduce your stress. A movie, a song, a vacation, talking to someone, it could be anything.

3. **Try Managing Your Stimulations** – It is common sense that no one can work in a proper way if they are under a lot of stress. If you are a hypersensitive person, it is possible that you already know what triggers you. So, when such a situation occurs, try taking control of your situation so that you can manage your stimulations. If you don't allow yourself to get too carried away, you will be better equipped to handle all the situations that you face.

Dealing With Sensory Overload

At times it might feel that the world around you is too harsh as people around us are generally not equipped to deal with sensitivity and emotions. But you cannot hide your reality, and neither should you change yourself. So, it is better to learn some techniques that will help you deal with the sensory overload when you do feel it.

1. It is advisable to try out different approaches that work for you while handling your emotions. Don't feel pressured to stick to any one method. Remember, it is your life, and you should do everything that suits you best.

2. Do not stop till you find out a solution that works for you. It is absolutely all right to try and fail, but it is not all right for you to stop looking. Remember that you shouldn't give up on being happy. Whatever works, keep on doing that.

3. Learn about new things and about how to deal with situations that you otherwise find difficult to handle. The more you educate yourself, the better equipped you will be at dealing with your life and also with people who get on your nerves by being insensitive.

4. Make sure you have such people around you, be it your family or your friends, who are aware of your situation and are sensitive people who respect others so that it becomes a little easier to deal with the world around you.

Lastly, you need to realize that you have nothing to feel guilty about or be ashamed of. You have done nothing wrong by being hypersensitive, while on the contrary, you are much more compassionate and loving than others as you can truly sympathize with others in times of need. All you need is a little knowledge and help to deal with the situations that you will face in life so that when the world around you is harsh, you have people and yourself to fall back on.

Chapter 11: Aura Reading

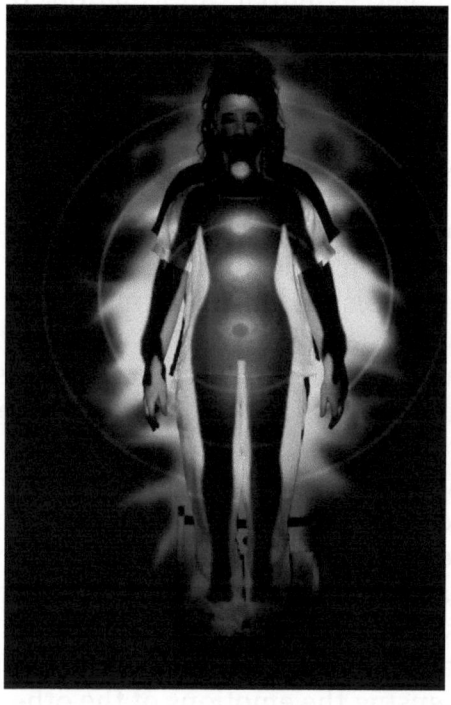

Did you ever get a nervous feeling just after meeting with someone, but you do not know the reason behind your unnecessary nervousness? Or, just the opposite. Like, you were feeling relaxed immediately after coming to someone's presence. Were you ever able to guess what your friend or the person opposite to you thinking about before speaking out? If you ever have come across such moments, then the feelings that you were experiencing were simply the reaction to the opposite person's energy. Many of you may also possess certain other experiences such as seeing flashing lights or colored spots, getting an odd or creepy feeling inside the stomach, hearing the sound of ringing in the ears, etc. Well, you need not worry at all about all such situations. A lot of individuals may refer to this as reading minds, but it is actually related to nothing other than aura. People who are aura readers can notice or feel the energy of other people on an auric field.

Here, you will get essential information related to aura reading, layers and colors of the aura, and a lot more. So, have a look!

What are Auras?

Whenever people refer to 'aura,' they are actually pointing out an unnoticed spiritual field of energy. It surrounds all types of living organisms, be it human beings, plants, or any other animals. In simpler words, anything that is alive possesses an aura. But, a lot of experts in this specific field believe that the energy field of human beings is more complex than the others as humans are much more evolved. It is the energy that is radiated by the people who are around you. Some individuals have the energy to make you feel nervous, whereas others may emit a positive energy that may help you in relaxing. A person's energy helps others to realize whether he/she is excited, confused, or very upset, overjoyed, or angry, even if they do not utter a single word. Aura helps in sensing the emotions of the other person.

Human beings emit a very small amount of electricity, which is better referred to as an electromagnetic field. The medical systems of the ancient age hold a belief that this particular energy is revealed in a total number of seven different layers. Every single layer interacts with different elements of mental, emotional, physical, and spiritual health. Another fact that is quite interesting is that all these layers can interact with each other and thus assist in influencing the overall health of an individual.

The colors of aura can be noticed only by a minority group of individuals. According to the studies of metaphysical believers and practitioners, the different colors of aura are generated by vibrations. The aura consists of vibrational frequency, or you may say vibes in short. Every single atom, as well as the molecule of this entire universe, converts into specific patterns. Those patterns emerge or radiate out of the body in the form of vibrations. It is possible to train the human eyes to perceive such vibrations as various colors. You will be able to sense the vibe or frequency of other people. A person feels attraction or repulsion from other people depending on the frequency that works between them.

Many experts state that seeing the colors of aura may not always be possible with your naked eyes, but you may feel them easily if you train yourself and keep trying with patience. Thus, it is possible to feel the warm, friendly, and affectionate vibe of some people as well as feel the negative energy of others. It is all because of the aura. If you are able to feel such energy, then it will prove to be beneficial for you. The main purpose of an aura is to protect a person's physical body as well as help you to stay away from negative vibrations that have the potential to cause harm.

A person's auric field or aura also possesses information about his/her own life, like mental and emotional thoughts, memories, and beliefs. One more interesting fact about the aura is that an aura cannot be exactly similar to the other. It is because a person's thought patterns keep changing, and thus the vibrations also keep on shifting continuously. If you are feeling down for any reason or your energy is lacking, then your aura will fall off naturally for reflecting your mental state. On the other hand, when you feel very happy, your aura will naturally develop as well as radiate positive energy outwards. Thus, people feel more interested in happier people and turn away from those who emit negative energy. But, if someone possesses negative energy, then, of course, he/she will get attracted to people who are also negative. So, a famous saying does exist – if your wish is to demonstrate or lead a happy life, you need to stay in touch with happy and positive people.

Seven Layers of an Aura

The aura of every single individual is composed of a total number of seven different auric layers, which are also referred to as planes or bodies. Each layer represents a different aspect. The layers of your aura are correlated to various features of your emotional, spiritual, physical, and mental health. Think about the vibrant layers of an onion; link the one in the middle with your physical body. Isn't it interesting? Now, it is time for you to know about the perfect breakdown of all the aura layers.

- *Physical aura layer* – The first layer, or you may say the layer that is nearest to your physical body, is this one. The physical plane is also referred to as the etheric layer. As you can see from the name, this aura plane represents a person's physical health. Therapists can see this layer at the time of treatment. It has a connection with the base chakra and sits at a distance of about four inches from your physical body. Thus, it is the closest layer to the skin. Professional aura readers, as well as many therapists, state that this layer is visible as violet or faint grey mist.

- *Emotional aura layer or plane* – This particular layer of the aura is correlated to a person's emotions. The emotional plane sits just outside an etheric body and extends up to three inches. It is known to connect with the chakra and is thus linked with your feelings and sensitivity like sorrow, joy, hate, and love. If you are feeling contented or excited, the emotional aura layer will show it. The color of this plane alters as it is totally dependent on a person's mood. It will turn out to be smudged or dull if a person experiences any sort of emotional disturbances.

- *Mental aura layer or plane* – The plane that is present outside the emotional plane is nothing other than the mental aura plane. It extends from three to almost eight inches from your physical body. It is linked with the chakra of the solar plexus. The mental plane consists of every single thought process of an individual, such as judgment, discipline, reasoning, logic, rules, and regulations. It is usually displayed by using yellow color.

- *Astral aura layer* – The fourth layer deals with the spiritual health of a person. It extends up to one foot and has a link with the heart chakra. An attractive rainbow color represents the astral body. You might be astonished to know that the capacity for care and love is stored in this layer. It even plays the role of a bridge between the higher spiritual vibrations and the lower physical plane vibrations. The astral plane is that place where everyone holds their beliefs like selflessness and self-compassion.

- *Etheric template* – The extension of this layer is approximately two feet, and it has a connection with the throat chakra. A person will be able to find his/her psychic abilities in this aura plane. People who possess a very clear etheric template find it helpful to understand other people's energy and connect properly with people of the same wavelength. The appearance of this layer is similar to a photograph's negative as it represents your physical body's blueprint. Your aura will shine brighter and gradually grow when you choose to share, engage and teach other people on a divine level.

- *Casual or celestial layer* – The casual plane has a close connection with the third eye chakra and has the potential of extending to nearly two feet. It is in this body where an individual's spiritual connection and the enlightenment procedure start. Every single person's intuition and dreams are nicely stored here. If the celestial layer of a person is strong enough, then he/she may have a tendency to be highly creative. It may even assist you in gaining an excellent and intense awareness level.

- *Spiritual aura layer* – The last layer of aura possesses a connection with the crown chakra along with an extension of almost three feet. The other six layers are protected and coordinated by this layer. This aura plane is highly essential as it helps people by guiding them on their life's path as well as stores all the experiences. The frequency of vibration of the spiritual layer is the highest. It is represented by an outstanding golden or white light.

Aura Colors and Their Meanings

Now, you might be wondering what you will do by knowing about the meanings of different aura colors. The reason behind studying the meanings is because every single aura color possesses a specific purpose. If you can understand those meanings, then it will assist you in telling important facts about yourself and other people. Expert aura readers are also able to listen to the opposite person's thoughts even before the thoughts are expressed verbally. Thus, the colors of aura are also helpful in detecting whether a person is lying or not. It is impossible to fake the colors. Aura colors are also beneficial in detecting mental disorders, health imbalances, diseases, etc.

Let us now learn some crucial meanings of a few aura colors.

- ***Red*** – The red color has an association with passionate feelings as well as sexual desires. If a person has this color in his/her aura, it means being both psychically and emotionally balanced or grounded. It is also the root chakra's color and connects with your physical body and the real world around you. This color is known to appear in the auras of those people who are fearless by nature and also understand the physical reality very well. Individuals who have the shade of red in their aura love to experience dynamic adventures in their lives and are unapologetic about it. Their restlessness and passion help them to stay active in life. Such people are usually not afraid of birth, death, sensuality, over-indulgence, or activities that induce adrenaline. The brightness or saturation of any color present in your aura may signify different things. If the red color is dark, then the indication is such that the person may be feeling frustrated, angry, or going through a traumatic situation. It may also indicate exhaustion or low energy.

- *Orange* – When the aura consists of this color, it signifies that the person is leading a happy life with his/her family, friends, etc. If your aura has plenty amount of orange color, it means you are quick enough in making and keeping friends. It has a connection with the sacral chakra, the one that deals with sexual energy and creativity. Usually, people who have this color in their aura have a tendency to learn lessons from their personal experiences and not from theories. Such a person is excellent when it comes to teamwork because of his/her ability to be sociable and relatable. Those who have orange color in their aura find it quite difficult to sit still because they always tend to seek a thrill. They crave sensation and newness. But, if the frequency of this color is low, it may lead to trouble to commit in relationships or addiction.

- *Green* – While learning about this color, a lot of you may feel surprised to know that the frequency level of both pink and green is the same, but pink does not indicate self-love. Whereas, green which is the color of mother nature, signifies self-love. If this color exists in your aura, it has two meanings: you are very kind and have a loving heart, or you have fallen in love and balance it nicely. To be definite, love and kindness towards plants, animals, family, friends, and life. This color has a connection with the heart chakra, which is the core place of healing and personal growth. A person having a green aura radiates unconditional love, which is felt by almost every being. That is why, if someone has a consistent deep green aura, he/she is drawn towards animals and nature and also has a nature of self-healing. If you come across someone with a green aura, it will definitely be a restful and peaceful experience. Such people are also responsible enough and self-assertive at the same time. Besides this, they also remain extremely focused, with aspirations and high ideals, and are creative individuals. Expert aura readers claim that no other people are as balanced as the ones with green in their aura. This aura connects the physical and spiritual worlds together. But, if the green color is a bit murky or dark, the person may have his/her focus on envious feelings. In such cases, the person may feel like a victim and thus view others' comments as criticism.

- *Yellow* – This aura color is an indication of the balance and inner happiness of a person. Thus, it is related to the chakra of the Solar Plexus. Besides signifying happiness, it also indicates high intellect and self-esteem, spiritual awakening, playful spirit, personal power, etc. People who exhibit this color emit vibrations of high confidence and also possess the ability to inspire other people to achieve greatness. Their energy level is very high and plays the role of natural leaders by motivating those who are opposed to them in the best possible way. An individual with a yellow aura supports and encourages others, just like the sun gives out light to all. Analyzing complex concepts is also another ability of such people. When the shade of this color glows or is bright, then it indicates the person is full of generosity, inner joy, warm, radiant, and attracts others naturally. But, when the aura exhibits a dense and darker yellow, that individual may experience perfectionism, self-criticism, ego, and over-confidence. An aura of lemon-yellow shade indicates that the person is scared of loss. It can be the fear of losing anything such as family, career, love, etc.

- **Blue** – As blue is connected to the throat chakra, this color relates to self-expression and communication. If any of you have this color in your aura, it reveals the fact that you enjoy being in a state of calmness and meditation. You also prefer protecting those people about whom you care a lot. Thus, this kind of person plays the role of being a strong support system for both their family and friends. They are also able to speak out the truth, no matter what the situation is. It is because they give importance to clarity and honesty at the time of communication. Individuals having a blue aura are fond of gathering and sharing wisdom. Thus, they can be excellent philosophers. If the blue color of a person's aura is lighter, he/she will project more positive and peaceful energy. They also have faith in their feelings for deciding what is correct, and they do not feel the necessity of any sort of outside data or facts for substantiation.

- **Purple** – It holds the highest position among all other chakra colors. So, those who have this aura color are intuitive as well as love guiding other people so that they can achieve the highest potential. They are charismatic, dynamic, and even possess strong personalities. Such individuals' main mission or task is to inspire humankind to build a new life of happiness, wholeness, and prosperity. They always feel the urge to do something that is important and may bring a positive change in the life of a maximum number of people. If someone around you has this color, you will realize that they possess great hopes and high ideals for their future and are visionaries. As they have both intuition and knowledge, so they have the potential to view the greater picture of almost all situations. They also crave connecting with others and love to introduce themselves as wide-open books. The speed of purple vibration is very high, and it signals an intimate connection with various unseen energy forms and the universe. At the same time, they are talking about open-minded judgment, progressive ideas, and innovative thoughts. People with purple in their aura show high levels of originality.

- **Pink** – Light pink is one of the rare colors displayed in an individual's aura. Baby pink or bubblegum pink aura indicates that the person is of gentle nature and radiates loving and pleasant energy to almost every person who comes in touch with them. Such people are extremely sensitive and prefer embracing the ethics and values of pure romantic love. They even possess the ability to manage their romance well-balanced and keep it alive in their relationships. The vibration of this color is of a similar frequency level as green. The people of the pink aura heal naturally and are creative by nature. They are uplifting and bubbly as they correlate with the heart chakra directly. Many of you might think that such energy has a connection with feminine characteristics. The best part is that people who have this color in their aura are capable of healing others who are facing difficult times or challenges, just with the help of a smile, a glance, one kind word, or simply by their presence. If you stay in contact with such people, they will help you realize that everyone should behave gently with human beings and other creatures of the earth.

- **White** – It is an energy-producing color, and if it exists in a person's aura, it actually has two meanings. First of all, it may indicate that he/she is more bothered about any sort of spiritual matter taking place on the earth. Secondly, it may signify that such people are not at all concerned about materialistic needs or possessions. This color may even indicate that the person is very healthy.

In case you are unhappy or unsatisfied with your aura colors, you can opt for various techniques of energy cleansing such as sound therapy, chakra work, meditation, etc. It will help in changing the colors over time.

Myths About Auras

The profession of aura reading invites many myths and theories. As it comprises myths, so people often find it very difficult to determine or rather to distinguish between facts and fiction. Though a lot of myths exist related to aura reading, here you will get to know about some of the popular myths.

- ***Chakras and auras are similar*** – Both chakras and auras are indeed connected to each other. They also have the potential to leave an impact on each other. But that does not mean that these concepts are similar. The energy produced as well as emitted by your body is referred to as an aura. It radiates out of a person's body and then influences almost everything in the surroundings. On the other hand, a series of a total number of seven different gates that are present inside the body as well as control the overall energy circulation is known as chakra. The alignment of these seven gates is basically perfect. Besides this, the energy flow through the gates is uninterrupted and smooth. Possibilities of chakras getting misaligned do prevail, which in turn may interrupt the energy flow.

- ***Aura is fixed or unfluctuating*** – The truth is that aura is not at all static by nature. It gets influenced by an individual's lifestyle, diet, mood, relationships with family, professional life, etc. As so many factors are responsible for influencing the aura, so it can never be static. For example- if you face any sort of problem in any aspects of your personal or professional life, the color of your aura will change a little for reflecting imbalance and distress. Professionals in this field often suggest solutions for cleansing the aura as well as restoring its balance and natural color.

- *It is possible to influence your aura deliberately* – Many people who have a doubt aim to verify the genuineness or effectiveness of aura reading as they think differently. To test its validity, a skeptic may feel entertained by attempting to have thoughts that enhance his/her anger. They do so just to influence the aura. But it will be of no help as the outcome will be faulty. The base of that person's emotion would be amusement and not anger; thus, the camera or aura reader would simply pick up that feeling. Thus, it is always recommended to pursue a session of aura reading with an open and crystal-clear mind. It is not possible to influence or alter your aura deliberately.

- *A person's aura is a solid color* – Now, this is known to be one of the oldest myths of this world of aura reading. First of all, you need to understand or rather realize that every individual possesses multiple layers of personalities and different types of motivations. Expert aura readers believe that the reflection of such a flexible and versatile nature can be observed in the aura of a person. Even though a person's aura will have any single dominant color, yet it always has multiple shades. Before providing a reading, the professionals will not only study your aura but also consider all the colors and gradations very carefully.

- *Obscure and special treatments are required for aura cleansing* – The truth is just the opposite.

There is no necessity of pursuing multiple obscure treatments for aura cleansing. In reality, you will be able to bring the aura back to its positive track by bringing a slight change in your lifestyle and practicing a few great habits. For example – you will be able to develop your mental, spiritual, and physical health by meditating and exercising on a regular basis. These kinds of practices will surely influence your aura directly and also clear the imbalance gradually. You will also be able to cleanse your aura by taking aromatherapy soaks and baths daily.

Several such myths are present related to aura reading. In case you have any sort of doubts and are willing to know the truth, it is better to communicate with an experienced and trustworthy aura reader. You will receive honest advice from them. Rumors and myths weaken a person's ability to realize this concept.

How to Read Auras?

Those of you who are trying or rather willing to read auras may certainly do so. But, if you think that you will be able to read or sense it on the very first day of your attempt, then you are holding a wrong thought. You will surely learn to read the aura of other people, and your sense will improve with time. Once you grab this technique of reading auras, it will prove extremely beneficial in understanding the people just next to or opposite to you and also yourself. So, have a look at the small guide on how to read auras.

First of all, you must try to read your aura. For doing so, you need to wear comfortable, simple clothes and then choose a wall of neutral color so that you can stand against it. You need to select a wall that is just opposite to a mirror of full length. In case you do not have such a mirror at your home, you may also use a handheld mirror of good size. If you are willing to read someone else's aura, make sure that your subject dresses up comfortably and then make him/her stand in a similar place like yours. A plain wall is always preferred as the aura colors are seen best when an individual stands against it.

Now, your next task is to check whether you are getting the perfect light needed for reading auras or not. Expert aura readers state that the best way is to use natural daylight. If the wall you have chosen is on the eastern side, try to pursue the early morning reading. But, if the exposure is on the western side, go for the evening time when the sun is about to set. If anyone of you fails to capture the natural daylight, your task will be recreating the same effect by using candles and soft lamps.

You might find the next step to be quite funny. The principle that is applied for seeing auras is not focusing your eyes. It is because if you fix your stare on any single detail too much, the aura that you are trying to read will disappear. But, if you do just the opposite, that is, waiting quietly and staring into any middle distance, slowly, the colors will start becoming apparent. You must not look straight at your chosen subject. All you need to do is pick up a spot that is nearly a foot away from your subject and wait for one or two minutes. Gradually, your exterior vision will begin to pick up the aura colors. Meanwhile, you need to trick your brain by thinking that your focus is just on the chosen spot of the wall. At the same time, you are supposed to remember the colors that you have seen and that too by not staring directly at your subject.

If you find none of the above-mentioned techniques to be fruitful, you must not lose hope and stop feeling disheartened. Try to fix your stare straight at your subject and focus hard for about sixty seconds. Just after doing so, blink your eyes very quickly and keep looking at the vacant wall next to your subject. This procedure is helpful in providing a clear after-image. Such an image will enable you to pick up those colors that you get to visualize around your subject and that too with little pressure.

In case you forget, note down everything that you get to see immediately. Just as you spot any color, remember jotting it down. Sometimes, it may assist you in drawing quick sketches of your subject. You may also draw patterns of different shades or colors that you see using watercolors or colored pencils. After this, your task is to decipher the exact meanings of all the colors that you have visualized.

Many people can see the aura with the help of their basic senses. You can also try to identify an aura through intuition. To read the aura with intuition, you need to be comfortable at first. Now, place both your palms at a level that is approximately 6 inches from the head. After that, slowly move the palms downwards and then upwards, covering your body's length. While doing so, you need to keep the distance constant, that is, about 6 inches away. Now, you must allow yourself to feel your energy as well as taking proper care to notice the aura colors. Before trying out this technique, you may rub both your hands vigorously as it is very helpful in opening up your hands' sensitivity.

Aura Anomalies

If light rays are present in a person's portrait, which is usually white, it signifies that he/she has a direct connection with the source of energy, spirit, the universe, and the divine. It even displays to be in a channeled and guided state. Such a ray of light also indicates that the person is growing through a conscious state and is ready to receive or accept any sort of messages, signs, downloads, as well as energies from various other beings, dimensions, realms, or frequencies.

Proficient aura readers state that such light bars are a form of helping energy that comes out from any external source. Those bars take an entry from the exterior part of an aura and then feed the chakras. The chakras require different types of energy. You will be surprised to know that these rays or energies can arrive from distinct sources. Friends, mates, family members, teachers, or any other individuals who care and love us send such energies either unconsciously or consciously. The energy can also arrive from those individuals that prevail on alternative vibrational levels. Lastly, these rays can also be sent by entities you have come across in this lifetime or any other.

So, by now, you might have realized that everything that we see around us is a form of energy, and every single living being is composed of energy too. The energy of all individuals is highly sensitive and is also affected by a lot of factors. Aura is an interesting and beneficial manner of knowing the energetic state of those people whom you deal with or come across in your personal or professional life. One thing cannot be denied that your body and mind are intimately connected. Experts believe that your aura is a fine way of representing this connection. Gaining knowledge about your aura as well as reading other people's aura may take time. You need to get one thing very clear that aura is not at all exact science. But it assists in becoming conscious about your energy, the way it influences you, and the people around you. The aura colors will help you interpret for providing an overall view of your patterns, inclinations, and personality. Once you get to read auras, you will find it to be quite interesting. So, give it a try and observe the magic!

Chapter 12: Telepathy

Telepathy comes from the Greek word *"tele"* which loosely translates to "distant," and *"pathos"* or *"patheia"* which means "feeling" or "perception." What telepathy can be defined as is "the purported vicarious transmission of information from one person to another without using any known human sensory channels or physical interactions." Suppose we try to understand this in a simpler language. In that case, we could say that telepathy is a means of communicating with someone else without actually speaking or being within the vicinity of that concerned person. There will be a successful transmission or exchange of information without any means of known modes of contact or communication. Then, it will be solely based on the powers of the minds. As there is no convincing mode of evidence to prove that telepathy exists, it can be treated as a form of pseudoscience in the language of the scientific community.

History of Telepathy

We can trace back the origins of telepathy as a practice to the late 19th century as far as Western civilization is concerned if we are to go by the claims of historians like Roger Luckhurst and Janet Oppenheim. It was during the same time that the Society for Psychical Research was also formed. During this time, there was a lot of significant advances in the field of physical sciences, and as a result of that, scientific concepts started being applied to areas of the mental phenomenon as scientists had the hope that this will be a way in which a certain understanding of the paranormal phenomenon could be made more sense of. In this very context, the modern idea of telepathy, which we now know of, came into being.

There have been certain mentalists and magicians during the 19th century, like Washington Irving Bishop, who would perform acts of thought reading based on only unconscious bodily cues, which he claimed was due to him having muscular sensitivity. Stuart Cumberland, another famous thought reader, was famous for his blindfolded acts. He claimed not possessing any psychic abilities and owing to his success through the help of muscle sensitivity. These people were in huge conflicts with the Society of Psychical Research as they were negating the existence of telepathy and advertising muscle sensitivity.

In the field of parapsychology, telepathy, often paired along with precognition and clairvoyance, is defined by means of extrasensory perceptions, which we can also term as ESP known as "anomalous cognition." Parapsychologists usually believe that this communication that is done in telepathy and these other modes of unique transfers are done through hypothetical psychic mechanisms or what is known as "psi." Parapsychologists usually use certain methods to test a person's telepathic abilities through the use of Zener cards and also the Ganzfeld experiment.

From the time of its origin till date, there have been suggested various kinds of telepathy, namely, Latent telepathy, Retrocognitive, Precognitive and Intuitive telepathy, Emotive telepathy, and Superconscious telepathy. Some other forms of telepathy also exist, like Dream telepathy and Twin telepathy. Latent telepathy, which can also be termed deferred telepathy, is when there is a transfer of information with a lag of a certain amount of observable time between the transmission and the reception. If there is a telepathic transfer between two sources about information of past, future, or the present state, then it is called Retrocognitive, Precognitive and Intuitive telepathy. The kind of emotive telepathy can also be defined as a sort of emotional transfer or remote influence where kinesthetic sensations are transferred through the altered states. What we understand by Superconscious telepathy is when there is a use of the supposed superconscious in a person to get access to the wisdom of the entire human species for knowledge.

It is extremely interesting to know that telepathy is not restricted to human beings only. There is something called animal "telepathy," where there is a predisposition of thoughts biologically in animals. For example, we have all noticed a kind of organized and synchronized behavior in birds as they wheel together. There seems to be a very quick inference from each and every bird present in that flock as they turn simultaneously. This can be considered very similar to what we know of telepathy. This was taken up by physicist Jure Demsar and another computer scientist in 2017, and their study led to the conclusion that there has to be certain built-in logic to this unanimous mass behavior in the birds, which is not necessarily transcending the laws that nature has but yet, this behavior has got to have some rule-based computational system, which proves the presence of telepathy in animals.

The entire concept of telepathy is also a very famous genre in the world of fiction, be it in modern fiction or science fiction, where characters are made to have telepathic qualities, adding important tangents to the main story.

The Science Behind Telepathy

The science behind the entire concept of telepathy can be explained by ESP, known as the extrasensory perceptions. Extrasensory perception refers to those outside the five sense organs that human beings have, including clairvoyance and knowledge of future events and telepathy. Many people are of the belief that since these phenomena cannot be seen or measured as such, they might not be true, and they don't have any base. However, modern research has been exploring these areas for quite some time, and they have come up with possible biological mechanisms that can be put behind such a phenomenon.

- **Mirror Neurons** – The science of telepathy refers to modes of communication outside the five sensory organs. Certain studies have shown that it is indeed possible to read the minds of the other person or understand what is going through in their mind at that point in time because we have certain neurons in our minds that acts almost as automatic mirrors and help us grasp the emotions and intentions of the other person. Gregor Domes, a psychology professor, back in 2007, had found out that this procedure can be enhanced by oxytocin, which is nothing but a kind of hormone that increases our trust and social approach behavior.

- **Long-Distance Communication** – Here, we refer to a concept where we travel a few years ahead to, say, 2014. A psychiatrist known as Charles Grau conducted a study where he went ahead to justify telepathy even further by proving in his work that brain-to-brain communication was indeed possible via the internet. He demonstrated with his work that it is actually possible for the information to be transmitted over long distances if we take the internet as the highway that connects the two concerned people.

- **Invisible Communication** – In 2005, Rupert Sheldrake, a biologist, wanted to research this field further. Along with his associate Pam Smart, they hired almost 50 experimental volunteers for a survey. They also hired four emailers. What they did was arrange for a fixed time for all the volunteers, and they made them guess as to which emailer, according to them will mail them during that time. Had the number of correct guesses been less, things could have been explained through mere chance and coincidence. But surprisingly, the percentage of correct answers was almost 43%, which is simply too high a number to be explained through mere chance or kept aside as a matter of coincidence.

Further researches have been conducted in this field for a long time now to prove the mechanism behind telepathy. In 2008, a mentalist, purportedly telepathic, was taken as a volunteer by psychiatrist Ganesan Venkatasubramanian and some of his colleagues while conducting a study on brain-imaging, and another volunteer was taken who was a controlled subject. It was seen after the study that the person who was a mentalist was able to recreate an image that was earlier prepared for him with a lot of accuracies, unlike the other controlled subject, who couldn't guess it at all. Further studies into the cause of this showed the scientists that while the mentalist was working, the right parahippocampal gyrus, or also known as the PHG, was highly activated in him, but the case was not that with the controlled subject. Quite contrary to the mentalist, for the controlled subject, the left frontal gyrus was activated.

All these studies and historical experimental data tell us that our brains have a weird ability to quickly take up many such subtle signs and social cues that are necessarily not communicated through the traditional modes. It also says that our brains have the ability to reflect automatically certain intentions as well as emotions while others are present. We are all aware of the communication system through frequencies that the internet uses. There has to be something very similar with our brains in order to get information exchanged or to have successful communication without the apparent methods. Our brains must get dialed into similar frequencies, which helps us communicate so, even without the sensory organs. Suppose we are to take telepathy as an established fact. In that case, it will also be true that certain individuals are more capable of doing it than others due to the above-mentioned frequency system, as some will get the frequency right over others. If we talk biologically, it has got to be the hippocampal and the parahippocampal regions of our brains that will be involved with telepathic communication. That is so because it is these two regions that otherwise are involved

151

in integrating memories and also with certain aspects of communicating language. And finally, telepathy has got to do with knowing the other person well. The more you know the person with whom you want to communicate, the easier it will be while transferring thoughts and emotions. Basically, the frequency will be stronger if the sender and the receiver are well-acquainted.

Signs That You Have Telepathetic Abilities

At the very beginning, it is very important to understand that there is a huge difference between having "psychic" powers and having "telepathic" powers. They are not the same and thus, shouldn't be confused. Let us try and understand that how a person can know whether they have telepathic powers in the first place. What are some of the signs with which a person can understand their own powers? Many times it might so be that we take things for their face value, considering them as luck or coincidence, while in reality, it is much deeper than that, and it has telepathic connections.

- **Telepathy and Intuition** – All of us at some point in time has experienced this thing called intuition which is nothing but getting a feeling in your gut that gives you a kind of premonition about something that is going to happen, and you start having a prior idea about the outcome of it before everyone else. Now, many a time, we might neglect this feeling as a mere coincidence, but it usually is not so. This might be a very potent sign for you to have telepathic abilities.

  Let me give you an example. When I was a kid, I often used to walk back home from school by a rive that was on the way home. One night I got a nightmare in which I saw a man who was cycling beside me on that road lose balance and fall in the river. I was so frightened of that thing actually happening that I was skeptical about even going to school that day. Yet, I went to school, making myself believe that it was just a dream. To my utter surprise, as I was coming back that day, I suddenly saw that a man is riding on a cycle right behind me, going towards that road by the river. I couldn't stop myself from stopping him and telling him not to ride his bike but instead walk through that road as it might be slippery. My feelings were further strengthened when we both saw that surprisingly that road that day was indeed very slippery, and an accident could have easily happened had I not given him a warning.

The thing about telepathy is that it often gets neglected by adults as mere whims. But that is not the case with children. They don't neglect such intuitions, and they act upon them as they haven't yet been conditioned by society to always think a certain way.

- **Telepathy and Dreams** – The dream world is one of the most interesting things that ever existed. How our unconscious and subconscious mind works are truly one of the most fascinating as well as one of the most complex things for us humans to experience and analyze. When we are sleeping, frequencies of our minds are much more receptive, and our brain waves are easily welcoming of any incoming data that our awake mind would not have allowed otherwise. That is the reason telepathy has got to do a lot with the dream state in us humans. It is in our dreams that many a time we receive a lot of telepathic information. But what happens most of the time is when we wake up, our brain refuses to take it seriously, neglecting it as mere dreams that don't have any basis.

What we need to realize is that time is not linear, unlike what we would like to believe. Time is like a cycle where our past, future, and our present are all connected, and each event has a connection with another event. It might not seem to be related at present immediately, but it is most definitely connected with events somewhere in our past or in our future. Every word that we speak, every word thought that we think, and every emotion we feel are all held together in a circle that plays its own game. As a result of that, many a time, our telepathic powers start acting in our dreams, giving us prior ideas about things yet to happen. If you have such recurring dreams, it is better to think and analyze them rather than ignore them.

- **Sensations in Your Third Eye** – Did you ever notice some weird sensations around the center of your forehead, or do you ever feel a sharp pain in the region between your eyes? You will be surprised to know that unlike what we commonly think this to be like something related to some eye problem that we have or migraine or whatever, this could actually be a sign that you have telepathic abilities. This place that we mentioned is where our third eye is located, and it is one of the most crucial chakra points in our body.

So, suppose this area is aching at times or having a tingling sensation. In that case, the chances are that your third eye is expanding or that you are developing telepathic abilities. You need to understand that you need to accept your reality and not shy away from it. Whether you choose to practice it is completely upon you. But before that, you need to accept what it is. So, as and when you accept this and embrace your reality, this pain will automatically subside.

- **You are Empathetic** – Some might get confused between what Telepathy is and what Empathy is because they are so very similar to one another. As we all know that empathy is the ability that many of us have to genuinely feel what the other person is feeling or is going through, and telepathy is when we have an acute understanding of what thoughts are going on in the minds of the other person. If we think properly, they are not exactly the same, but they do have many similarities. They both deal with the thoughts and feelings of other people and understanding in detail what the other person is going through.

If you are an empath, you will obviously have these deep feelings of understanding for other people's needs, their character in general for you to know what they are going through and to get a prior understanding of what steps they might take next given you understand how their mind works. These are very similar to how the mind of a person, who has telepathic abilities, thinks. So, it might also happen that the empathetic powers in you give rise to telepathic powers over a certain period of time.

- **Connection With the Spirit World** – Many a time, it can happen that a person who already has telepathic abilities in him\her might not be fully awakened to that truth due to various reasons or modes of distraction. But even if you haven't been awakened to the truth, you need to ask yourself certain questions like whether you are drawn towards your spiritual self often or whether you feel a deep sense of connection with your ancestors. Is it so that you find a lot of peace and comfort in practices like meditation or activities of mindfulness? One of the most potent reasons for this is that you have telepathic abilities which are yet to be discovered. This happens because your inner consciousness knows the truth that lies within you and your being, and these are just mere signs of that which are helping you to be awakened to your truth.

- **Picking Up Lies** - Have you noticed this ability to easily understand when someone is lying or not? If that is the case, then this could be a potential sign for you to have telepathic powers. Telepathic people can easily get a feeling in their gut of something that has not happened yet or when something is unnatural and not in the way that it is supposed to be. People who have telepathic abilities have this inherent tendency in them of being able to communicate with their minds, so it becomes easier for them to instantly catch people who might be lying. That something is unnatural and that the other person is hiding something can be easily understood by telepathic people as the normal frequency starts getting disrupted.

- **You Have a Tendency of Receiving Thoughts Directly From Others** – This happens with time when someone has been practicing telepathy for a long time and has honed the skills with a lot of practice. With a time of prolonged practice of communicating through telepathic methods, it might so be that you are now able to directly "hear" thoughts of others without much effort, or with time your gut feeling has become so strong that you just "know" things for sure now and can act upon them with complete confidence. It becomes easier for people with telepathic abilities to know things and hear thoughts with regular practice and an honest acceptance of their truths and welcome their powers.

- **You Can Easily Send Messages to Others** – Telepathy is not restricted to only hearing thoughts and getting a premonition or a kind of gut feeling about something that is going to happen. Telepathy is also about the transmission of thoughts. That includes both receiving and sending information accurately with others who are equally adept at telepathy. That is the reason a person who has been practicing telepathic powers for some time now, and they have honed the entire mechanism of this practice, along with receiving information, also becomes adept at sending information accurately to others. All it takes is a bit of regular and diligent practice from your part if you do have the powers so that they might not go to waste and can be put to proper use.

How to Practice Telepathy?

Telepathy, like all other forms of psychic abilities, needs a lot of honest and diligent practice on our part. If we are ready to accept our truth and welcome the powers that we have, then just known about them superficially won't help at all. It is equally important to build up our strength and skills so that we can internalize the art of telepathy and use it to accurately transmit information, that is to properly receive and send information. While at the same time, we become more confident in our intuitive abilities. Let us then see some of the methods by which we can practice telepathy.

- **Practice Meditation** – It is absolutely imperative for anyone who wants to practice telepathy to learn to meditate and do it diligently every day. Unlike what most people will believe, meditation is not sitting at one place with your legs crossed and arms folded while you chant "om." It is much more than that. Meditation will help you learn what your thoughts are capable of and how you can bring them together and use their powers. Meditation teaches a person to redirect their thoughts in the right direction, and it helps a person to learn how to focus on something without allowing anything to distract them. This is what is needed in telepathy. You need to be able to focus on the transmission of your thoughts and feelings without getting distracted, and meditation helps you achieve that.

- **Understand Where Your Strength Lies** – It is also crucial to learn about your mistakes, your weaknesses, and your strengths. Only then will you be able to avoid further mistakes and get better at your job. That is why, while you are starting your practice of telepathy, analyze your methods and try and understand what your strength is. Is it sending, or is it receiving information? Based on that, further your practices and focus more on improving that quality. This will help you remain focused and improve your confidence.

- **Practice Receiving Information** – This is a very good way of practicing telepathy if you have the powers. While you are talking to anyone, try and listen to what they are thinking more than what they are saying out loud. Try to focus more on what they are feeling at that moment and try to understand their emotions regarding what is being discussed rather than what they are saying through their words. This will help you slowly strengthen your receiving powers. You will slowly but steadily become more comfortable and confident with your own emotions. Initially, what must have come to you as only a feeling will now become more specific. You can do this while talking to strangers, and it will be even better if you do this with your family and friends as you already know them, so the entire process will become easier. But just a note of caution, do not try this with someone who is a skeptic. Those people are never open or honest about their thoughts and feelings, and it will only confuse you further.

- **Practice Sending Messages** – It is as essential to practice receiving messages as it is sending them. It is exciting and tricky as you start practicing. Try this initially, that when you visit someone or greet someone with a "hello" maybe, while you are saying that "hello" out loud, say "goodbye" in your mind. If you see that their facial reaction changes slightly, it means that they are confused and they have received your message.

- **Exercise Regularly** – Once you have understood the entire situation and gotten information on all the necessary things, you need to start practicing your skills, and at the same time, you need to exercise regularly to perfect all your abilities. Find yourself a willing volunteer who will participate in your mind exercises as you receive and send messages. You can start exercising with tarot cards, or you can also use an oracle deck. Create small hurdles for yourself to conquer, like increasing the physical distance between you and your exercise partner.

Remember that the more you practice your skills, the better they will become. If you have been gifted with telepathic abilities, you should not let them go to waste, and instead, you should try out different methods of getting to know more about them and finding ways of practicing them for perfection.

Chapter 13: How to Stop Absorbing the Energy of Others?

If you are an empath, then the chances are that you are constantly bothered by other people's energies, even when you do not want to. However, although that is almost unavoidable, that is also very tiring in nature. This is why, if you identify as an empath, it is really crucial that you learn and practice ways in which you safeguard your energy.

Here are a few ways in which you can try and stop absorbing other people's energy and can also get rid of negative energy –

Identify Any Unresolved Issues You Might Be Having

A lot of times, in order to repel negative energy, you need to focus on what is going on with you before you can turn your attention towards other's energy. You have to identify and fix things within yourself before seeing how other people are disrupting your energy and how those can be avoided.

A lot of times, when you are interacting with someone else, you might get easily triggered by something they might have said or done, and it would immediately strike a nerve with you. You might want to lash out at them and take all your anger out in one instant. If this sounds like something which happens to you, then you need to take a long look at your own triggers and issues as, in the longer run, that would help you stop absorbing the energies other people give out the energies which are bothering you.

Completely Express Yourself

Allow yourself to express completely without any feeling of remorse or guilt. What can happen when someone is interacting with you for hours, draining your energy, and making you feel exhausted, but you do not want to raise a concern just because you do not want to be rude? You are only hurting yourself that way by remaining silent. You are turning yourself into a sponge, absorbing everything people throw at you without caring for your energy.

This way, you are completely neglecting your authenticity as you are not letting yourself be at your full potential. Once you can really express your 100%, by subtracting guilt from that equation, you are becoming more transparent. This will only go on to help yourself become the best version that could be.

While growing up, a lot of us functioned on the principles of *reward and punishment*. This functions in the following way – if you are doing something right, your parents will give you some rewards, so that good behavior is reinforced, and if you are doing something wrong, then something is taken away from you so that you are conditioned to not repeat your behavior. All of these lead to repressing your own feelings right from your childhood. This leads to repressing your true self. Once you start unlearning this behavior, you take better care of yourself and your energy.

Find Your Inner Environment

It is important that you build a very healthy inner environment so that your positive energy could flourish. It is not always about the outer environment; although the outer environment is important and affects you a lot, if you help build a healthy environment within you, no matter how the outer environment is, you would be able to protect your energy. Our environment is of such importance because it affects and even alters your DNA. However, even more than your environment, your perception of your environment alters your DNA. how you see and understand yourself in relation to your environment greatly influences the time of the person you become and how you interact.

This is why what you witness with your own eyes, as well as how you perceive what is inside you, becomes a clear reflection of how you are feeling. Once you build a better environment inside you and nourish positive feelings, you will reflect that in your actions and invite more positive energy. Eventually, there would come the point when you would have a perfect sense of inner harmony. This is when you would start to let go of other people's energies and start manifesting the positive energy that resides inside you in the environment around you.

Do Not Assume Responsibility for Others

Remember that you have no control over how other people choose to react and respond to you. You also cannot control or change how others feel for you or act towards you. A lot of times, assuming responsibility for others is how you deflect acting upon your own self. Let yourself get rid of those accountabilities. When you do this, you are freeing yourself of the burden of carrying the guilt and accountability of someone else's actions on your own shoulders. You learn to create a boundary between what you can have a say on and what you cannot and can thus divide the personal from what is clearly not under your purview. Once you let yourself be free of these responsibilities, you stop absorbing the energy given out by other people.

Eliminate Your Need for Validation

All human beings function on a clear need for validation. Remind yourself repeatedly that you do not essentially need external validation; instead, you need selfless help and support. When you live your lives striving for external validation and approval, you start to absorb their energies, as you would feel angry, hopeless, and frustrated if you are not getting the validation back that you are expecting.
When you are trying to become the best version of yourself, you let go of the expectations that you need others to validate

you and your energy. What other people feel for you or say about you does matter, but it is not too significant that it has to completely take over your feelings. You need to be self-aware and reflect on how much the opinions of people should matter to you and how they might help you improve.

Come up With Ways of Protecting Yourself

There are various ways to protect yourself from negative energy through the use of shields and barriers. A convenient form of protection many people use- including professional healers themselves- is developing a shield in the form of an envelope which gives out white rays of light around your body. When you are visualizing this envelope, imagine it as something which acts as a filter- it filters the negative energy out and allows only positive external energy to get inside your body. For example, you feel like your brother is about to blow up and is destructively angry, but you do not want his anger to affect you in a drastic way.

What you can do in this situation is to imagine that there exists a foolproof barrier all around your body that will repel the negative, angry energy that is coming out of your brother, and before that energy can even touch you, it is being repelled by this barrier. Shielding is a very useful technique as it helps set up a frontier of deliberate defense. It helps protect and guard your feelings instead of blocking them out or repressing them. Therefore, it lets you healthily process your feelings as well as helping you preserve yourself without affecting how you are letting yourself function.

Learn How to Practice Vulnerability

A very important tenet of spiritual practices is to learn how to actively be vulnerable. This is the exact opposite of building a shield for yourself, and this form works better for some people. Use only the strategy which works the best for you, and if the best mode of protection turns out to be no protection at all, then so be it.

It could be extremely liberating to let down all your guards and allow yourself to take in all that comes your way, and then letting your energy select for itself what it wants to attract. This way, you are not deliberately shutting down any energy interactions but are learning from trying and testing what works for you and what does not. Assuming a stance that is vulnerable in nature will feel a lot safer in the long run as you do not always have to worry about building defense shields for yourself at all times. Being vulnerable is a life-long practice, and it needs a lot of courage and a lot of practice; and if you think you can commit to that for the longer term, then it is highly recommended.

Walk Away From Sources of Negative Energy

In order to keep negative energy at bay, you must learn how to walk away from people who you do not have a good feeling about. For example, let's say you are at a seminar. You met someone there, and the both of you started chatting, and you immediately feel as if negative energy is seeping out of them. It is not a feeling you can clearly justify, reason with, or put your finger on, but it is a feeling you feel very intuitive about. In situations like these, make sure to trust your gut feelings and excuse yourself from a situation like this.

Often, what happens is that you let other people absorb your energy because we are afraid of sounding rude and want to be polite and formal from our side. But we must remember that we cannot tend to anyone by sacrificing our mental peace and empath energy. Risking your own well-being just so that you do not come across as impolite to someone else is not a healthy practice; it will only drain you further. Allow yourself to make a smart, swift exit at situations like these. Physically remove yourself from these tricky situations before you get too emotionally invested as if that happens, then removing or detaching yourself might become trickier and harder.

Meditate

Meditation is one of the healthiest practices that you can develop so that you are better in charge of how you are managing your energies. Meditation helps you strengthen your inner bond and hold your grounding in place no matter what the situation is that you are in.

The best way to practice meditation - especially if you are new to it - is to get into a daily habit of taking some time out of your day and dedicate it to practicing and improving your meditation techniques. You can start with meditating for only a few minutes and can then increase the duration. The technique you have to follow could be very simple- you just need to follow your breath and be active about how your body is regulating energy when you inhale and exhale. As and when thoughts come to - like they most definitely will- you need to navigate the spaces between the thoughts, as that is where your spirit is waiting to be discovered. Help yourself silent get familiar with your spirit, and do not force anything on yourself; you do not have to learn too fast or take too long, discover your own pace and go with the flow, as that is how your spirit would also be most comfortable with in terms of how it is interacting with you during meditation.

Try all of these techniques out when you start feeling overwhelmed. Some might not work for you at all, but if that happens, then do not get discouraged. Try the other tips out and take some time with it. One of them will work out for you, and once you recognize which one does, make sure you stick to it since if you are an empath, you will need to recharge your energy. The best way to do that is to keep negative energy at bay, and that is what this article is to help you out with!

Chapter 14: A Step-by-Step Guide to Protect Yourself From Energy Vampires

All of us need protection against energy vampires because they do a very good job at draining you of all your life force and energy, be it intentionally or unintentionally. They have the power to leave you emotionally incapable, and that is why we need to find active ways to firstly know who these energy vampires are (we shall talk about that in detail later in the chapter), how can we identify them, and what are the best ways to deal with them and protect ourselves against them.

Who Are Energy Vampires?

Have you ever felt that there are people in your life who, when you talk to, you start feeling low? Are there people who make you feel unworthy or unloved? The chances are that they are energy vampires and whether knowingly or unknowingly, they make you feel unloved, uncared for; they do a good job at pointing out your mistakes all the time, without even once acknowledging the good in you. It is in their nature to always look at the negative things. Or even when they are not doing that, they have an inherent way to turn any situation uncomfortable for you so that you are left feeling emotionally drained. Energy vampires are good at "taking" things from you without giving anything in return, be it your energy, your spirit, your enthusiasm, or something else. Let us see the different types of energy vampires so that we are more aware of them because they could be anywhere. They could be our family, friends, colleagues, neighbors, clients, or even strangers. That is why we need to be aware at all times.

- There is a kind of energy vampire who could be termed as "jealous bees" who are of the habit of never being happy with anyone's success or even happiness. No matter how close that other person is, they have this inherent jealousy in them that restricts them from being happy for others, and they make it a point to make you understand that.

- The next is the "blamers" who have their unique way of putting the blame of everything on you, whether or not you were a part of that work. They never take responsibility for anything that they do and slyly make their way out of all situations without any remorse or sense of responsibility.

- Then there are the classic "fun haters" who simply cannot tolerate fun. They won't let you have fun no matter how good in a mood you are in. they make it a point to say something inappropriate or make you uncomfortable in some way so that your mood is ruined and you don't have it in you to have fun anymore.

- The "guilt trippers" use guilt as a weapon to darken the mood and make any happy situation into a gloomy one. They use guilt to get whatever they want.

- We also have the "insecure ones" who are always fearing their own place in a person's life, and as a result of their own insecurity complex, they tend to bring down others along with them so that no one else can be happy.

- And finally, there are the "Debbie downers" or the "whinners" who complain all the time about something or the other; they are gossiping all the time, making sure they turn one person against another, and they are very good at creating drama.

These are the various kind of energy vampires who literally suck the happiness and energy out of you in different ways as they cannot see anyone else happy besides themselves. The basic fact is, they might take whichever form they want to, but their ultimate motto in life is to suck out other's means of sustenance in order for them to go on. Like leeches, they tend to latch on to the positivity that others radiate, and they feed on the life forces of others so that they have enough for themselves to go on while their host is left with nothing and their life is filled with negativities and misery. These kinds of people are really dangerous, and they should not only be identified but also avoided at all costs.

How to Identify an Energy Vampire?

There are few things that you need to look out for in a person. Notice whether they do these things, and you can get a fairly good idea about whether or not they are energy vampires.

- *They Avoid Taking Accountability* – Energy vampires are usually very charismatic. They know how to such out all the energy from you and yet slyly come out of the situation, without taking any responsibility for what they have done, while all the while making you feel guilty for something that you haven't done in the first place. They can be very charismatic that way. They refuse to take any kind of accountability for their actions. They very craftily pin problems at others in case of any kind of disagreement or problem, blaming others on the way.

- *They Create a Lot of Drama* – Energy vampires live on drama. They do this very well. They absolutely love creating a scene so as to completely ruin the mood of everyone present. They make it a point to prove to others that they are victims of every situation as they tend to find themselves surrounded by catastrophe all the time. They love creating chaos, and if by chance you happen to be around, they will make sure you are a part of that drama as well. And then they quickly turn the tables on you, saying that it was not their fault but somehow yours.

- *They One-Up on You* – Energy vampires are narcissists, and probably that is why they cannot tolerate when others are happy. They have the tendency to steal the spotlight at every opportunity that they get. They cannot stand the fact that someone could be happier than them or more successful. They need to be at the top no matter what the situation is. That is why, when they see someone doing better than them, they try to one-up that person by whatever means possible.

- *They Like to Play Up Their Problems by Diminishing Your Problems* – As energy vampires like to make everything about themselves, so it is very natural for them to try and bring themselves to the center of any discussion that is taking place. It can so be that you are trying to talk about your problem, and they instantly start talking about their own problems in a way that makes your issue seem frivolous and their own of grave importance. They talk in a way so that everyone present gets distracted from what you were saying and fix their attention him\her specifically. They have their way of making things such that you might feel that their problem is more important than yours.

- *They Act Like Your Savior* – One of the most common ploys that energy vampires use is to act like a martyr so that they can feel good about themselves. They tend to brag about whatever good they have done for someone over and over so that they can create a good image of themselves in other's minds. They use this ploy to portray how superior and good a person they are so that people will talk about them, and that in turn boosts their ego.

- ***They Use Guilt to Their Advantage*** – This is a favorite with energy vampires. They often use guilt trips and ultimatum to their advantage to get what they want. They target people who are compassionate and kind, and they know that with these kinds of people, shame works really well. That is why they use this as a weapon. They try to engage a person's attention by the use of ultimatums in order to make them do things that they otherwise wouldn't have done.

Energy Vampires in Workplace

Energy vampires can be present everywhere, and we need to be aware of them at our workplaces as well so that we can do our work in peace while at the same time not fall prey to such people. Let us look at some of the ways by which we can identify the energy vampires at workplaces.

- Look out for those people who tend to constantly ask for your help even when they clearly do not need it. If you are an employer, notice if all your best employees are giving a relatively poor performance. It could be because an energy vampire is around. Such people make it a point to target those who are more capable as they simply cannot tolerate others being happy.

- Look out for such people when you are having a meeting in the office. Meetings are literally hunting grounds for energy vampires as they get so many people who have come together to discuss something positive and productive. Look out for people who make it a point to act in a way that hampers the meeting, be it by making irrational points or trying to keep the attention on themselves somehow.

- Be aware of people in your workplace who bully others and who take the help of intimidating ways to get what they want. If you are an employer, make sure such people are not around, as it will invariably hamper the work culture and bring down the performance of the entire team.

- If you find that your office is having a lot of drama lately, try and found out the cause, and you might be surprised to see that the source of these dramas are such energy vampires who, when they see any progress in people apart from themselves, go out of their way to ruin the mood.

What Does an Empath-Vampire Relationship Look Like?

Empaths are fixated with their attitude of helping others and being compassionate all the time, even at the cost of their feelings. They genuinely want to help others as they can easily feel the pain that others are feeling. Energy vampires, on the other hand, cannot tolerate the happiness and success of others. They go out of their way to bring others down by destroying their spirit and by criticizing people, pointing out their mistakes so often that they don't have enough spirit left to go ahead. Naturally, a relationship between an empath and an energy vampire would be problematic and toxic, to say the least.

Any relationship flourishes when both the partners are taken care of, and they benefit mutually with the shared love and care. However, in such a case as we are discussing now, the empath will continue trying their best to make sure that all the needs of this other person are looked after while the energy vampire would be on the receiving end of all the care, giving nothing in return and sucking out all the happiness and enthusiasm from the partner. Such a relationship will never be balanced and will only cause misery to the empath partner and others around them.

The empath, with their need and desperate want for love, will never complain even if they feel something is wrong, and the energy vampire will have a gala time getting their twisted psychological nourishment by sucking away the spirit of their partner. The relationship will become stagnant after a point as the energy vampire will not let the empath move forward or develop in any way, and the empath will continue satisfying the energy vampire all the time. The empath already feels insecure about themselves and thus the constant need for love; on top of that, the energy vampire, knowing all the weaknesses of the partner, will simply take advantage of that, adding to their misery. Such a relationship is indeed unfortunate and problematic. The empath will have difficulty coming out of this as they will try not to give up on the partner. The energy vampire would want not to come out of the relationship because they are getting all the nourishment that they need. It's a completely win-lose situation for the vampire and the empath, respectively.

How to Handle Energy Vampires?

There are many ways in which you can shield yourself from potential energy vampires. As intimidating energy vampires might sound, there are ways to protect oneself from them.

- *Practice Self-Awareness* – If you can identify who the energy vampires are around you, it becomes easier to protect yourself. Many-a-time what happens is that we remain oblivious to their charisma, and we might also choose to ignore them because they might be close to us. But, we need to be self-aware all the time so that we instantly recognize who they are and take necessary measures. No matter how close these people are, we need to avoid them.

- *Take Back Control* – The thing with energy vampires is that due to their charisma, they tend to hold a lot of power over us. If you can recognize them, then you need to make sure that you take back the control in your hands. The lesser control they have, the easier it will be for us to not get affected by what they are saying.

- *Practice Self-Care* – Energy vampires can do a very good job at bringing your morale down, and they can suck out your spirit. As a result, you might feel bad about yourself and inferior, which is what the vampire wants. What you need to do when you have such a person around you is to practice self-care. Just because someone told you something doesn't make that the truth. Know your self-worth and hold it close.

Dealing With Energy Vampires at Work

- **The Melodramatic Type** – There might be colleagues at work who have no sense of personal space and don't respect your privacy. They tend to bother you all the time with their drama expecting help.

  Be kind to them but maintain distance. Do not entertain them after a certain point. Limit their entrance to the point that doesn't affect your work.

- **The Egomaniac Type** – These kinds of people will make it a point to suppress you just because they want to. In order to satisfy their ego, they can even try to turn your colleagues and boss against you.

  Try to understand what has hurt their ego. Knowing the actual reason will help you deal with the problems they come up with. It will help you stay detached without getting personally involved in it and find a solution.

- **The Dependent Type** – This person will be a constant nag. They will come to you for every small

173

and big issue making sure you lag behind your job at your office. They would ask for help with silly things.

The chances are that this person needs your reassurance for everything, so give them the necessary positive feedback at the very beginning so that it satisfies their psyche, and they go. But if that doesn't work, be stern with them, reminding them of their boundaries.

How Can You Set Your Boundaries With Energy Vampires?

The first and foremost thing to protect yourself from energy vampires is to set firm boundaries that don't let them come very near. Let us see what some of these ways are.

- *Listen to Your Gut Feeling* – Understand that your body is never wrong. It will always give you the correct signals. It might so happen that you don't even know who these energy vampires are in your life. That is why listen closely to your body. If it ever happens that you start feeling fatigued and pessimistic after talking to someone? If so, keep that in mind the next time you meet them. If the same thing happens, understand that they are energy vampires. Keep these people out of your circle.

- *Remember to Keep Control* – The moment you lose control with an energy vampire is the moment they get a better grip on your spirit. Do not let that happen. Tell yourself constantly that you are in control and keep holding on to it. That will prevent them from coming too close and messing with your mind.

- *Take a Non-Confrontational Attitude* – One of the best ways to deal with energy vampires is to be completely straightforward with them and to take a non-confrontational attitude. Suppose you have to have a problem with people like them. For the sake of your mental health, be straightforward and tell them to back off. The more you entertain their advances, the more they will claw their way in. It is necessary to keep them at bay.

- *Take a Break* – Dealing with energy vampires can be extremely exhausting and for all valid reasons. At times avoiding them is also not an option given if they are someone very close to us or someone like our boss. In those times, you need to take regular and meaningful breaks so as to replenish yourself from time to time. No matter how much you try to avoid them, they have their own ways to get under your skin. So, if you have to, unfortunately, deal with such people, be kind to yourself and take breaks so that you can get in control of all your thoughts and regain back the energy to start a new day.

- *Cut Them Out Completely if Needed* – This might be a very difficult thing to do, but if necessary, then you need to do exactly this. We understand that cutting someone off from your life is a pretty difficult thing, and it takes a lot of courage. More so if that person is close to you. But having said that, it is your life, and it falls on your shoulders to make it better. If for that you need to take this action, so be it.

I hope this chapter has been helpful to you in getting information on energy vampires. They are genuinely problematic people, and it really takes a lot to deal with them. But there are ways in which such situations can be handled, and I hope you have got some idea regarding the same through this chapter.

Chapter 15: The Art of Clairvoyant Healing

Clairvoyant healing is a spiritual and psychic process of directing energies. All living bodies consist of energy. We are made up of and surrounded by energy at all times and are constantly affected by these different energies – sometimes when we are aware of their presence and impact, and sometimes when we are not – in ways that go on to shape our lives in major ways. When these different forms of energies transform, move around, shift forms, and release and restructure themselves, a process of change takes place in our mind, body, emotions, as well as spirits. This process of change is known as healing.

Common Techniques of Clairvoyant Healing

There are many different techniques that you can resort to if you are looking to get started with clairvoyant healing. Through these techniques, you would essentially be facilitating several ways of spiritual healing and transformation.

Some of these methods which have proven to work with many people include acupuncture, touch, sound, prayers, chantings, and so on. A lot of times, these techniques – and the effects they generate- come along with some degree of visualization. If someone is getting started with clairvoyant healing, it is only natural for them to visualize what they want, desire, and intend for. For example, if you are a clairvoyant healer and you are feeling hungry, you might be very easily able to visualize a sandwich in front of you. It is easy for you to get lost in what might seem like daydreaming – for the lack of a better word – but it is actually a manifestation of the visualization powers that come with your clairvoyance abilities. However, even if you do not have the clearest visualization abilities, you could still be causing powerful transformation in yourself or in another person through your powers as a clairvoyant healer. Although visualization is a part of the process, it does not define it and is not an indispensable realm of clairvoyance.

If you want some very basic tips on how to get started with clairvoyant healing, then we have got you covered. Follow the steps listed below to guide you through any attempts in general at healing:

- **Creating a screen for healing:** Any activity which deals with clairvoyant healing needs you to access psychic information, and for doing this, you would need a designated place where you could display the required information. This is where a healing screen would come in handy. Setting up a healing screen for your clairvoyant activities will help you just like a television screen would help out in seeing TV programs and other related broadcasts, or a desktop monitor would help you out to browse the internet and access information. When you are performing healing, you would have your eyes closed, and from the inside of your head, you would have to imagine that you are looking outward using your third eye, and this image is being projected onto a screen which is situated a couple of inches out of your head. It is up to you to decide what the screen looks like and to settle on its specific details.

  The screen could be any way that you want it to be. It could be as large as the screen at a movie theatre or even as small as the screen of your tablet device. There are no restrictions, you create your healing screen, and you get to decide its details. Notice the minute borders of your healing screen as well- notice if it has a border, and if it does, how does the border look like, what are its dimensions, what color is it, and so on. Also, notice for yourself if you can spot something unusual about your screen or not. Before you consciously create an image – any image – and project it on the screen, it might help to just notice how the image looks at first, rather than trying to actively project it. If you try to notice that for a significant amount of time and you are still not sure of how the image looks, then you can make a conscious decision to create your image in a certain way.

- **Grounding your healing screen:** Once you have set up a healing screen, it is up to you to keep any negative energy away from affecting your screen in any possible way. This energy might also include the energy that could be interfering between you and your attempts at visualizing and focusing on your screen. Steering clear of this negative energy will help your clairvoyant healing practices at large to a great extent. You can achieve this by trying to create a grounding cord. This can be done by forming a connection between your body and the center of the earth; however, when it comes to the screen, the grounding cord needs to connect the center of the earth with the screen through a column of energy.

  Again, since the screen has been born completely out of your imagination, it is also up to you to imagine what this grounding cord would be like. It can look like an anchor, the trunk of a tree, or even like a steady metal pole. Once you have managed to secure your healing screen using its grounding cord, call out whichever foreign energy might there be present, which is obstructing your vision. To execute this, you can imagine a certain color being sucked by the earth's gravitational pull through the cord and then imagine the planet absorbing it completely. After you do this, take a look at your healing screen, and you might be able to notice that some things about it and the images projected on it have been transformed.

- **Creating a viewing receptacle for healing:** Now, after you have created a screen and made sure that you have protected your healing screen from negative entities, you would have to shift your focus to creating a viewing receptacle that you can place on the screen. This receptacle is where any energy or information which you want to read will appear. In a way, a healing screen acts as a dining room table. You have to sit down at the table, and on the table, you have to place a bowl, which would act as your receptacle. If you pour your food directly on the table, then it will spill over everywhere and will create a mess. Similarly, if you create a screen without a proper receptacle, then the entire act of clairvoyant healing will be nothing but a mess in itself. In this case, it would not just be uneasy about eating your food this way; it would also take you a lot of time and effort to clear it up. The same thing will happen to your energy as well if a viewing receptacle does not take the place of a disposable bowl on the dining room table that your healing screen ends up being.

  You can imagine the receptacle to be in the form of any neutral object. This object can be a flower, a balloon, or even a candy. A lot of established clairvoyant programs suggest that you pick the image of a rose to act as your receptacle. This is suggested because a rose can be very easily visualized, and they also come in various colors, shapes, and forms. Since the rose, like any other flower, grows directly from the earth, it is easy to set a grounding cord for it as well.

- **Grounding the viewing receptacle:** Once a viewing receptacle has been set up, it needs to be grounded. For this, imagine that you are looking at your healing screen. Visualize yourself placing a receptacle onto your screen. Notice the shape and size of the receptacle. Notice its details; notice how it looks and appears against a blank canvas that your healing screen is. In case you are facing any difficulties visualizing the object that you have chosen to be your receptacle, imagine a strong grounding cord around it, which might help you situate it better. Connect your receptacle with the center of the earth and let it absorb its energy through the cord, and make sure you let the earth naturally suck up the negative energy, which could be causing problems for the process of your visualization.

However, if you see that your receptacle is behaving in an unusual way or even taking up a life of and on its own, do not worry! Remember that if something is happening to your receptacle, you can use your clairvoyant energy to intercept it and control what is happening. If it was not important, you would not have been able to recognize it at all in the first place, so try your best to direct your energy towards controlling your receptacle.

- **Inviting energy into your receptacle:** Finally, after your healing screen as well as the viewing receptacle have both been set up, you would have to call energy into your receptacle since the ultimate purpose of performing clairvoyant healing is for you to access some psychic information from an external, often spiritual, source. For you to do this, you need to have a clear goal and/or set of questions laid out in your mind so that you can direct this information towards your viewing receptacle. The question can be simple or very layered or complicated, that does not matter so much, and it can revolve around other people or you. You might want to know why and how certain energies concern you or affect other people or feel a certain way- all of these questions can be answered through a process of healing.

Through an intake of energy, the questions which are there in your mind would be solved. Any act of clairvoyant healing is quite simple- it basically is simply about opening yourself up to accept forms of energy into the viewing receptacle that you have set up for yourself, and then, you need to request your receptacle to display the answer for you through a sequence of images and colors. There are three methods through which this can be done, and you can try all of them out to figure out which one suits you the best.

- o Create the image of your receptacle over the screen, study it closely, and imagine it connecting to your inner aura. If this imagination makes the image change, focus on the change and try to find the answer to your question through the ways this change has taken place. Once you have done this, destroy the image you had created into a thousand pieces, and discard it.

- o Create the image of your receptacle over your healing screen. Notice its shape and size and study it for a while. Next, situate that using its grounding cord and ground the image towards the center of the earth. Project the image to be a representation of yourself and make the cord absorb any energy which you are ready to release yourself. Once you have done that and feel any change occurring, end the exercise, following which you need to destroy the image of your receptacle by pretending that it is being dissolved into a fire.

- o Repeat the starting exercise, and this time, have the receptacle represent a part of your life that you would like to bring into existence (it could be a new job, an opportunity, or even happiness). Do not manipulate the image. Just observe it closely and see if it shows any changes or not. After doing it for a few minutes, you are most likely to notice something unusual which you did not intend to create. This aspect is the one you need to highlight and use to find the answer to your queries. Once you are done, make sure to destroy the image. This time, imagine that you are sending it away to a divine being so that it can serve a better and larger purpose.

Now that you know the techniques to perform clairvoyant healing, here are some of the ways in which you can prepare yourself for a session of the same:

1. **Communicate your expectations:** Before conducting a healing session, both parties should be very clear about what they are signing up for and what they seek to gain out of this session. There must be clear channels of communication between them so that the experience can be an enriching one for everyone involved in the process. Discussing each other's experiences is a very ethically and morally sound practice, and if you are being charged (or inversely, if you are paying) for this session, then financial details should also be looped into the discussion that you are having. If these discussions are not out in the open, then there would be unresolved anxiety on either one of the party's minds (or even both), and this tension would prevent a proper healing session from being conducted.

2. **Find the correct location:** It is really important for you to find the right location before you even plan to conduct a healing session. This location ideally needs to be quiet and have as few distractions and external disturbances as possible. However, it must also be a spot that makes you feel safe and secure, as you might be sharing that spot with another person, even a stranger, so ensuring personal safety is absolutely

integral (if you do not feel safe, you do not allow the healing to be a safe process as well, and it is not likely to serve its purpose in such a case).

3. **Keep track of time:** It is very important for someone to keep track of time, which can easily be done by keeping a timer, watch, or even a digital clock around the place of the healing. The sound of a timer might be too distracting or startling for some people, so it might be a better idea to have a larger clock at the display, which just needs your visual attention and would not interrupt the concentration that is needed to conduct a successful session of clairvoyant healing. Having a clock or a timer on you will help you monitor the passage of time, and at the same time, it might also help the person at the receiving end of the healing session to come back to reality and accept that the session has ended.

4. **Start with a set intention:** Before you start a session of clairvoyant healing, it might be actually useful to pick up a few things which you will try to work on during the session. Having a clearly defined intention will help serve as a reminder that both the healer and the person who is being healed are important and that healing acts as a process of growth for everyone who is involved. Often, the person being healed tends to assume more importance in the process, which might leave the healer feeling drained and tired. Having an intention set for them to achieve as well helps cope with any such feelings.

5. **Practice meditation before healing:** Before you start a session of healing, it is widely advised that you meditate for around 15 to 20 minutes on your own. Meditation would do away with all the negative, exhausting thoughts and energies you might be holding within yourself, all of which would pose an obstacle for the healing to effectively take place if they were not properly taken care of. You would also be

less susceptible to negative external entities if you flush yourself out of similar negative energies, which might act as a magnet for these.

6. **Establish clear boundaries:** Like any other interaction, it is absolutely essential that you set boundaries when it comes to clairvoyant healing sessions as well. When you are acting as a healer, you would often feel that even before you are allowing yourself to be receptive to the receiver's energy, it would be approaching you, sometimes even in an invasive form. This can happen very unintentionally as well, and can throw you off guard, making you apprehensive and nervous since it feels like taking up more than you had signed up for.

   Sometimes, healers carry out an individual session before the other person arrives so that they feel less nervous and more equipped to deal with such situations. That is very much discouraged as it turns the session into a mere performance. Instead, what needs to be done is regularly sharpening your psychic tools so that it is enabled to take on more than it could initially do.

7. **Do not allow just anyone in the room:** When a session is going on, it is in the best interest of both the parties involved that nobody other than the two of them is allowed in the same room (or spot). This is because a third person's presence might emit energies that would disturb the healing process, and you can even start reading them and not your intended receiver if this happens. Besides this, clairvoyant healings tend to be very personal sessions, and a lot of intimate information – which should not be shared with other people indiscriminately – might come up during the session, so it is also advisable that other people are not allowed inside the room so that the receiver's privacy and confidentiality are maintained at all times.

8. Set up a healing routine: Set up a routine for yourself. Greet your receiver, introduce yourself to them, show them around the room where you will conduct the healing, cut down on external noise, etc., by drawing the curtains or shutting the door. Having a set routine creates a sense of professionalism, which in turn often helps to set healthy boundaries between the person who is healing and the person who is being healed.

Troubleshooting Any Problems That Might Arise During Clairvoyant Healing

In case you are trying your best at clairvoyant healing but are still encountering some unexpected problems, here are some easy and actionable solutions that might help you fix those:

What to do if you are having trouble visualizing your screen and viewing the receptacle?

For this, you need to start with visualizing simple, smaller objects before moving your energy and focus on larger exercises. Do not let yourself be overwhelmed by the dimension and scope of the things you want to visualize. Start small by studying things from your household – like a fruit or a book or something else you are very familiar with, master how to visualize that without external help, and once you are absolutely skilled at it, try and move on to larger things. If you are still unable to visualize properly, just postulate that you are doing so and work ahead with it.

What to do if you cannot invite the needed energy into your viewing receptacle?

There is a very concrete justification behind everything that you can and cannot see. So, if you are trying very hard to visualize something and all you can see is black- a giant blob of darkness – then it might mean that you are not patient enough with your visualization. So, a good place to start is to fix that and to try and be more patient with things. Watch the void and ask it to show you what it truly stands for, and continue to watch and observe it. If nothing comes out of this, try readjusting the screen using its grounding cord and repeat the exercise.

Another problem might be that you might be asking the wrong question, which is why you are getting a futile answer in return. Some questions do not really have any answers, and for some others, it is not possible for the process to give you a suitable answer. Try to better select and formulate your questions so that you can get appropriate answers to them. For this, you can start with framing very direct, to-the-point questions which are not vague or confusing to deal with.

What to do if you keep falling asleep during clairvoyant practices?

If this happens to you, then there might be a few obvious explanations- the first one being, you are simply tired! To avoid this from repeating, schedule your sessions during a time when you feel naturally energized and fresh and are not being burdened by any other stressors which might take your attention away from the healing session. Also, try and get a good night's sleep regularly if you are practicing healing sessions so that the energy you are losing in the process can be regained in a timely manner.

You might also try practicing healing in a different position or at a different location. Make sure to distance yourself from locations where you rest or relax during these sessions, as those can pose distractions otherwise.

Can it Heal Your Relationships?

Relationships – like individuals – cannot be magically healed, all of their problems done away within the blink of an eye. That is simply an unrealistic expectation to have from any healing session, no matter how used to the process you have become. However, if done with proper care and consideration, healing can help your relationship achieve its truest and best form, even if that means the termination of the relationship. When relationship healing is carried out, the partners involved also need to be ready to assume some responsibility and carry out some of the work to mend the relationship on their own. Otherwise, no external intervention can fix a human bond that needs human effort to grow and thrive. The healing will definitely push the partners towards the desired path, but if and how they choose to walk down it is a decision they will have to consciously make.

People are constantly being influenced by a lot of different energies (both positive and negative) which are not under their control. This would include the energies they are regularly absorbing from friends, family members, co-workers, and other people in general. A collective form of these energies affects the way their relationship functions, and regardless of how aware these other people are of the relationship, their energy ends up playing some part in how the partners interact within and drive a relationship.

Clairvoyant healing is a spiritual process that holds a lot of potential in bringing about positive, life-affirming changes in people's lives. In this chapter, we went over not just what clairvoyant healing stands for but also the basic techniques of carrying it out and preparing for it, how to troubleshoot when common problems come up during these healing sessions, and so on. If you are a beginner to the world of healing, then I am sure this chapter cleared out a lot of questions you might be having and motivated you further to participate in a healing session yourself (but remember to do it with the utmost care and to steer clear of negative energies)!

Chapter 16: A Guide to Intuition

Human species by nature are bestowed with five senses – sight, taste, smell, sound, and touch. These senses send signals to our brain, and with the help of them, we perceive the workings of the world. Each of these senses works independently and cumulatively to give us an overall experience. The other sense, often called the sixth sense, which is not directly connected to any of these five senses, is present in all human beings. It works very differently from the other five senses. Our five senses have their limitations. For instance, our smell receptors work to a certain extent, or our hearing abilities or visual senses may weaken, and its capabilities can be measured. There is no concrete way to determine how our 'sixth sense' really works because, unlike the five senses, the source of it is not known to humans. It works unconsciously.

This 'sixth sense' or what is called intuition in simple terms may be defined as an inner knowing or feeling without any contemplation. We are often faced with situations in our daily lives where we neither have prior knowledge nor do we have facts available at that instant to think through and make the best decision. At times like these, we use our gut feeling or intuition to obtain an immediate perception of the situation and make a decision that is devoid of rational or strategic reasoning.

Try and think of a few similar situations you have faced in life like the following –

- You could tell who could have called you just by hearing your phone ring without a glance or who could have visited you when someone rang the bell of your house.

- When you just knew you could trust a person at first glance, or maybe you had an inkling that something was wrong just by looking at someone.

- Maybe you had an inner feeling about changing a plan that you have decided on after many thoughts like changing your career or a similar important decision in life where you had a hunch that it is not the right thing to do.

The majority of the human population has faced a similar situation in life where they can feel some kind of guidance from within without thinking much about it. If you, too, have had a similar experience and were wondering what it was, it was probably an intuition. Intuitions prove to be more helpful at certain times than a mind that has been trained with all the knowledge available in books as it enables us to see and perceive in a manner that cannot be achieved by thinking. It may initially be difficult to trust, leaving behind the assurance and confidence that our assembled knowledge provides us with and accept something outside the parameters of reason but, our intuitive minds complement our rational minds even though their tasks are different.

Intuition vs. Psychic Ability

Psychic experiences are related to intuitions and are often regarded as mystic experiences. They are a subtype of intuitive experience, and they are not completely the same. There are many different ways you can get an intuition, that is, get information without logical reasoning. Here is a list of some of the varied ways you may have an intuitive experience –

- Suppose you are struggling with a project at work, and your experience at that job gives you intuition as to how you can creatively solve the problem.

- Another kind of experience may be just knowing something instinctively. For example, when you know that you need to do a particular thing because you have an intuitive feeling in your body.

- Intuitive experiences that one might have when in a zone. Like a team intuitively knows what to do when they meet a certain situation.

- A psychic experience is a kind of intuitive experience. An example of it is when you have an intuition about what the other person is thinking.

Many intuitive people may not have ever experienced a psychic intuition which is just another way of obtaining information without logical reasoning.

Some may question if there is a relation between intuitions and spiritual experiences because of how uncannily one might receive guidance, but it feels all spooky and mysterious because we are trained to think practically and often do not pay conscious attention to it. Every human is gifted with intuitive abilities, but only a few choose to use them consciously, which is what makes some people more intuitive than others. It is very similar to how every child is bestowed with the same faculties but sharpening a particular aspect makes some become artists while some athletic.

In many cultures, however, intuitions are considered elemental to a spiritual and religious experience as we cannot physically determine the existence of God. Therefore, our belief or faith and the voluntary act of worshipping may be viewed as an intuitive experience that led us to do so. It is also important to remember in this context that even people who do not practice any kind of organized religion or are atheists may also, in a different way, have intuitive experiences.

Here are a few instances that will help you understand better if you are by nature more intuitive or you have psychic capabilities –

- Intuition is when you are stuck on an idea, but suddenly a different approach comes to your mind that will make your work better.

- When you try to concentrate or meditate holding an item that you have found to know more about its owner is you trying to exercise your psychic ability to obtain information.

- If in a situation you know exactly what your friend would say even though it is the first time you may be in that spot, that is your intuition.

- When you hear voices from within telling you more about a person or thing you have no previous association with is a psychic ability.

Your psychic ability develops when you consciously work on your intuitions; it requires practice. Anyone can enhance this ability by paying attention to it though many are naturally blessed with it and do not require any extra attention to intensify it.

Both these faculties may be acquired through specific senses – direct knowing or claircognizance, clairvoyance, clairaudience, and clairsentience.

Strengthen Your Intuition

As mentioned before, intuitive experiences are common for most people globally, but not too many people consider and act on them. We tend to seek outside help when we encounter any kind of setback in life. We either consult our family or friends or try to receive professional help during such times, which is great, but we must also be aware of our capabilities to help ourselves when the need arises. We forget to seek out what can prove to be the most powerful and accurate faculty of ours, our intuitive minds. It works just like our memory or intellectual capabilities; our intuition is a faculty of the mind that we can make use of to create a successful path for ourselves and better ourselves. Our subconscious mind is the greatest source of genius, which though invisible, always helps one with the exact knowledge we need to make the best decision. This is not only experienced by those who believe in the power of psychic or intuitive abilities but also by those who do not consider themselves gifted to experience one.

You may follow the ways listed below to enhance your intuitive abilities and make wiser, better decisions in your life –

- **To be able to realize when your intuition speaks to you** – Some people think they are not intuitive solely because they fail to realize when their intuitive minds are sending them a signal. Therefore, the first and most important way to develop your intuitive capabilities is to realize when you are being spoken to. You have to be attentive to catch such signs. Intuitions are mostly soft and subtle and are not always easily perceivable. Here, your five senses come into play. Use them optimally to activate your sixth sense and make it receptive to signs.

  These signals are transmitted to different people differently –

  - Some experience visual signs like that of flashing images or visions that are not decipherable at once but unfold gradually.

  - Some might get face emotional uneasiness or feel confused as if their logic and reason are being bypassed and they are being pushed to a thought or feeling they have not occurred to them before. It may feel almost like an epiphany or a sudden realization. This feeling of being led on a path usually makes people feel joyous and peaceful.

- o Sometimes it may be feeling like a voice is guiding you or you are being spoken to like a hunch, and if you manage to recognize it, you may be able to get clarity by entering into further dialogue with whatever you may be hearing or feeling.

- o Intuitive signals may also be sometimes felt by the body, such as feeling goosebumps or a chill in your body or a sudden sour taste in your mouth.

- o Intuitions may occur to some, just like deep-rooted confidence or a sense of certainty where you know something from your core or gut.

- **Giving importance to dreams** – These subtle signs, when received while our conscious mind is at work, maybe missed out on by one as they overrule one another. Our subconscious mind is at play when our conscious mind, too along with us, falls asleep. It is therefore important to pay attention to dreams and analyze them as our subconscious mind might give out hidden signs or intuitions in them.

- **Questioning** – You need to be actively trying to get answers out of your intuitive mind by asking specific questions. You will get more clarity on your situation if you ask clear and specific questions. That way, the guidance you will receive will be wiser.

- **Keeping track of the answers** – Intuitive experiences are always not loud, and as science suggests, they are likely to disappear within less than a minute. Therefore, they must be taken into account before they disappear. You will see a lot of clarity in your thoughts as well as clear signs if you make a habit of writing down every day in the form of journals. It has been proven to be helpful by neuroscience.

- **Acting immediately** – One must act immediately on intuitive signs that they receive as it is the way one will be able to create a channel for such signs to work together with your conscious mind and get more strong intuitive messages for them to be able to hear easily and clearly.

- **Meditate** - An effective way of connecting better with your intuitive mind is to meditate, which, when done regularly, will help you to avoid distractions, will calm the mind, thereby increasing chances to recognize such subtle internal signals. You do not need to spend hours of your day meditating, but setting aside fifteen minutes or so daily will clear your mind and augment your intuitions to take a central spot.

- **Engage yourself in creative tasks** – It has been proven through science that occupying oneself with creative tasks helps to calm down our busy and stressed minds creating an opportunity for the unconscious to communicate better in the form of intuitions. Try crafting, painting or journaling, dancing or playing a musical instrument, or anything that helps you to relax your mind.

- **Taking a break** – Our busy lives tend to clutter our minds with stress and various unwanted thoughts. Going on a holiday, spending time in nature, taking time off from your hectic daily schedule to unwind outdoors away from the technology we are always surrounded with may help us to notice the soft, intuitive signs that otherwise get overlooked due to our bustling lives.

- **Making time every day to slow down and focus on your thoughts** – In the rush of everyday duties, we often miss chances to slow down and allow our minds to think freely. Sometimes we need to consciously make a position for our intuition to speak to us as the wisest thoughts come to us when we are inclined to receive them. Take all your life decisions rationally as you may, but it is also important to consult our intuitive minds before deciding a path as it will show you your inner self, enabling you to make a true choice.

- **Prioritizing feelings over thoughts** – Our intuitions are mostly feelings while our mind keeps actively thinking, second doubting things, hesitating. Focus more on how you are feeling regarding a matter than what your logical mind is telling you. You may then be able to tell better if you are acting on your intuitions or logic of your rational mind.

- **Being in line with your morals** – Our cognitive mind thinks pragmatically and does not consider our morals into thinking, but our intuitions are always based on what we believe in or what our morals are. If you know your values well, you will know which is the thought of your rational mind and which is your intuitive feeling.

- **Putting your intuitions to test** – If you are an intuitive person or are trying to find out if your intuitions work, try and test them. You may do so by writing down whenever you have a hunch about something, maybe an intuition about your favorite team winning the match or your friend reacting a certain way to a situation or a feeling about the future. Then when the time comes, cross-check with what you had written to find out how often your intuitions were correct.

- **Practicing to intuitively guess what people are like before knowing them** – An easy exercise to practice intuitive thinking is to guess at people's personalities and how they are before getting to know them. Observe them and try to find out if you have a hunch about their personalities. The more observant and attentive you get, you will see that your intuitions may tell you a lot more than your rational mind.

- **Be open to learning from previous experiences** – All of us have experienced some unfortunate situations in life that we could have prevented had we paid more attention to minute details regarding how we felt before it. Perhaps our intuitive mind gave us some feeling which we overlooked. Think of such an event and try to remember your feelings before their occurrence. Collect as many minute details as possible, and it may tell you a pattern as to how your gut warns you so that you may have better reception and identification of them in the future.

- **Taking help of tarot cards** – Those who believe in tarot reading may try this out. Take a deck of tarot cards and try reading into it without consulting a handbook to check if your readings were on point.

- **Learning more about intuition** – Read books, articles, journals available to you to have more concrete knowledge about intuition, its workings, and ways to develop them.

- **Try breathing exercises** – Breathing exercises also calms one's mind as much as meditation and relaxing exercises. Manipulating your breath into various rhythmic patterns may help quieten the mind, thereby increasing your intuitive powers.

- **Do not oppose what you feel** – Human minds can be pretty manipulative and may make you rationalize your feelings and ignore them. Try and refrain from doing so. Trust what you feel to be able to make wiser choices.

- **Believe in yourself** – Having belief in oneself plays a big role in not just creating the opportunity to be open to receiving intuitive messages but also it enables one to confidently act on them. It is like how one trusts or believes in themselves in life situations to manifest their desires. Similarly, the more trust one puts in themself, the better the outcome will be, as trusting intuitions is all about having trust and believing in oneself.

Not everybody is equally decisive in life, or decision-making comes easily to them. Our rational mind constantly doubts, judges, and reconsiders the decision we make, but with time and the above-advised exercises, you may be able to clear your mind, eliminate any such voices within confusing you and achieve better communication with your intuitive mind.

Ego vs. Intuition

We are often advised to intuitively make decisions as they are considered the best in most situations, but it is not always possible to decide with intuition as there are several voices in our heads- what our gut says, what our rational mind says, and our ego. With so many voices running simultaneously on our minds, it is very likely for our minds to go off track and lose the intuitive voice. We have already learned what intuition is, so let us now understand what ego is.

Our ego is that part of our mind which is constantly oscillating between the conscious and the unconscious that constantly tries to maintain a notion of personal identity and assessing emotions against real life. Our ego is vastly impacted by our environment, the experiences of the past, hurtful events, and our worries. Our ego feeds off these factors to acquire a big shape. Therefore, all our thoughts are manipulated by our ego, which is why we often get held back as it tries to protect us emotionally. This may deter us from choosing the right path by scaring us into irrational fear of failure. Our intuition, on the other hand, is opposite to our ego. Our intuitions are supposed to boost our confidence in choosing the right step. Unlike our ego, which can be detrimental, our intuitions guide us to our highest capabilities. This is why we must learn to differentiate between our ego and intuition to make decisions confidently.

It is very difficult to eliminate our ego, but knowing how and when it is at work may take away its negative power. Following are few ways by which you may know that your ego is acting up –

- If your inner voice is being anxious and fearful, be sure it is your ego because your intuition is supposed to convey something that you know already, therefore, having nothing to do with fear.

- It is not your intuition if your thoughts are continuously see-sawing as intuition is unchanging and stable.

- A feeling of insecurity or inferiority is your ego at work, as intuitions are supposed to give you confidence.

- If you feel that your feelings by your mind are being justified by a catalog of reasons, be sure that it is your ego. Intuitions are supposed to come naturally to one. They do not need any justification.

After you begin to understand the difference between thoughts guided by your ego and those by your intuitive mind, your intuition will become more intelligible to you. They will become more clear and easily noticeable, leaving you with a peaceful mind.

The 4-Part Meditation Technique for Intuition Enhancement

The list above suggesting ways to improve intuitive receptibility mentions meditation to be one of the most effective ways to have better access to your intuitions. Meditation is an exercise that allows the human mind to be trained in a way where a state of consciousness can be generated. Mediation has manifold benefits like reducing stress, calming the mind, healing, improving concentration, and also helps develop qualities like patience, driving away any kind of negative thoughts. Meditation has also proved to be beneficial in connecting one to their inner minds, thereby helping to develop intuitions. Practicing meditation by concentrating on the breathing pattern, listening to soft music or chants can help to become mindful of your present moment by relaxing the mind.

Different kinds of meditation bring about different results like some help to calm the mind; some give energy to the body while practicing some can benefit the body physically. The 4-part meditation is a combination of a few forms and is the best to enhance intuitions. It is quite easy to practice if you follow the steps explained below –

1. The first step to meditation should be to prepare for it physically, mentally, and environmentally –

- Make sure to not sit to meditate on a full stomach or when you are worn out completely, and you are not under the influence of any kind of drugs. Always be dressed in comfortable clothes.

- Prepare mentally as well before you start meditating, either by watching something motivational or reading up something, or listening to something that inspires you.

- The place you meditate in is also important. Choose a quiet place that will not interrupt the process in any way.

  Take care of your sitting position as well. Sit wherever you feel comfortable. You could choose to sit either on a chair or the floor, keeping your back straight and with your hands placed on your lap in a relaxed position. Take a few deep breaths, use your nose to inhale and mouth to exhale. Gradually take more relaxed breaths, and you will see that your breaths have become relaxed and rhythmic.

2. Use a candle, any point on a black wall, or a religious object if you like, and focus your mind on it. This process is called repetition, which helps to clear out the thoughts of the conscious mind, which still may be at work. This is an important step of meditation, and you may practice it either with your eyes open or closed. Most prefer to keep their eyes closed as they believe it helps them to concentrate better. If with eyes closed, you cannot focus on a phrase that you like, which could help you relax and concentrate. If you were to simply take the word 'relax,' breathe in at 're' and exhale at 'lax' and think of it continuously without letting any other thought disrupt it. Focusing on it at once may be difficult, but you will begin to see a better-disciplined mind with regular practice.

3. After practicing the previous step for a few minutes, you will feel your mind sinking into a receptive mode. If you have had your eyes open for the previous step, close them now. With your back straight, both palms placed on your lap facing skywards, keep your mind relaxed, free from any conscious thoughts. Allow your mind to openly feel any images or sound pattern. Do not try to think about it. Assess all of it that is coming

to your mind in the form of visuals or sounds from a passive stance but if you see that you are beginning to think along, stop and try to focus again. It usually takes some time, but once you have mastered this role of being an observer, you will attain a calm of mind.

4. The last step of this meditation must end with a feeling of being in a warm, protected environment. Finish the last step by folding both hands into fists and try to imagine a white light encompassing you. This should make you feel protected and in a guided place. With this, the mind that you have so long trained to open up the core of your consciousness will now close down. This step is powerful, and you might want to think of a goal you want to achieve to visualize it and then manifest it in real life.

Post meditation, you will begin to be aware of the wisdom you hold within yourself, which so far has gone unrealized because you often fail to connect to your inner mind. You are not required to meditate for hours, but only fifteen to twenty minutes of it daily can help you enormously. If you are a beginner, divide the practice into segments and divide the time accordingly so that it does not seem too long. You may also want to try out each method of breathing, movement, or focus meditation individually than the mixed method provided above to see what you can practice more easily.

Meditation will help you to focus better and train your mind to focus on the thoughts of the inner mind. Attaining the ability to listen to your intuitive mind will help you not only achieve your goals in life, those related to your career or personal matters faster but also in life it will always direct you to the right path enabling you to have an overall aligned experience of life.

Chapter 17: Guided Meditation

Psychic empaths are intuitive and deeply sensitive, which often leads them to unconsciously get soaked up in other people's emotions. Therefore, what otherwise is a gift, that is, to see through situations, may prove to be burdening. One may feel overworked from being receptive all the time. Meditation is one way for psychic empaths that helps them to draw boundaries and choose what they want to feel and what they don't—meditating regularly, even if for few minutes, helps one to connect better with their energies and mood. It is important to clear the mind by practicing relaxation and be conscious of one's present. It will help them strengthen and steer their energies to their present, enabling them to be less troubled by the energy around them.

What is Kundalini Awakening?

The word 'kundalini' is a Sanskrit term meaning coiled snake. The base of the spine is considered to be the place where all divine energy in a human body is created. Kundalini then works to uncoil this snake and guide us to be one with our divine essence. Kundalini was previously an ancient form of study of energy and spiritual philosophy, and spiritual masters in ancient times delivered sermons educating the royalty about Kundalini. Bringing Kundalini to the western culture, where now it is practiced and known by many as an amalgamation of ancient science and practicality of modern times, can be credited to Yogi Bhajan.

We practice yoga to help us attain a state of higher consciousness or a state that practitioners describe as joyous, light, and unbounded love. Kundalini, which may be understood as a form of internal power or the vital force of life from where all our creative and spiritual energy stems and the supreme feminine energy, when practiced, enables us to draw up all of our slumbering energies that lie from the crown of the head to the base of the spine and align our chakras.

All human bodies are bestowed with this energy or Kundalini, but not all of us have felt it awaken in us. There are several ways to awaken Kundalini, but the cause of Kundalini awakening remains unknown to the world. For some, it takes committed practice for several years, but some are lucky to experience it unrehearsed. Although in both cases, it occurs unpredictably. Therefore, it means that we cannot control the occurrence of this awakening, but several practices may act as catalysts to guide or speed up the awakening. Yogis prepare for this with the help of various holy practices that have their roots in Hinduism. You may consider practicing the following to help in your journey of Kundalini awakening –

- Daily meditation helps to quieten the mind making it possible for the energies to freely flow in the body.

- Practicing pranayama and breath control exercises will further be effective in attaining stillness. This is because focusing on breathing patterns helps to make the mind collected, composed, and concentrated.

- Practicing tantra is another way of cultivating spirituality. Tantra mainly seeks to interwork the masculine and feminine energies, and ways to do so are through tantric sex or practicing tantric yoga.

- Kundalini yoga or any other form of yoga can be practiced to help in this journey of spirituality.

- Focussing on your chakras and working on them is another method. The second and third chakra in our bodies keep are designated to the rational senses of our body; therefore, training them will help us move beyond the material world.

- Working on your energies and fostering love is a suggested way. The more love that you give out in the world, it comes back to you doubled.

- Take the help of sound to heal yourself. The third chakra of our body is in close relation to the throat chakra so try using chants or mantras and other different kinds of sounds whose vibrations can soothe the mind.

- Living a grateful and open-hearted life

- Engaging in physical activities like dancing

After your Kundalini awakening, your life will have completely changed, and you will witness long-lasting positive changes. The benefits are usually manifested in an all-over-life improvement.

- After your Kundalini awakening, you will feel a rise in your spirit, mind, and body. Your energy levels with shoot up higher than you have ever felt which will bring about a change in your path of life.

- You will notice that you have been calmer, at the highest peace of mind, and will feel bliss.

- With a calm mind, your creative levels will bound to be at their best. The calmness of the mind will help you to solve your problems better and effectively, which an otherwise cluttered mind always hindered.

- Your feelings of compassion and empathy will have increased. You will feel more spiritually connected.

- Your psychic abilities will have grown than before and intensified.

- Kundalini awakening has a therapeutic effect on one and brings about an effective change in one's life as it helps to improve and enrich oneself.

- Spiritual understanding may dawn upon you.

- It brings you to realize your inner self, your soul.

Beyond the above-mentioned benefits, many other positive changes occur differently for different people like some have chosen a different career path or some have experienced changes in their relationships or even have changed their lifestyles to suit their new energies and a new way of life. It brings about an overarching change in one's way of living.

Signs That You Are Going Through Kundalini Awakening

People often tend to confuse between a Kundalini awakening and a spiritual awakening. Not all spiritual awakening is Kundalini awakening, but a Kundalini awakening may be understood as a kind of spiritual awakening. Kundalini awakening is a natural process; therefore, only those who seek don't need to be able to experience this. Practicing for it may help one to enhance their spirituality, and it may so happen that one does not feel the awakening because their practice has made them balanced and aligned that they have become neutral to such a feeling. Listed below are few indications that can help you know if you are undergoing a Kundalini awakening –

1. One of the strongest signs is a feeling of liberation from the material world and your ego that always seemed to hold you back.

2. Before you realize the positive energy working, it may feel like your life is in a state of complete disorder. Things you were dedicated to before may feel to wear out, like certain relationships or old habits. This initially can frighten one, and they may find it difficult to adjust to these changes, but all that is not aligned with their energies will slowly be removed from their lives. It will be the beginning of a happy path.

3. Your concentration levels will seem to have increased, enabling you to focus better on a task or idea at a time.

4. A feeling of ecstasy and delight will take over you, and your mind will be at peace.

5. You will be free from the constant doubt that your mind was in for so long and will realize that your reality is what you believe in.

6. Some may feel like on an emotional roller coaster as they may experience a feeling of deep emotional despair, much of what would feel like depression. The gush of energy that will flow in your body may feel like anxiety, and some may even hyperventilate. This happens solely because the nerves are not used to this sudden burst of energy. These signs are not so prominent for those who experience it at a steadier pace. However, it is more important to correctly direct these energies in a proper direction to benefit one than to simply be tormented by the signs.

7. You will begin to see yourself as an innate part of the whole, and feelings of compassion and love also increase in one.

8. Your past experiences that were negative and traumatic will no more trouble you anymore than they would before. Your memories of them will remain, but they will seem far from causing emotional stress.

9. Your mind will be at a higher level of consciousness where your ability to perceive, observe and understand things will be better. You will see that your ability to read into happenings will have improved, and you will be able to reflect upon incidents of your past life. It will give you a better perception of your present life.

10. The awakening will bring you to realize your inner self. Your intuitions will have intensified, and now that you can see through the eyes of your soul, the relationships that you grow hereon will be stronger and deeper. You will rely more on yourself, and therefore what people say about you will no more have a similar effect on you. You will be able to listen to only what you need to hear and do away with negative energies.

11. Your awareness will not only be limited to yourself but will also encompass the happenings of your environment; therefore, empathetic feelings may be noticed to have increased. The awakening brings about an awakening of the mind, soul, heart, and body, which allows you to be more compassionate to the outer world, which will automatically make you want to serve those in distress. You will have the profound realization that all beings are connected in the world, and you would want to fulfill your purpose through your service. Along with caring for the self, caring for the world will also become an important lesson that you will learn in this journey of this wisdom.

12. There will be a noticeable rise in your creative ability.

13. People tend to become more sensitive to external things that they could never indulge in before. A change in food palate may be noticed in many. The people around you, the media you consume are some of the things that might change, too, as one is more sensitive than before. You might detest being in large crowds, watching violent shows on the television, or might need to move in alone where you can focus only on yourself.

14. The physical sensations you feel will now be more pleasurable; they are often more sensual than sexual.

15. You may grow a bit of an adventurous spirit where you are no more afraid of trying new things. You will see yourself making changes in essential aspects of your life, from your career to relationships that you thought you never would. An increase in confidence and a feeling of vigor will help you make these changes in life without being afraid or doubting yourself.

16. Once you have put your mind to make these changes and embrace the ones taking place in your life, almost like a miracle, you will see that things will come to you like never before. It can be meeting the right person for a certain thing or landing up at the right place at the right time. What you need will present itself to you organically.

17. A significant indication of Kundalini awakening is a budding sense of purpose. Yogi Bhajan, who popularized Kundalini Yoga, calls this destiny. According to him, the Kundalini awakening makes us more close to the divine, and now that we have learned to clear our bodies of every energy that was hindering us from choosing the right path, we are more close to choosing our destiny. This fulfillment of our destiny automatically brings about a sense of purpose, making us more headstrong to achieve what is meant for us.

18. When the Kundalini rises in your body but is not yet awakened due to incorrect alignment of your chakras, it may show signs like inexplainable shaking in the body, insomnia, or sometimes a feeling of the spine getting heated up.

The Kundalini awakening empowers us to journey to the world that destiny has composed for us, to have a better understanding of our real selves, and to live as one spirit and body. Do not limit yourself in understanding the meaning behind the symptoms you may be observing in yourself rather, focus on working with these energies and practicing to clear any blockages that are disrupting their free flow all over your body. Make use of them to make any uncomfortable symptom disappear and help in an all-around improvement.

Let not the intensity of the signs of a Kundalini awakening prevent you from practicing it. Not everybody undergoes a similar experience as it depends on the lifestyle of a person. Some may experience a super positive and blissful awakening, while for some, it may initially feel like an overwhelming experience one might have after intake of drugs. People have been practicing it safely worldwide for years now, and it is not completely impossible; however, practitioners always advise not to go overboard with intensive practices but focus on the enriching journey.

Chakras and Kundalini

Beyond our physical bodies that are visible to us, there is our energy or what is also known as the astral body. For the uninitiated, acupuncture is a good way to understand how the energetic body works. Acupuncture is a system of medical science where needles are used which are inserted in the skin along the lines of energy or what are called meridians in medical terminology. It helps cure both underlying mental and physical conditions. Meridians or energy points are used to chart the energetic bodies and treat conditions accordingly.

These channels of energy called meridians are called 'Nadis' in the yoga terminology. These 'Nadis' are like lanes or passages that lead to larger areas where energies are concentrated. Imagine these larger areas as towns that again meet at other major cities. These larger centers of energy are called chakras. In Sanskrit, chakras mean wheel, and they are called so because these energies are constantly moving and are never static.

These chakras are located at certain places throughout the length of the spine, and they are like whirlwinds that are constantly moving in a circular pattern. It is said that there are seven chakras in our body, beginning at the bottom of the spine. This is the first chakra which is located below the pelvic area. Some believe that it is only partly presented in our body while the rest of it is rooted in the ground, and it connects us to the earth spiritually. Moving up from the spine, these chakras are distributed up to the head where the last or the seventh chakra is situated. Like the first chakra, some believe that the last chakra, too like the first chakra, expands beyond the head. It links up to space where the universal energy or God for those who believe in resides.

From the above section, now that we have managed to grasp the concept of chakras, let us now proceed to understand their locations in our energetic bodies, their names, and their relation to Kundalini –

1. The first comes the **root chakra,** which is situated at the bottom of the spine near the tailbone. It symbolizes our fundamental needs to survive like money, shelter, food, and everything that makes us live a safe and secure life. Most of us are lucky to have a decent lifestyle where we have a place to live, but we are still constantly insecure and worried about it. We are seldom able to live in the moment and relax. This chakra helps us to work on meeting these basic needs as well as helping us to take care of ourselves.

2. The second chakra in our energetic body is the **sacral chakra** which is situated around the naval region close to the sacrum bone, and its main function is to rule over our overall well-being, including creativity, pleasure, and sexuality. It is believed that this chakra is also a median of emotions; therefore, it also governs our feelings and the quantity in which we want to feel them. It facilitates us to deal with experiences that are new to us. It gives a better understanding of our desires and our present situation in life.

3. Then comes the **solar plexus chakra,** which can be pointed to be present at the naval. This chakra looks over self-confidence, self-esteem, and self-worth. If this chakra is aligned, you will have a strong determination to achieve things in life. For those

whose third chakra is not balanced, you are likely to be someone who is work-obsessed and find it difficult to slow down and relax. Those on the other hand who procrastinate and, compared to others, are slower, which means that there is a deficit of energy movement in this chakra.

4. The fourth chakra located on the vertebral column is called the **heart chakra** which is found at the center of the heart. It is also known as the fulcrum chakra as it forms the center of the chakra structure with three chakras located above and three chakras located below it. This chakra is responsible for governing our happiness. When aligned, the energy in the chakra permits us to feel delighted and joyous.

5. Right above the fourth chakra is present the **throat chakra,** and its name suggests its location in our energetic bodies. Presented at the throat, it controls our communicating abilities; therefore, as linked to communication, it governs the expression of our ideas and helps us to express ourselves better.

6. The sixth chakra, which is present between the space occupied by the pituitary glands and pineal glands and the area up above our eyebrows, is called the **third eye chakra**. The function of this chakra is to guide our wisdom, intuition, thinking abilities, imaginative faculties, and the capability of decision making. When in a position of alignment, one might witness an increase in their potential to see things through and have an overall vision of things. It gives us the vision to perceive what we need in life. For those in whom this chakra is not balanced, their minds usually tend to be conservative, they lack insight, and often end up missing chances in life. There may be a feeling of being stuck in the same mental space; they tend to overthink and hang onto old habits.

7. The seventh chakra at the highest position is called the **crown chakra** and is believed partially to be located in the head, and the other part is located outside the body connected to the sky, where the supreme power resides. Some have this belief that this supreme power is God, while some simply consider it as the energy that binds the whole universe together, guiding it all.

Our Kundalini and these chakras are connected in the sense that the Kundalini energy resides at the base of the spine, and this energy moves upwards and downward through the seven chakras located through the vertebral system. When the energy can flow freely without any blockages on either end of the spine, the Kundalini awakening happens after the flowing energy has caused the awareness and consciousness in us to intensify magnanimously. Chakras can be balanced the best way by the process of Kundalini to facilitate the flow of energy through the chakras without any hindrance. Some fail to understand the benefits of healing through the Kundalini process and focus more on healing their chakras, often doing yoga asanas or taking the help of mantras and crystals.

Practicing Kundalini Meditation

No one knows when and where the Kundalini meditation began, but it is beneficial as it works on the energies to awaken them, free them and harness them. It has since the 1960s become quite popular in the western world with thousands of practitioners now who seek awareness of the body and mind, spiritual connection and as a method of de-stressing, and all the other benefits that have been discussed above. Kundalini meditation falls under Kundalini yoga which assists in moving the energy in the body through the seven chakras. This process makes for an arrangement of connecting the soul, mind, and body that ultimately helps to attain spiritual awakening.

Kundalini meditation is not a faith but a method that enables one to be close to their inner selves. Yogis who practice Kundalini yoga regard it as a way to purify or decontaminate our minds, and it uses the circulation energy technique to do so. It is also referred to as a form of meditation that makes use of the inner breath. After a hectic day when you are stressed, Kundalini meditation will help you rejuvenate, undoing all the stress and bring about an alignment of the energies in your body so that you take action with a sense of purpose rather than passively reacting to your ecosystem.

Kundalini meditation is a harmless method to activate the Kundalini energy, which, when it reaches the seventh chakra in the head, grows. This form of meditation is also believed to have abilities to enlarge the chakras of the body.

It takes some time to master this branch of meditation, but with regular practice, it begins to show signs of improvement early on in your body, mind, and spirit. Following is a list that will elaborate further on the benefits of practicing Kundalini meditation –

- Kundalini meditation makes sure of sound health and body, and it helps align the soul, body, and mind.

- It creates an awareness of the body as well as your inner self.

- It helps release stress, anxiety and gives you a feeling of tranquillity.

- The breathing technique that it employs needs the practitioners to practice deep inhalations and exhalations, which improves the oxygen flow in the body, getting relieved of the toxins in the body.

- Since this meditation focuses on breathing pattern, your will learn to breathe properly, and it will cause your lung capacity to expand.

- It helps to improve cerebral functioning, and you will be better at cognitive tasks.

- The chemicals released in the brain, such as melatonin and serotonin during meditation, uplift our mood, reduces depressive tendencies, and it helps solve any trouble that you might be facing with sleep or your sleeping pattern.

- It prevents your concentration from wavering, and therefore your thoughts too remain aligned.

- A healthy body ensures an improvement of mental health too. The meditational process gives us an insight into the workings of the world and grounds us to our purpose.

- The meditation helps us to remove any feeling of us that makes us doubt ourselves or makes us feel unworthy and helps boost our self-esteem.

- The inner peace that dawns upon one through the Kundalini meditation helps them to relax.

- It causes an improvement in creative faculty, enabling one to handle situations in life better.

- It will bring about a change in your daily, hectic schedule and rejuvenate you.

- It will bring about a change in your brain pattern, and your emotional balance will thus be increased.

- Kundalini meditation is also beneficial in improving sexual energies. Improving sex lives is not meant to benefit one with pleasurable orgasms, but it helps to free the mind to concentrate on the present and thereby heighten the senses.

Kundalini meditation makes a being more aware than before of their inner and outer selves, which is integral to one's spiritual journey.

Kundalini Yoga

Kundalini Yoga is practiced to aid the waking of the Kundalini energy, which helps humans to achieve a sense of awareness, facilitates progression into the journey of spirituality by getting rid of the ego. This form of yoga entails breath exercises, chanting, singing, and repetitive poses. Kundalini yoga guides the movement of the Kundalini energy from the base of the spinal system through the seven chakras that bring about spiritual wellbeing. Practicing Kundalini yoga may lead to your Kundalini awakening.

Kundalini yoga is a unique branch of yoga and differs from the yoga forms we are more familiar with, like the 'Hatha' or the 'Vinyasa yoga,' both of which are practiced through several body postures. Kundalini yoga is a more spiritual practice, and it is more repetitive and accurate. Other yoga forms create a flow in our body with our regular breathing pattern, but Kundalini yoga is practiced through chants, songs, movements, and breathing in specific rhythms and patterns. It works with mudras, mantras and kriyas.

The Kundalini yoga has six main essentials, which are done in the order as described below –

1. The opening chant is the primary thing with which each session of Kundalini yoga begins. It is also called tuning in.

2. Then comes pranayama, which helps you to warm up. Pranayama mainly aims to focus on your breath control. It requires practicing breathing exercises and stretching the spine through certain postures.

3. Next comes kriya, which may be understood as a series of body movements making certain postures, mudras or hand gestures, and pranayama. There is no strict time prescribed as to how long kriya should be practiced; therefore, it depends on your instructor, who will decide the intensity and duration of your kriya.

4. Following the kriya is a stage of relaxation where you do nothing and simply relax to allow the reactions of kriya to be absorbed by both the mind and the body.

5. The fifth stage of this practice is meditation, for which you will again have to depend on your instructor for guidance. This stage aims to help generate awareness.

6. The last part of this practice is the closing chant with which every session gets over.

Kundalini yoga is an ancient practice; therefore, some of its benefits have been passed down the ages only by word of mouth, but since its popularization, Kundalini yoga has been studied, and their benefit has been scientifically confirmed.

- According to 2017 research, it was found that Kundalini yoga brings about a positive change in how we perceive our bodies and which leads to an acceptance of the self. Observing nine women suffering from bulimia nervosa and anorexia nervosa, both types of eating disorders caused by body image issues, it was found that Kundalini yoga helped them overcome their problems. Therefore, it was concluded that this yoga helped generate a better perception of the body and cause such sufferers to love and accept their bodies.

- Kundalini yoga has proved to be a great stress reliever and, as a result, helps to reduce anxiety. Of many studies that have been conducted to find out the effects of Kundalini yoga, one such was conducted in 2017 where a group of people participated, and just one session helped them release the repressed stress in their mind and body. It proved to be more beneficial for those who chose to continue it for another three months. In 2018, similar research was conducted for eight long weeks, and the participants have noticed a similar effect. All of them reported having lower stress levels than before. According to what the researchers inferred, Kundalini yoga could be an effective way to help patients suffering from GAD or generalized anxiety disorder.

- Kundalini yoga has shown results to enhance cognitive functions. A research was conducted in 2017 which studied eighty-one patients with light cognitive disability. They were divided into two sets where one set practiced Kundalini yoga while the other set was treated with techniques that help in memory enhancement for twelve weeks. At the end of these twelve weeks, the patients were checked upon again, and it was found that both groups showed improvement, but the group that practiced Kundalini yoga showed both short-term and long-term improvement in their memory functioning. Their problem-solving capabilities, their reasoning, and cognitive functions were better than the other group. This group also showed lesser signs of depression by the end of the study.

- Kundalini yoga facilitates spiritual awakening, but science cannot measure it. Therefore, our only trusted source is the gurus who have practiced this and achieved spiritual enlightenment themselves or the words of ancient masters. They have observed that Kundalini yoga creates a unity of the mind, body, and soul, which, when achieved, shows benefits such as an increase in empathetic feelings, creative improvement, more energy, which positively impacts the charisma of the person, and brings about inner peace.

Try out the following yogic poses for the beginner level and see the benefits yourself.

- **The Lotus Pose** – It is a seated posture for which you will need to sit on the ground with your legs stretched and a straight back. Move to a cross-legged position placing your feet on the opposite thighs and then holding the pose, breathe in and breathe out.

  This pose will help you get rid of any stiffness in your hip region.

- **The Cobra Pose** – To do this, lie down facing the ground. Your feet should touch the floor. Place your hands below your shoulder. The arms should be parallel to one another and lift your chest stomach from the ground with its support while breathing in. Hold this pose for half a minute and then release while breathing out.

  It is believed that this posture helps awaken the Kundalini.

- **The Archer Pose** – This is a standing posture where you need to place your right feet at a 45-degree angle on the outer side of your body. Bring your right foot behind and straighten it. Then making sure not to go beyond your left foot, bend your knee. Stretch out your arms to the height of your shoulders and roll your hands in a fist only with your thumb pointing upwards. Then you will need to move your body on the left side and bring your right hand backward near your right armpit. Only the upper body should be turned leftwards, and your face should face front. In this position, breathe in and out for about two minutes or a little more. Repeat the same posture on the right side now.

This posture which by its name is that of a warrior, will help you improve your confidence levels.

Kundalini awakening may be achieved through various ways, of which yoga and meditation are the most common ways. With the help of the instructor, when practiced, it may produce multiple overarching benefits in your life and bring about a divine spark in your mind through the consciousness it imparts. Therefore, the goal of practicing Kundalini should not only be at the result but importance must be given to the journey, which in itself is an enriching experience.

Chapter 18: Basics of Dream Interpretation

People dream about 4 to 6 times every night. You must be thinking that there's no way this is correct, but it is! People forget 95% of their dreams. People usually dream throughout the night. The dreams that we remember and the most vivid dreams usually happen during the REM (Rapid Eye Movement) sleep. The thing you are dreaming about might be influenced by something you thought right before going to bed, or it can also be influenced by something that you have experienced while awake. Dreams can also be based on your anxieties and things that you want to avoid or escape from. Dream interpretation dives deep into interpreting the meaning behind your dreams and figuring out where it is rooted from.

A Brief History of Dream Interpretation

Several current and ancient cultures think of dreams as a communication form, and they believe that there is a meaning behind these dreams. Nowadays, people analyze their dreams based on their personal experiences, but it wasn't the same back then. The ancient Mesopotamians thought of dreams as messages sent from the gods. Therefore, they kept very detailed records of the themes and the symbols. A method by the name of "incubation" was used by some cultures where the people slept in sacred places and waited for the gods to send them messages in their dreams. Previously, only the well-respected and intelligent members of a society who had high positions in the medical community or in the church were allowed to interpret the dreams. There is a lot to learn from these ancient civilizations about how they used their dreams through ancient notes and poetry.

The "Epic of Gilgamesh" is probably the oldest literary work that has been preserved. In this, we can see that punishment was given to a cruel king by the gods. The gods created a man who became very close friends with the king. After a few days, the gods made that man die due to a severe illness. Gilgamesh was left heartbroken and left alone, only to mourn the loss of his close friend. He then started having several intense dreams throughout the entire story. He went to his mother and to his friends so that they could help them interpret his dreams. His dreams were often interpreted as previews that were yet to come, whereas sometimes, his dreams had no link with his actions.

Dream analysis started taking on a new role around the late 19th and 20th centuries. Carl Jung and Sigmund Freud hit the scene, as a result of which, dream interpretation got a new direction and outlook. Both of them believed that dreams tell people about themselves, but their opinions varied when it came to the dream's underlying purpose. Freud suggested that dreams are all rooted in a person's repressed desires. According to him, a dream is the only place where a person can be honest with themselves without having to worry about societal pressure or embarrassment. On the other hand, Jung suggested that dreams are more than just expressing unconscious desires. He believed that dreams might have several different interpretations. He gave more importance to the symbolism than he gave to the outright subject. According to him, dreams could be amazing sources of creativity and might even predict future happenings.

Types of Dreams

Some common types of dreams and their probable meanings are as follows:

Daydreams

Daydreams are very common—everyone daydreams, especially when they do something mindless like waiting or working. Daydreaming can also be referred to as mind wandering. People don't sleep while they daydream, but they do enter an altered state of mind. It is almost like meditation or a hypnotic trance. It is kind of a visual experience where people imagine themselves in certain situations. Several studies have suggested that people spend 50% of the entire time they are awake daydreaming. There is nothing to worry about if you tend to daydream a lot. Some studies even suggest that people who daydream a lot usually have a high-functioning memory. Usually, daydreams involve other people. Some studies suggest that if you daydream about people to whom you are close, it is a sign of positive well-being. On the other hand, if you daydream about people to whom you aren't that close, it is a sign of worse well-being and loneliness.

Normal Dreams

Normal dreams refer to the regular run-of-the-mill dreams. Normal dreams might comprise several dream elements that I am going to talk about a little later.

Nightmares

Nightmares refer to scary or negative dreams. The term "mare" is an old English term that means goblin or demon. Having nightmares is pretty normal because that is how your brain processes things. People suffering from sleep apnea, migraines, anxiety, or depression are more prone to having nightmares compared to those who don't suffer from these.

Causes of Nightmares

Some of the possible causes of nightmares are:

- If you have sleep disorders like narcolepsy, nightmare disorder, sleep apnea, and so on

- If you are sick (fever, etc.)

- It can be a side effect of some medication you took

- If you eat right before going to bed

- If you are sleep deprived

- If you read or watch something scary

Some of the common themes of nightmares are:

- Being hunted or chased

- Physical violence

- Death

Night Terrors

Severe forms of nightmares are known as night terrors. They are way more intense compared to normal nightmares. Sometimes, the night terrors can also involve screaming, talking, or sleepwalking. If you have a night terror, you might find yourself waking up terrified. People usually forget what they dreamed about after waking up from a night terror.

If you have a night terror, you might find yourself waking up:

- Unsure and disoriented about where you are or what is going on

- With an increased heart rate

- With difficulty in breathing

- Sweating

- Moving, kicking, or jumping violently

- Screaming

Lucid Dreams

Do you ever find yourself wondering, "Am I dreaming?" in the middle of a dream? That is exactly what lucid dreams are—being lucid means being aware of the fact that you are dreaming. Once you become aware of the fact that you are dreaming, the dream doesn't last very long after that. In most cases, you wake up right after realizing that it is a dream. You can actually practice lucid dreaming. In case you want to control your dreams, you can try practicing lucid dreaming.

There are several advantages of being aware and being able to control your actions while dreaming. They are:

- You can meet your favorite celebrities

- You can travel to amazing places

- You can practice certain hobbies or skills that you enjoy doing

- You can experience something that you can't experience in your real life

- You can practice how to face your fears in a non-threatening and safe environment

Recurring Dreams

If you notice that the same story is coming up again and again in your dreams, then you have recurring dreams. In recurring dreams, a few details might get altered, but the main storyline and the concept remain similar. Certain recurring dreams have themes like being late, teeth falling out, flying, being chased, etc. Having recurring dreams is a little unusual, but you don't need to worry about it. That is because a certain amount of your dream content is likely to be repetitive. So, there is nothing to worry about if the same thing pops up again and again. But, if you are dreaming the same thing every night on a regular basis, there must be something more to it. It might be because of stress. It is still not fully clear as to why stress induces these themes to come up again and again in your dreams. But, in case you have recurring dreams frequently, try to do something to reduce your stress.

Some of the common themes of recurring dreams include:

- Freezing with fear

- Falling

- Being chased or attacked

False Awakenings

If you see that you are waking up, doing normal things, and suddenly things get unrealistic, then you probably have false awakenings! False awakenings are dreams in which you dream about waking up. For example, you woke up, had your meal, got ready for work, opened your door, and see that your house is floating up in the air! False awakenings are quite scary and disorienting, as they are very realistic. Finally, when you realize that something is not normal, it takes you quite some time to figure out that you are dreaming.

Precognitive Dreams or Prophetic Dreams

It is a type of dream that not everybody experiences. Even if someone does experience precognitive dreams, he or she might forget these dreams. Precognition is all about seeing your future or seeing snippets of certain events that might occur in the future. It is not yet clear how people see these things, but it is perceived as some kind of extrasensory perception. Precognitive dreams usually show you events that are going to happen in the future. Obviously, you won't be able to understand whether your dream last night was a precognitive dream or not right after waking up. You need to wait and see if things turn out the same way you saw in your dreams.

Healing Dreams

There isn't enough scientific information available on healing dreams. Healing dreams can be described as the dreams that:

- Make you feel at peace and joyful

- Make you reconcile

- Give you a sense of purpose, meaning, or connection

- Bring harmony or balance

Vivid Dreams

If you have a vivid dream, then you are most likely to wake up during your REM sleep. Your dreams are the most vivid during this time, and it is way easier to remember vivid dreams than to it is remember other dreams. Vivid dreams are usually very intense, and it feels very realistic. Sometimes, being stressed out or being pregnant might contribute to having vivid dreams.

Some Common Elements and Themes of Dream

Dreams usually vary from person to person as they depend on a lot of factors, like – your emotions, the people present around you, your stress, etc. But there are certain common elements and themes that pop up in people's dreams very often. They are:

Spiders

There is a well-known link between fear and spiders. According to certain studies, the spider is considered to be the most feared by children. A lot of people fail to outgrow this fear even after growing up. That might be because they have had some scary incident involving a spider, or they might be simply scared of how it looks. People see spiders almost every day, so it is quite common that they might appear in your dreams as well.

Some Positive Meanings of Seeing Spiders in Your Dreams

- Tenacity

- Art

- Creativity

Some Negative Meanings of Seeing Spiders in Your Dreams
Sometimes, seeing spiders in your dreams might also indicate some real-world anxieties, like:

- Worrying about an aggressive and a strong female

- Feeling like someone is hiding something from you

- Not being able to see the bigger picture

- Having a feeling of being trapped and not being able to figure out how to escape

Snakes

Snakes are also feared by many. Several studies suggest that people's brains associate some shapes with fear and danger. The shapes of spikes, claws, and teeth all fall under this category.

Some Common Positive Meanings of Seeing Snakes in Your Dreams

- It might be a sign of new beginnings.

- If you see a shedding snake, it might indicate a transformation or a change.

- It might symbolize wisdom.

- It might be a sign of creativity.

Some Common Negative Meanings of Seeing Snakes in Your Dreams

- If you see yourself getting bitten by a snake in your dream, then it might indicate that you have a toxic person in your life.

- If you see a talking snake, then it might indicate that there is someone who has bad intentions (from a religious perspective).

- It might also indicate that something is happening behind your back or in the darkness.

Teeth Falling Out

It is a very common theme and is surely a horrible one! It might signify certain things, like:

- You are very concerned and conscious about your physical appearance.

- You are not able to communicate properly.

- You are losing your self-esteem or personal power.

- You have a fear of being embarrassed.

Running Away

Running away without any aim is even scarier than being chased. That is because here, you don't even know what you are running from and why you are running. These kinds of dreams usually signify that you have a strong desire to escape from something or someone. So, you need to pay close attention to what is the thing that you are running from. It might be some animals, some people that you know or don't know, or might even be some entirely unknown entity. If you see yourself running away from animals, it might signify that you want to escape your own passions, anger, or fears. If you see yourself running away from someone you personally know, it might signify that you have some unfinished business with this particular person that you want to avoid. If you see yourself running away from an unknown person, it might signify some old wound or childhood trauma. If you are clueless about what you are running from, then it might indicate that you have a fear of the unknown and have a feeling of helplessness. Seeing these kinds of dreams might also have a positive meaning. It can mean that you are leaving all the negativity behind yourself.

Flying

Everyone has a desire to fly around freely. It happens quite often in dreams. Seeing yourself flying in your dreams might signify a sense of freedom. Sometimes, it might also signify a strong desire to escape reality. You need to notice whether you are fearful or happy while flying. You should notice whether you are looking towards the grounds or you are looking at the sky and the clouds. Also, you need to pay special attention to whether you are controlling your flight or is it not under your control.

Some Common Positive Meanings of Seeing Yourself Flying in Your Dreams

- Exploration

- Joyfulness

- Freedom

Some Common Negative Meanings of Seeing Yourself Flying in Your Dreams

- Being Someone else's puppet

- Having a strong desire to change a situation

- Wishing to be somewhere else

- Having a strong desire to escape the reality

Falling

Seeing yourself fall or having that sinking feeling is the scariest, and it happens quite frequently in your dreams. It might be a sign that your subconscious mind is trying to give you. You need to notice whether you are falling off of something or not. Notice whether you are into something, or you are being pushed, or you lost your balance. Generally, falling signifies the feeling of being out of control.

Common Positive Meanings of Seeing Yourself Falling in Your Dreams

- If you see yourself falling towards something bountiful and beautiful, it might signify abundance.

- If you see yourself jumping willingly, it might signify freedom.

Common Negative Meanings of Seeing Yourself Falling in Your Dreams

- It might signify being out of control

Vehicles

You need to pay attention to exactly what is happening with the vehicle because the meaning entirely depends on it. If it is a car crash, it might signify some repressed feelings or anxiety. If you see a stolen car in your dream, it might mean that you have a fear that someone might take something away from you.

Paralysis

If you dream about yourself being in a situation where you are not able to move, it might indicate that there is something in your life that you feel out of control about.

Being Late

If you dream about being late, it might indicate that you have a fear of being embarrassed, or you have a feeling of panic.

Infidelity

These kinds of dreams are usually triggered by bad experiences in the past. For example, if your partner had done something unfair to you in the past, you might have these kinds of dreams. These dreams basically reveal your innermost fears that you tend to hide.

Sex

Having sex dreams is quite natural. In fact, it indicates that your body is functioning normally and is completely healthy.

Killing

If you find yourself committing murder, it might indicate that you have repressed anger. These dreams might also be a side effect of watching something violent on television or playing violent video games.

Death

If you see yourself dying in your dreams, it might mean that you are ready to leave everything behind and start afresh. It signifies rebirth and new beginnings. If you see someone else dying in your dreams which hasn't yet passed away, then it might mean that you love them and you worry about losing them. In case you feel like something is wrong, or if you worry about something, it could be a precognitive dream. It might remind you that you need to express your love and gratitude to them. It might also be a reminder for you to start living in the moment.

Loved Ones Who Passed Away

A lot of people have had lost someone they truly cared about. If you see someone in your dream who passed away, it might simply mean that you miss them. If you think about your lost loved ones a lot, then you might relive those memories in your dreams. A few people think that their loved ones are conveying some messages to them from the other side via these dreams. You need to notice the context closely. If you feel happy and see yourself spending good time with them, it simply is a recollection of your loved one who passed away.

Some Common Positive Meanings of Seeing Someone Who Passed Away in Your Dreams

- Missing someone you lost

- Spending time with someone you lost and reliving the precious memories

Some Common Negative Meanings of Seeing Someone Who Passed Away in Your Dreams

- Warning

- Premonition

Being Naked in Public

It is a very common theme a lot of people dream about. It signifies deep humiliation or embarrassment. It might also indicate a fear of being judged, alone, or separated. It might also mean revealing your true feelings and personality.

Dream Interpretation

Some common theories of dream interpretation are as follows:

Unconscious Mind Theory by Freud

Sigmund Freud, in his book named "The Interpretation of Dreams", suggested that the dreams people see are somehow related to fulfilling their wishes. Freud believed that the things that people see themselves doing in their dreams are nothing but their unconscious wishes. The four elements of this process are:

- **Condensation** – In this, you see different concepts and ideas within a single dream. In other words, all the information is condensed into one image or a single thought.

- **Displacement** – In this, the important part of the dream or the emotionally significant part of the dream gets sidelined by insignificant parts of your dream. As a result, you get confused.

- **Symbolization** – In this, you see symbols that act as metaphors to your real-life situations.

- **Secondary Revision** – According to Freud, this is the final stage where all the bizarre elements are recognized for making the dream comprehensible. As a result, your dream's manifest content gets generated.

Archetypes Theory by Jung

Although Carl Jung's theory has certain similarities to that of Freud, Carl suggested that dreams were not just about expressing one's repressed wishes, but way more than that. According to Jung, dreams reveal the personal as well as the collective unconscious. HE suggested that dreams usually compensate for those parts of your psyche that are not fully developed in waking life. According to Jung, the archetypes, like the animus, the shadow, and the anima, are the symbolic figures or objects that symbolize some of your attitudes that your conscious mind represses.

Cognitive Process Theory by Hall

Calvin S. Hall suggested that dreams are nothing but a part of the cognitive process. According to him, dreams are "conceptions" of certain elements of your personal life. He analyzed multiple dream diaries of the participants for studying the dream patterns and themes. Eventually, he created a quantitative coding system capable of dividing your dreams into several categories. Hall's theory suggested that it is important to know certain things for interpreting one's dreams. They are:

- The dream's outcome, transitions, and setting

- The interactions that are taking place between you and the other characters present in your dream

- The figures and objects present in your dream

- Your actions within the dream

The main goal of this kind of dream interpretation is to understand the dreamer and not just the dream. Hall revealed through his research that the traits that people exhibit while they are awake are similar to the ones they exhibit while they are dreaming.

Walking Life Theory by Domhoff

A prominent dream researcher named G. William Domhoff suggested that dreams usually reflect the concerns and thoughts of your waking life. He also suggested a neurocognitive model of dreams. That model shows that the dreaming process usually results from a system of schemas and neurological processes. He suggested that these cognitive processes are responsible for creating the dream content.

The Popularity of Dream Interpretation

Dream interpretation started gaining popularity in the 1970s. The 1974 book named "The Dream Game" by Ann Faraday outlined several ideas and techniques that can be used by anyone for interpreting their own dreams.

In the upcoming days, dream research is going to grow further. According to G. William Domhoff, you should forget your dreams if you don't find them artistically inspiring, intellectually interesting, or fun. Other dream experts like Kaszniak and Cartwright suggested that dream interpretation is responsible for revealing things about the interpreter than it is for revealing about the dream itself.

The Effect of Biases on Dream Interpretation

Michael Norton and Carey Morewedge have studied the dreams of about 1000 people from South Korea, India, and the United States. They observed that a few of the college-going participants had a belief that their dreams were a result of their brain's response to certain stimulations. At the same time, Freud's notion suggested that dreams are responsible for revealing one's unconscious urges and wishes. They also discovered that people's biases hugely affect the importance and the weight they attach to their dreams. If you have a negative dream involving someone you already dislike, you are more likely to remember this dream.

Similarly, if you have a positive dream involving your loved ones, you will remember this dream as well. So, you will interpret your dreams based on your pre-existing beliefs about the world, about yourself, and the people present around you. Several studies have suggested that things like self-serving bias and confirmation bias can hugely impact how you respond to your own dreams. Some researchers also suggest that these dreams might become a self-fulfilling prophecy, as people are more likely to take their dreams seriously. For example, if you dream about failing a certain exam, you might feel reluctant to study and give your best because you are so sure that you will not make it no matter how hard you try. You might even get so stressed out because of your dream that it affects your performance in the exam.

Some dreams have meanings, and some dreams don't. Interpreting one's dreams has gained so much popularity that some people even make big life decisions based on their dreams.

Chapter 19: Astral Level Techniques to Help With Your Psychic Abilities

2021 hit Netflix show *Behind Her Eyes* made the concept of astral projections a popular and widely discussed one. Based on Sarah Pinborough's best-selling novel of the same name, the show follows the story of a single mother who gets into an affair with a man and, at the same time, also strikes up an unusual friendship with his wife. The wife delves into her part and teaches our protagonist the art of astral projection, and the story takes off from there, where we are shown how the women use techniques of astral projection to control each other's bodies and meddle in each other's lives! Sounds spooky, right? Give the show and watch and decide for yourself. However, although the show is a work of fiction, astral projection is a very real thing.

In this chapter, we will first go through what astral projection is and then discuss steps to practice astral projections and how that is connected to our psychic abilities. However, it is understandable that trying this out is not for everyone, but if it sounds like something you would be interested in dipping your toes into, then dive right in!

What is Astral Projection?

Astral projection is basically the belief that while we are sleeping, we can escape our physical bodies. Although this might sound far-fetched and a little unreal, there have been many cases where instances of real-life astral projections have been successfully documented. During the course of an astral projection, one's soul (or their *astral body*) leaves their physical body while they are either asleep or in the state of deep meditation. Once their soul is out of their body, it is free to travel wherever it wants to! This is why astral projections are also often known as 'out of body experiences

(OBE), although it has been suggested that there are some differences between the two concepts.

Healthline suggests that while astral projections are planned occurrences, OBEs are mostly unplanned. In an out-of-body experience, what happens is that a person's soul – or their consciousness – simply floats above and around their physical body, whereas in the case of projections, the consciousness is guided actively to travel to someplace else. Secondly, while astral projections are widely regarded to be largely spiritual practices, out-of-body experiences have been mostly recognized within the domain of medicine.

The idea of astral projections is not a recent one. In fact, its inception can be traced back to ancient times all across the world. Groups of people, such as the Shamans and the New Agers, believe that astral projections have been practiced for many years for the purposes of both spiritual healings as well as self-care among several people belonging to different beliefs and cultures. Although practiced for centuries, astral projection is also something that needs to be done very carefully and with strong intent, as otherwise, people might end up losing their sense of control while projecting astrally, and that might lead to disastrous results at times.

A common question that is asked by a lot of people is whether the astral projection is safe or not. The answer is the same as it is when it comes to any adventure sports- if done with enough care, precaution, and prior knowledge, astral projections are completely safe. However, yes, astral projections can be unsafe as well. With adequate education and awareness, astral projection can be absolutely safe and even quite rewarding! But suppose you want to get into something which you have not invested enough time in learning. In that case, it might end up with you getting severely hurt – both physically and mentally, as astral projections involve both your body and soul.

How to Prepare Yourself for It?

You can think of astral projection as a form of sport or something similar in terms of its accessibility. Almost anyone – if they want to – can prepare themselves to astrally project and can execute it with enough caution and practice. Just like success in any sport depends on how much effort is put into it, the same goes for astral projection as well. Similarly, some people are naturally more gifted when it comes to astral projections- like in certain sports- and hence, they are required to invest less time and effort compared to others to master the same.

If you are wondering how to get started with astral projections and how to start getting prepared to carry it out, the following tips might come in handy –

1. **You are patient:** this is the most important thing you need to keep in mind- patience. There will be times when you would have understood some parts of astral projection and would be keen to practice it in real life, but you will still need to hold on to your instincts and wait it out until you master all of the intricate details attached to astral projecting. If you do not have enough patience to let yourself guide through the entire learning process multiple times, then astral projection might not be the right thing for you to pursue in the first place!

2. **You have enough time:** Learning how to astral project will take you quite some time. You will have to study, practice, and experiment with different techniques, and you will not get things right on your first go. However, it is very important that you set aside time for specifically practicing this every day or week. The chances are that you will learn how to project the right way if you choose to stick to it instead of just going through it once or twice. Therefore, you would need to make sure that you have enough time

to devote to learning the art of projections, as otherwise, it might not benefit you a lot.

3. **You are young:** Studies have shown that younger people – between the ages of 13 and 18 years – have a natural advantage when it comes to astral projecting. However, that does not mean older people cannot learn how to project; it just means that younger people tend to have a more open mind comparatively, which is why it is naturally easier for them to suspend some disbelief and acquaint themselves with astral projections.

4. **You are open to experimenting:** Even after you know the details of what astral projection is and how to execute it, there are chances that no matter how much and how hard you try, you might not have a lot of success in actually projecting. This is why you are needed to experiment and try your hand at different techniques, strategies, and so on. Do not feel discouraged if your initial attempts are not showing any success. They are not in vain. They are merely preparing you for the next stage – when you actually manage to guide your soul out of your physical body. The only way you will learn how to do something properly is by getting to know what are the ways in which you should *not* do it. When it comes to astral projections, there are many incorrect ways, all of which you need to steer clear of, and regular practice and experimenting are your best friends for figuring this out.

5. **You are dedicated:** Nothing can replace a very strong desire to project. If you are truly intent and dedicated, you are more likely to learn how to project faster. You can follow the path others have set out for you, and in no time, you will be able to accomplish what you want for yourself. The path- for you- might be difficult, frustrating, or even unattainable at times. However, it all boils down to the fact that if you *really*

want to learn how to astrally project, you can. Your true desire to learn it is what would keep you going when you are frustrated or tired with how your effort might not be showing in practice. But do not worry, you will surely get there if you keep at it!

6. **You have an open mind:** This is also one of the main requisites to prepare yourself for astral projections! You need to have an open mind when it comes to learning how projections function and how you might participate in it yourself. If you believe something to be absolutely impossible even before you start delving into it, then it is better that you do not try your luck out with projection at all. There are many phenomena that people do not believe in completely, and yet, all of them hold to be true. The case with astral projections is quite similar. If you advance with certain pre-conceived options about how astral projections are not real, and you are trying it out only to confirm your suspicion, then you would not be able to succeed at it. This is because you do not actually want to succeed in these cases; you just want to disprove something thousands of people place their faith in. On the other hand, if you walk into this with an open, broad mind, and you allow yourself to learn and practice new things, you are a lot more likely to project.

Steps to Practice Astral Projection

Next, other than preparing yourself and your mindset towards astral projections, you also need to set up and prepare a proper environment where you can carry your projections out. Here are a few easy tips which will help you set a suitable environment up for projections –

1. **Choose a location:** You need to first get started with the very basics- where do you think you will project the most frequently? Is the particular space somewhere you feel safe? How easily can you access

243

it? All of these are questions you need to actively ask yourself in order to determine a location that works well for you when it comes to both practicing and carrying out your astral projections. Here are three of the most commonly selected locations – all of which come with their own advantages and disadvantages – which you can consider for yourself as well:

- **Your bed** - Your bed is perhaps the most comfortable location for you to project. Your body will not be cramped up here, and it is a location you already are very well acquainted with and know that you would be comfortable functioning out of. Moreover, a lot of people tend to practice projections right before they go to sleep, which is another reason why beds are a great option. Other than that, if you are in your bed, you also do not have to worry about your body falling out of position during the process, as might be the case with some other, more restrictive locations you can project from.

  There are also some cons of you projecting from your bed, which also need to be kept in mind. First of all, if you are trying to project before you go to sleep, then you might be conditioning your body to fall asleep before it can separate itself from your soul in case you are doing it from your bed, which is a location your body automatically associates with the act of falling asleep. Besides that, if you share a bed with someone else, it might not be the ideal location, as they can disrupt your attempts at projection knowingly or unknowingly.

- **Your couch** - Your living room couch can be a good idea for the location you project from, primarily because if you are choosing this location, then you can program it to be your location of choice. This means that you can form a psychological association with the location in a way that your body feels like each time it is lying down on the couch, it is preparing itself to project. This is not something you can achieve if you are projecting from your bed. You also would not have a partner sharing this space with you, which means there would be minimal distractions.

However, a problem that might arise is that you will need to make sure your couch is a very comfortable place for you. If you have hard, uncomfortable pillows, or an alignment that hurts your back, then your couch might not be an ideal location. In this case, try switching pillows, tucking a blanket in, and shifting things around a bit so that you can make it as comfortable for you as possible before you start to project.

- **A chair** - If you do not want to project lying down, then your chair can be a good alternative from where you can project while sitting up. It is actually a great option because if you are projecting from your chair, you are not going to fall asleep since you are sitting up. Plus, you are also most definitely going to be alone in your chair, so you do not have to worry about unnecessary traffic in that area or any external disturbances from other people that might interfere with your projections.

Having said all of that, there are also some serious disadvantages when it comes to projecting from an upright chair. In this position, chances are higher of your body falling over, which will force it to get out of the state of a projection and will place your astral self back into your physical body before you choose to do so. Other than this, your head can also flop forward around the neck, which would mean that you can potentially be cut off from a stable source of oxygen, which, if continued for a longer time, can cause serious breathing problems.

No matter which of these three (or even a different option) you choose, the focus is to pick a location that you are comfortable in and which can help your astral self get in and out of your body as and when you would like it to, without causing any external interferences or obstructions.

2. **Start maintaining a logbook:** When you get started with astral projections, it would be extremely helpful if you also start recording your experiences in a logbook. You will have to be careful and meticulous with maintaining this. When you have an astral experience, make sure to write down all of the following details and maintain records of the same so that you can use them later to notice any patterns and to improve your ability to project -

- To begin with, write down the date and time of the projection. When did it take place? Was it during the night or the day? What did you do immediately before or afterward projecting? Did you try it out on the weekends or on a weekday? Writing all of these down will help track what could be the optimum day and time for you to execute your most successful projections so that you can more carefully pick the times for your future attempts at projection.

- Also, write down what the precursory events and conditions were prior to your projection. What happened right before you tried? Had you just gotten out of bed, or were you meditating? Had you passed out from a night of heavy drinking? Had you recently listened to some music – and if you had, what tracks were you listening to? If your projection was a good one, then you can perhaps try later to recreate these conditions and attempt to have a similar experience while projecting.

- Make sure to note – in as much detail as you can – what happened during your projection. Write down a detailed account of what happened and about how you felt. Did you feel any changes in temperature? Was there any tingling sensation? Did you hear a high-pitched sound or any external voices, or did you perhaps feel someone else was climbing into bed with you? You might have even seen other entities while you were projecting. Noting down all of this helps regulate your experiences and ensure that your projections are not being intervened by any harmful external bodies.

- Note down how you managed to return to your physical body. Was there any disturbance? Did you feel the presence of any negative entity, or did a guide safely put you back? It will help your future projections if you can make a note of all of these, as it would help you out immensely in the future to keep track of what works for you best and how you can channel those better to perfect your projections.

You do not need to maintain a logbook forever. Do it for as long as you feel that you are still getting used to things. Once you have somewhat become more accustomed to it, you can just jot down very short notes. Remember to not completely give up the practice, but you can do it more quickly because, by that point in time, you would most probably know what time, location, and other conditions would work the best for you.

3. **Take control of your environment:** You can also follow some of the following tips to control your environment better so that you are more in charge of your astral projections -

- **Turn your alarm off:** The first thing you should do is to turn your alarm off. It would be awful if you were finally in charge of your astral self, and then you are snapped out of it just because of the annoying sound of your alarm. If this happens, your body is going to absolutely startle, and your attempt at projection – no matter how hard you have tried to execute it – will fail.

- **Control the noise in your house:** Besides your alarm, what are the other sources of noise in your house? Do you have a grandfather clock that goes off every day during midnight? Is your air conditioner – or any other electrical device that you regularly use – that is a source of the noise? Although you might have grown used to it, think about it separately for a minute to see if that would act as a disturbance to a third person. If your AC is causing a disturbance, try and use a fan for your projections instead, and it would also serve as a good source of white noise, which might aid your projection attempts. If your windows create a rattling sound, then make sure you seal them carefully so that they would not pose any problem later. Any possible thing which might break your sleep and snap you out of your projection needs to be taken care of, so give yourself some time to think of all such possibilities and deal with them beforehand.

- **Prepare the people around you:** People around you can be very big sources of disturbance, which you need to be very mindful of before you start projecting. Does someone in your family call you every day without fail at a certain point in the day? Is your flatmate prone to knocking at your door during dinner time for some errands? Does your partner like to cuddle you in the middle of the night unprompted? All of these are factors you need to think of how to deal with so that you can better direct your projections. Close your blinds, shut your door with care and inform other people as much as you possibly can to not interrupt you during certain hours of the day.

If you live in a house full of people and feel like they would not be the most considerate towards your needs, it might be a little more difficult for you to create a suitable environment for your projections. However, even in such a scenario, try your best to set up certain conditions which might help you to ensure that you have some quiet, alone time to yourself so that you can try projecting for even a short while regularly.

- **Take care of your pets:** Do you have any pets? If yes, then they can also pose a problem and hamper your projections. If you are used to sleeping with your pet dog curled up next to you in the bed, then without him, you might have some problems getting your body used to projection attempts from your bed. Some dogs are also entities that might react to any entities which you might be interacting with astrally. In case these might happen, it is best for you to keep your pets out of the area, which would be your projection zone, as to say. Make sure to keep them out of that place and to fasten your door so that they cannot come in and create any disturbance.

Tips for Safe Travelling

If you are traveling through astral projections, make sure you are taking care of yourself and maintaining precautions so that you can practice safe traveling. There are chances that astral projection might sometimes get out of hand, so make sure to follow a few tips which will help you prevent that:

Astral Shields

Astral shields are your main source of defense when you are navigating the astral plains. You need to be prepared while leaving your body and guiding your soul into other planes and also perhaps into other beings at will. There are many negative entities out there that have the potential to cause disturbances. These entities can not just hamper your projections but can also cause certain harm to you physically – preventing you from safely reentering your physical self. In these cases, you will have to create a shield around yourself to project your astral body. Every person has their own shields by harnessing their own sources of energy, and all shields look different from the others. You would feel a lot safer and more at peace and in control when you are traveling with a shield attached to yourself. An astral shield can be created by combining your intent, will, and strong vibrational energy, and it would go on to act as a protective shell around your soul.

Astral Weapons

Astral weapons come to your aid when defensive measures like astral shields are not enough to keep harmful entities at bay. In these cases, you have to actively learn how to create something which can be used in a way that deliberately dispels the energy given out by this negative being. You create these weapons in the same way you would create an astral shield by using your free will, intent, and positive vibrations.

Astral Guardians

Remember that you are not alone in your journey while you are astral projecting. You are always surrounded by people who are your spirit guides and people who have your best interests as their priorities to guide you in ways that would only help you. Spirit guides include archangels, guardian angels, spirit guides, and so on. Your astral guardians keep the astral planes in order, and they are also most likely to make sure that no harm is being caused to you during your journey. However, they cannot protect you from self-guided actions. If you act in a way that provokes other entities, then your guardians cannot do much to stop you from getting harmed. Therefore, make sure not to cause any mindless interruptions with other entities, mostly for your own safety.

Astral projections can be very tricky but also very rewarding experiences. This chapter has comprehensively covered the most important parts about preparing yourself, your surroundings, and your mindset so that you can begin to learn and experiment with astral projections. But make sure to follow the safety tips and be patient with your astral journey so that you make sure you are taking enough care of yourself because projections might also be harmful to your astral self if proper care is not taken.

Chapter 20: How Can Empaths Have Successful Relationships?

If you know someone who is an empath or if by any chance you are an empath yourself, you will have a clear idea as to how difficult it is for an empath to get into relationships or to maintain one successfully. It is ironic that the very things like trust, intensity, looking after one's feelings, things that are the base of any relationship, are the very things which, when done in excess, can ruin a relationship. Perhaps that is why when someone is sensitive to the emotions of others when they are aware of other's energy shifts and start to act according to that when someone tends to get invested emotionally very easily; it becomes difficult for that someone to find themselves a partner easily or to be in a relationship. All of these above things are applicable for an empath, and so it is not difficult to guess why empaths have a hard time finding a partner or love, for that matter.

People who are empaths are by nature extremely lovable and loving at the same time as they are sure to take care of all your emotional needs. They are compassionate, and they have very caring hearts that will go out of their way to cater to your requirements. But, it is this very nature of theirs that can backfire on them and become their worst enemies. Because at times, especially during close relationships, sometimes for a partner, it can become very overwhelming and can be a potent cause for the prospective partner to get cold feet.

However, the good thing is that there is no end to how much a person can improve, and there is always a way if the person has a strong enough will. We shall be talking about various ways in this chapter as to how can empath improve themselves and become more aware of their emotions so that they are more in control of themselves and the situation between their partner. As long as the partner is supportive and understanding, it shouldn't be a huge problem as to why the issues should not get resolved.

What Problems Do Empaths Face in Romantic Relationships?

Let us talk about what are the probable problems that an empath might face when considering a romantic relationship so that we get an idea of what we are dealing with.

- ***Fear of Intimacy and Getting Closer*** – It is very common among empaths to fear intimate relationships and getting physically and emotionally close with someone because they think that they might get overwhelmed with all the emotions that need to be invested, with all the energies of their partner that they will naturally absorb and also how comfortable they might get provide they need a lot of space and alone time to function properly. An empath often needs to retreat and recover so that they can calm their hyper-perceptive system from breaking down. They fear that not many people will understand this. Some empaths prefer staying alone, and that is completely fine. But for those who want to be with someone, it is important to know that a successful relationship should give both the partners abundant space to retreat and recover, and there is nothing wrong with asking for that.

- ***Prioritizing the Partner's Need Always Over One's Own*** – It is a very common thing for empaths to give more importance to what others around them are feeling. That tendency increases even more when that other person is their partner. In a relationship, which is supposed to be a two-way journey and a give and take from both ends, when only one's person's wishes are given more importance, the relationship becomes unstable. An empath tends to feel what the other person is feeling with a lot more intensity than what we do, and so they always want to match up to their energies, and in the process, they forget to think about themselves, and their emotions go unnoticed.

- ***Tuning in to the Partner's Observations*** – It is in the inherent nature of an empath to tune in to whatever others are saying or feeling. They tend to say yes to all the observations that the partner might be making, making themselves almost invisible in the process, and this makes the relationship stagnant and one-sided. What this will do is make the empath feel empty in the long run. They might feel the need to cater to prioritize others over themselves, but they will be left with nothing, and all their feelings will go uncatered. The empath is bound to feel neglected, and what is worse, it will be their own doing. Tuning in to the partner's thoughts will eventually make the relationship one-dimensional and stagnant, which could be a potent reason for the relationship to eventually dwindle away. If these emotions are positive, then still better, but if by chance they are negative energies, the empath will take those in them as well, which will be eventually harmful to everyone.

- ***Trying to Manage the Partner's Emotions*** – What empaths do is they feel what the other person is feeling in their system, and after a point, they start mistaking their partner's emotions their own and try to control it. They feel, and rightly so, that they understand what their partner is feeling better than others, and so they take it upon themselves to manage those feelings and emotions. This can put the partner in the right spot, and it is not good for both the concerned parties who are in the relationship. The empathetic partner needs to stop feeling responsible for the other person's emotions as that will make both the partners feel overwhelmed and burdened to an extent, and ironically that will be the empath's fault as they did this to themselves.

Things Empaths Should Keep in Mind Before Dating

There are certain things that an empath should keep in mind before they start dating, which will make things much easier for them in the long run.

- *There Are Two Sides of Having a Big Heart –* If you are an empath, you naturally have a big heart. And like there are always two sides of a single coin, this too has its own positive and negative qualities. By having a big heart, we necessarily do not mean how kind you are to people around you. But, it means that you have a deep sense of compassion for people, which is surely going to be very important for a romantic relationship. Any partner would be lucky to have you as they will know that their emotions and problems are in safe hands. But, that being said, at times, this very thing can become a huge problem. That is because, on your part, you will always try to put yourself in their shoes and think of the situation from their perspective, and so much so that after a point, you will stop thinking rationally and start ignoring the red flags, if any. This will make you fall in trouble as you will be taken advantage of. So, before you commit to someone, keep in mind that you need to think neutrally and be conscious of reality.

- *You Can Become a Beacon for The Broken –* As an empath, have you noticed that people who are attracted to you are usually in need of emotional comfort, and they prefer being with you because somewhere they need your empathy and are not really invested in the relationship? This could be the situation because you being an empath is a perfect opportunity for people to come near you and help themselves heal. But in reality, this is going to be a one-sided relationship where your partner will be on the receiving end, and you will be left empty. So, before you date someone, rationalize the situation and gear yourself for something where you are also gaining something.

- **Understand How Valuable You Are** – As an empath, you are a master of self-sacrifice. You tend to keep everyone ahead of you, and most of the time, you give other's feelings more preference at the cost of your own. What happens when you bring this attitude in a relationship is that your partner if he\she wants to, can get the opportunity to take ample advantage of that where you will be on the receiving end of criticism and the giving end when it comes to all the emotions. What more, you will not understand the reality, and you will go with the flow. Your mental health and physical health can get terribly affected as a result of that. Before you start dating or even think of a relationship, be it of any kind, you need to first and foremost understand how valuable you are. How important your feelings and emotions are and how much respect you deserve. If you don't believe in it yourself, no one else will. Understand that you are irreplaceable, and your partner needs to understand that. Do not settle for anything less, and make sure you don't get involved in a relationship where there is no respect.

- **You Know What Might Happen Even Before Your Partner Does** – This is a thing with empaths that they usually get to know things much before their partner or anyone else around them does. That is because empaths have a very strong sense of intuition which makes them see and feel things in a much deeper way. If you are an empath, the chances are that you notice even the slightest change in a person's behavior or a situation that might occur next, of which your partner has absolutely no idea about. This leads to you and your partner being on different pages. You are emotionally ahead, and he\she is left behind, having the thought at every point that you are thinking and feeling something else. So, before you go for a relationship, understand that this is something that many people might not appreciate, and it could be a cause for you to have problems in your relationship. You need to stop your emotions from running ahead when your partner has started to barely walk so that a sense of stability and parity prevails.

- ***Learn to Protect Yourself*** – You need to make sure that you are all right emotionally and physically before you take any step towards a new relationship. Nobody knows this better than you how your emotions work and how they can very quickly turn serious and might cause you emotional turmoil. So, more than that other person who could be your potential partner, it falls on your shoulders to protect yourself. Before you go to meet someone new, make sure you are mentally prepared. Do not ever go with very high expectations and take things slow as that will help both of you to make the correct and necessary decisions. It is advisable to practice some breathing exercises before you go so that instead of getting overwhelmed and thinking a lot, you can be comfortable and actually enjoy the date. It depends on you as to how you want your date to be and eventually your relationship. Take it at your own pace, and remember that if you have the right partner, it won't be very difficult to be on the same page and take things at a pace that suits you both. Try not to give undue importance to things that don't matter at the end of the day, and you should be fine.

Here's How You Can Have a Healthy Relationship as an Empath

There are many ways in which you can have a very healthy, transparent, and beautiful relationship without having to constantly fear something going wrong. Let us look at some of those ways.

- ***Take Care of Yourself*** – You know it very well that you take care of others much more than you do if yourself. When you are an empath, you tend to give your everything without keeping enough for yourself, even if that something is you. Do not do that. Always remember that in order to have a healthy relationship, you will need to be all right mentally and physically so that you can contribute fully from your end while at the same time you can understand whether your partner is doing the same. For a healthy relationship to work, there has to be an effort from both ends. Your partner needs to cater to your needs, and that will only happen when you know yourself what you need and convey that. So, do not compromise on that. You are a human being, and like all of us, you need love, care, and pampering. It cannot be only one way as that will make the relationship stagnant after a point.

- ***Spend Time With Yourself*** – You need some alone time to get all your emotions in order. We all know that life can become a bit too overwhelmed at times and more so if you are an empath because everything is personal to you. When it comes to your partner's feelings and your relationship, in all probability, you will ignore what you need in the hope of providing more to the other person. But you need to remember that in order for your relationship to work, you will have to take some time off and replenish yourself. You need to do things that make you happy, be it a walk or your comfort food, or watching your favorite movie. It could be anything as long as you are happy and it is giving you enough energy to get up once again and take on the world.

- **Be Curious** – When you are an empath, you tend to notice everything in great detail. On top of that, your intuition makes you get a hinge of things before others. So, even a small change in your partner's body language is sure to come to your notice. Now, it might be the case that you already know what the reason for that change is. But, it might also be that you don't. In that case, instead of jumping to conclusions and overthinking about it on your own, it is always advisable to ask your partner what has truly happened so that you can both find a solution as soon as possible. What this does is, firstly, it helps you to stop overthinking and getting bothered by every little change, and secondly, it makes your partner realize how mindful you are of his\her emotions. It helps uplift the entire relationship. Your curiosity is sure to help you improve the bond that you and your partner share while not making you emotionally burdened.

- **Communicate With Your Partner Verbally** – As an empath, it is no surprise that you are excellent at picking up signs and understanding what is in the mind of your partner. You are naturally talented at non-verbal communication. You tend to understand the feelings in detail so many times there is no need to have a verbal conversation. But the reality is a bit different. Every good relationship thrives on good communication. As important as non-verbal communications are, verbal communications are equally important. Those will help you and your partner to clear things out in greater detail without having misunderstandings. It will help you both to clear out doubts which will improve the overall relationship and the balance that you both should have. So take out time to have proper verbal communications often.

- *Accept Constructive Criticisms* – We understand that it might be difficult to take criticism from others. Not everyone can take criticisms, and it is natural. The situation intensifies if you are an empath. The moment you hear someone criticizing you, you might naturally start thinking that this person doesn't like you and has some personal grudge against you. Well, the situation could be quite different from this in real life. The thing with constructive criticism is that it is meant to improve you and help you develop. You have got to understand the difference between abuse and criticism and more so when someone is trying to help you by being constructive about it. You need to make yourself understand that if and when your partner is giving you any constructive criticism, you need to not panic or overthink, but you need to see what he\she is trying to mean and accept it if they are right. It will only help you develop yourself, and it will help you strengthen your relationship for the better.

The Toxic Relationship Between an Empath and a Narcissist

Narcissists don't consider other human beings as individuals but as objects. They have a complete lack of empathy and an inflated sense of self-worth. People who are narcissists have great difficulty feeling any kind of emotion because they do not let vulnerability enter their system, and emotions and feelings for them are a means of weakness. Quite naturally, they lack the ability to love others, and relationships with them are mostly manipulative, where they tend to only take without giving anything in return. Empaths, on the other hand, are just the opposite. They have a deep sense of compassion, and they have the ability to love and care for others deeply. Empaths tend to give so much without even asking anything in return even for once, that the partner doesn't even need to initiate the process. Empaths tend to feel everything more, and so if by any chance the partner is a narcissist, it will just be a one-way journey of the narcissist sucking all the emotion and the empath allowing that gladly. Needless to say, such a relationship is extremely toxic.

Let us consider such a relationship and see what the dynamics could be. Firstly, the empath is constantly under the impression that they do not deserve love, that they are not doing enough, and that they need to put a little more effort to make the relationship work. On the other hand, the narcissist takes advantage of this very thing and constantly burdens the empath into giving more and more while not contributing anything. The empath is quite natural to feel that if they can make someone like the narcissist fall in love with them, as they are otherwise incapable of loving anyone, then they will be worthy of love. And thus goes on their unrelenting struggle to give more and yearn more even at the cost of submitting their everything to the other person.

Some might have the question as to why does an empath behaves this way. The answer could be many things, among which one is that they had been raised by narcissist parents who never gave them love and care. When they are in a relationship, they become of the mentality that if they don't receive love from their narcissistic partner, they will again fail in another sector of their lives. Thus they tend not to give up no matter how painful it gets. A narcissist is naturally oblivious of all these things, and they carry on their behavior. If you are an empath and if you have been raised by narcissist parents, the chances are that by now, you have unfortunately started associating love with pain. You think that only by suffering will you get love. That is why the toxic nature of your narcissist partner doesn't bother you as much as it should because you think that's normal. The truth, however, is very different. As far as the narcissist partner is concerned, it is impossible to change them no matter what you do. A narcissist won't change unless they decide to.

It is in the nature of an empath to thrive on helping other people. But the problem arises when in the process of catering to others, an empath ignores their own needs and rightful wants. A narcissist will never cater to others, be it emotionally or physically. So, in a relationship between a narcissist and an empath, it is the narcissist who is on the gaining side and the empath who keeps on losing all the time. All their needs go unnoticed, and they are never respected. This can very easily create an emotional void in the empath, one from which they might never be able to come out. That is the reason it is of utmost importance that such a relationship should not be taken too far, or else conscious decision should be taken from both ends to rectify the situation. Else this toxicity will keep on increasing to a point where everyone will be hurt.

An Empath's Guide to Dealing With Conflicts

There could be many doubts that can arise in the mind of an empath along their way to a new relationship or while maintaining an old one. Let us look at some of the ways by which such conflicts can be eased.

- Whenever you feel that that the conflicts are taking a toll on you, try to visualize your standing in an open field while the wind is rustling your hair. Try to visualize the conflicts rising up and going out of your body slowly. Try to feel that the wind is gently calming your soul and is taking away all the negative emotions.

- In order to lessen conflicts, you simply need to set boundaries – boundaries that will be flexible but firm, boundaries that will not be crossed by others, boundaries that will help you protect yourself and also maintain the basic professionalism needed to function in social affairs. And lastly, boundaries so that people won't get an easy chance to take advantage of you.

- Accepting yourself more is another way of dealing with your conflicts. For an empath, much of your conflicts arise because most of the time, you are not happy with yourself, and you find faults in yourself. You need to stop doing that, and you need to give yourself much more credit because you truly deserve that.

- Whenever you and your partner are having any conflict, be it internal or external, do not make the mistake of dealing with it all alone or of ignoring the issue. Talk it out. Trust your partner enough to respect your emotions and do the same yourself. Communicating will help you both deal with the situation better.

- Try listening more and strictly avoid jumping to conclusions. Listen to what your partner has to say and stop making a decision in your head at the first instance you get. It might so be that you truly understand human emotions better than others, but it doesn't take away the fact that your partner is also a mature adult who should be given his\her due share of responsibilities to handle.

- Respect what your partner is saying and feeling at that moment. As an empath, you can often get sidetracked by your overwhelming reactions to things, and in the process, your partner's thoughts might get misrepresented or misunderstood. Try not to do that as your partner might get hurt. Drop the defenses that you might have for the time being and try solving the conflict by being honest with each other.

- Accept your own worth. As discussed earlier, as an empath, you might be in a lot of internal conflicts because you believe in yourself a lot less than what you are supposed to. Accept that you are capable of love and respect, and do not compromise on that.

Your sense of self-worth will help you deal with a lot of difficult situations in a much easier way.

Beginning a new relationship or maintaining an old one can be really difficult as relationships by themselves are complex things. You might be an empath or not. You can have doubts, apprehensions, and fears regarding the same. I hope that this chapter has been helpful to you in many ways regarding clearing some of the doubts that you might have been having as an empath. I hope that if you are about to start a relationship, you will be much more confident and well equipped than before.

Chapter 21: A Guide to Embracing Your Gift As an Empath

It is normal for people who are empaths to get exhausted very easily because, as we all know, they tend to feel everything with great intensity, and after a point, everything becomes personal to them. As a result, getting exhausted is common for having to deal with so many emotions all the time. What can happen due to this is the feeling of being overwhelmed at times and the possibility of them being taken advantage of. What is needed then is to know of effective ways to turn this trait to one's advantage. If a person can truly embrace their trait of being an empath, they can easily turn things around for themselves.

How to Normalize Your Gift as an Empath?

Given whatever you have had to face in life for being an empath and some of those experiences have not been good or desirable, it might so be that you take your empathy as a curse which you think can only bring you problems. The truth is just the contrary. Empathy is a great gift that not many people have been endowed with. So, if you are one of the lucky ones, you can turn this trait of yours into a superpower and use it to your advantage. Let us then discuss few such steps which might help you cope with the world and normalize your trait of being an empath.

- **Acknowledgment** – The first step towards taking that burden off your shoulder is always accepting your reality. In the beginning, you need to accept and acknowledge that you have the trait of empathy in you. More than the world, it is you who need to understand all your trait for you to truly own them and then go out to the world. Understand that you were probably born this way to help people around you, to lighten the burden of many shoulders. If you are an empath, you are most definitely compassionate. Instead of being ashamed of that, be proud. Not everyone can be what you naturally are.

- **Trust Yourself** – If you are an empath, the chances are that you are highly intuitive. You can easily see and feel things that others around you can't. You need to trust this intuition of yours. You usually get strong feelings in your gut regarding people or things around you. Your intuition makes you see through people and understand what is lying underneath the apparent. Realize that not everyone has this gift like yours. In today's world, this is an extremely helpful gift that can take you to places. You can decide wisely for yourself, and you can give valuable counsel to others. This intuition of yours is a gift that you can use to your advantage at all times. So, instead of avoiding it and ignoring g what you feel, try listening to your gut feeling more.

- **Do Not Play the Victim** – Empathetic people often tend to feel that they are the victims of a particular situation. They don't get enough love or mostly because they are not reciprocated in ways that they expect. If you are an empath and you somewhere feel that you have a similar tendency, then you need to stop feeling this way. Self-victimising will not take you anywhere, and on the contrary, it will destroy your sense of self-worth and make you feel inferior, which you are not in reality. You have to understand that not everyone feels like you simply because they are not empaths. But that doesn't mean you are not appreciated enough or loved. People have their way of reciprocating, and you just need to find that out. Instead of victimizing yourself, own the fact proudly that you can feel things more intensely than others.

- **Have Boundaries** – Having said the above-mentioned things about different people having different ways of reciprocating, it is also true that some people are energy vampires by nature. They exist to demotivate people and out their energy. If you are an empath, the chances are that you will understand better who these people are. It can so be that, unfortunately, some of them might even be in your close quarters. What is important then is to set boundaries for yourself. No matter how close these people are, remember that if their effect on you is one of pain and anxiety, then it is not worth it to remain close to them for the sake of it. Interact with them only as much as you think is all right. When it comes to rest, set firm boundaries that they shouldn't cross to maintain your mental health.

- **Meditate** – Meditation is a very helpful and useful means for empaths to regain back their energy and mental stability. Meditation by itself is helpful for everyone and more so for empathetic people as that helps us to regain back our mental composure and calm all the anxieties that we must be feeling. Regular practice of exercise, even if it is for ten minutes a day, is helpful for you to settle all the storms that might be raging inside. As an empath, it is common for you to feel a sense of sensory overload, but if and when you take out time to sit and meditate, the load on your heart will lift, giving you ample opportunities to rejuvenate yourself and start afresh. Another way to rejuvenate yourself is to spend quality time with yourself and visit nature. When you are in nature, you will be enveloped in a protective bubble of positive energy that will take away the anxieties and worries.

- **Breathe**– Breathing exercises are very good for you if you are an empath and if you have a lot of pent-up stress in you. Sit with yourself consciously every day for some time and take regular deep and stable breaths. As you inhale, think of all the clarity that you want and the positive things that make you happy. As you exhale, tell yourself that all the negative things from inside you are getting outside, leaving you clean and free. Doing this every day will help you function better and manage your stress a lot better.

- **Transfer negative energy** – It is very natural for empaths to be surrounded by negative energy and to get affected by it because empaths tend to think a lot more about things, and as things become very personal easily, empaths tend to absorb all the energies that people around them exert. Be it good or bad. What happens as a result is that they can easily get anxious and depressed by being bogged down with so much negativity. That is why it is important to transmute all the negative energies that you might face as an empath if and when it comes your way. Try different methods like keeping plants around you, where you stay, and where you work. Plants can easily take away the negative energies, leaving you stress-free. You could use crystals as well. Keeping yourself surrounded by beauty is also very important. Beauty will add positivity to your attitude and help you deal with things that might otherwise hurt you. Another thing that you could try if you want to transmute bad energy is to start your day with a gratitude affirmation. That will make you realize all the good things that are there in your life, making you look towards positive things rather than focus on the negatives.

- **Appreciate your efforts** – No matter what you do, the first and foremost thing you have to realize is that as an empath, your priority is to take care of yourself and respect your feelings and emotions before you start doing that to others. Until you start giving due importance to how you are feeling, it won't be of any help to anyone. You can't go on trying to feel what others are feeling and helping them unless you help yourself. So, you need to realize how precious you are and sit with yourself every day and consider how you are feeling. See what makes you happy and what causes you pain, and act according to that so that you can lessen the sufferings from your life. Self-love is the most important thing for all of us to lead a happy life and to help others in return. So take some time to love yourself a bit more. Take some time to accept that you are a person who has empathy, and that means you will give some extra care to love and feel for yourself as you do for others. Own what you are and see how easy it becomes to deal with problems.

These were few ways by which you can normalize being an empath as you can stabilize all your emotions, and you can also have enough time left for yourself to do everything that makes you happy. Being an empath is just a way of being, and there is absolutely nothing wrong with being an empath. The faster you realize that, the easier it will be for you to go ahead in everyday life. And soon a time will come when negative energies will stop bothering you, and all you will have is more energy to do things you want, more positivity to give others, and more selfolove to make yourself happy.

Avoiding the Empath Trap

There is a thin line between deeply feeling for someone and getting trapped in their problems, thinking them to be yours, and being unable to differentiate between the two. Let us then see some of the situations which might make you realize if you, being an empath, is falling for the empath traps, as we call them.

Answer these questions with a simple yes or no, and you shall have more clarity.

1. Are you someone who gives more importance to how your partner is feeling than what you feel yourself? Do

their feelings seem more important to you than your own?

2. Does it so happen that during an argument, you get so lost in what the other person is saying that you forget what you had to say? Does your attention shift completely to the other person to the exclusion of yours?

3. When someone you love dearly is facing any problem, does it so happen that you get so worked up with that that their problem becomes yours after a point, and you start treating it as something that is your responsibility to solve?

If your answer to these questions is yes, then the chances are that you are falling into the empath trap, and you need to come out of it consciously before it is too late. Let us see some ways in which you can avoid this trap.

- Whenever you are sensing something like this, use that opportunity to focus on your feelings at that moment and not on others. Ask yourself how you are feeling. Pause for a while, take few deep breaths, and ask what you want at that moment.

- Once you know what the feelings that are underlying your outer appearance are, rationalize as to how much emotion you are ready to invest in that other person or in that situation so that you are left with enough emotions for yourself. Never let yourself go to a situation where you have given everything to others and left with nothing for yourself. Remember that will not be of any help to anyone.

- After you have rationalized your emotions, start taking necessary actions accordingly so that both you and the other person are well equipped to deal with the situation. You need to constantly keep in mind that a certain distance is required for you to remain neutral. Do not let yourself get so caught up that it becomes difficult to come out of it.

- It might so happen that initially, you are facing a lot of difficulty keep distance because you have become accustomed to falling into this trap. If that is the case, then at every point, you need to take conscious steps to change this. One of the ways is to change the way you communicate. Maybe your way of communication is making you feel more entangled. From now on, you can clearly state your boundaries at the very beginning to reduce all the miscommunications with the other person.

Every person functions differently; however, these are some of the common ways in which you can stop from falling into an empath trap.

Special Protection Strategies for Empaths

- Ask yourself pertinent questions often like whether the emotions that you are feeling are yours or do they belong to someone else. You might get caught up with a lot and get overwhelmed with all the emotions you are feeling. It is not unnatural to get confused with feelings. So, at every point, ask yourself about what you are feeling and why that is so. If at any point you feel that it is getting too much for you, start taking prompt actions and distance yourself when you still have the time.

- Continue with this strategy of rationalizing your decision at every point. It is very easy to get with the flow of letting all the different emotions enter you, and after a point, it becomes difficult to take a practical decision. That is why you need to do away with all the negative energy that might be surrounding you for you to think clearly. Try taking deep breaths. Slowly exhale and inhale and visualize for yourself that with every exhale of breath, negative energies are leaving your body. This will help you think clearly.

- The next thing that you need to do is make your boundaries firm. Learn to be firm and step away from things that you are not comfortable with. No matter how close the other person is, if you are not comfortable with what they are doing, tell them that and don't let them get away with it. For example, if physical contact is a limitation for you, tell that firmly and don't tolerate things for the sake of it.

- Empaths love water as immersing yourself in water can be an excellent way to detox yourself. You can always try taking a long nice warm bath when you feel overwhelmed. Try lighting scented candles and adding essential oils to your bathwater. The water will make you feel fresh, relieved and will take away the negative energies from within you, detoxing you of all the toxic emotions that you were feeling.

- You have to take out time for yourself when you are an empath. It is necessary for your mental and physical health. Take some time out every day to spend only with yourself and do things that you like. Invest your time in things that make you happy. Leave aside the world and everyone else for that time, and make sure you don't waste that time. This will help you rejuvenate yourself and feel more comfortable with all your feelings and emotions.

- As an empath, you need some time every day where you stay away from being online consciously. At this age of technology, the entire world is in the palm of our hands, and at all times, we are just overcrowded with news happening everywhere. As an empath, this is bound to become a concern as you will e more affected by this news than others. So take some time off from being online and give yourself a needed rest.

Dealing With Empath Anxiety

- **Keep in Mind Your Emotional Limits** – The chances are that people around you are invariably drawn towards you because they know how kind you are, and your empathetic abilities are a blessing to many. The problem, however, is that this might be taxing on your mental health and could be a reason for you to get anxious as you might feel that you are not catering to everyone equally. That is why, at every point, you need to be aware of your emotional limits as to how much you can take without harming yourself, and if you find that limit is crossed, do not give in to that.

- **Understand Your Feelings** – This is a very important thing for you to do if you want to deal with the anxiety that you are feeling as a result of you being an empath. Try and analyze all the different feelings you are experiencing and see what each different person is making you feel. If you recognize who or what are the sources of you being anxious, it will be easier to avoid them and take necessary actions to reduce your anxiety.

- **Look For an Outlet** – You need to remind yourself all the time that along with taking care of others and helping them deal with their problems, it is your foremost responsibility to help yourself. Do not put your feelings aside for the sake of others and look for an outlet. An outlet that will give you a break from all the anxiety that you might be feeling. An outlet that will help you breathe better. It could be anything that suits you.

- **Use Grounding Techniques** – This could be a very effective way to deal with empath anxiety. Whenever you feel that the emotions are becoming a bit too much for you to handle, do not resort to other human beings but try looking around your room and find any single object to put your focus on. Try concentrating on that object with all your might and study it in detail. What will happen as a result of that is that as you will be more aware of the features of that object, it will help you come outside of all the intense feelings that you were otherwise experiencing so far.

Through this chapter, I tried to give you an overview as to how you can deal with various problems that come with being an empath and as to how you can deal with it. I hope it has helped clear away your doubts.

Chapter 22: Train Your Third Eye

It is believed that there are seven chakra centers distributed within our body that are responsible for our overall well-being and for increasing our perceptions in general. These chakras are wheel-like centers of energy. The entire concept of chakra centers has been a part of the Indian culture and a system that dates back to almost 1500-500 B.C., and it has been written in detail in the ancient Vedic texts of India. Before that, it had been passed down through ages orally. Their mention can be found in yogic teachings as well. Let me give you a small idea of what they are; there are, as already mentioned, seven chakra centers from the top of the head to the root of the spine. These chakra centers reside and also correspond to those areas that have the vital organs in the body. It is in the nature of energy to move up and down with different effects from the environment, and that is why even the chakra centers in our body are never static, and they move up and down.

The seven chakras are "Root Chakra," "Sacral Chakra," "Solar Plexus Chakra," "Heart Chakra," "Throat Chakra," "Third Eye Chakra," and the "Crown Chakra." It is interesting to know that all the different chakras have a different color that corresponds to their energy and with their purpose. The root chakra is red in color, and the Sacral chakra is orange. Solar Plexus chakra is yellow, and the Heart chakra is green, the throat chakra is blue, the Third eye chakra is indigo, and finally, the Crown chakra is violet in color.

The third eye chakra is one such wheel of energy located in the region between our two eyes on our forehead. The third eye chakra center is also known as "Ajna," and it is known to be the sixth chakra center in our body. Placed in the middle of our two eyebrows, it is known to be intrinsically connected with our perception, our awareness capabilities, and also our spiritual communication. As a result of that, the third eye chakra can actively provide us with wisdom and increasing perception, deepening our insight, and it also helps us improve our spiritual communication.

When the chakras in our body are healthy, and we as a person is healthy mentally and physically, it is said that the chakra centers are "open," and simultaneously, if our body is not healthy and we are not doing well mentally, the chakras get blocked, as in energy stops flowing through them and that will invariably lead to us getting ill mentally and physically. Serious ailments might even follow if the energy gets blocked and remain so for a long time. So, it is important to learn to open the chakras.

Some Third Eye Basics That You Should Know

The third eye chakra is the main source of intuition in our body, and it also enhances our vision. It is the third eye chakra that helps enhance our imaginative qualities, and at the same time, it helps a person to vitalize their clairvoyance. The third eye chakra is located in the region between our eyebrows in the front of our forehead and what it does is help us look beyond the immediate environment that we live in. it helps us look beyond the material plane and connect with our spiritual core. It is very important and beneficial for us to train ourselves in ways that help us open our third eye chakra as that will help us get in contact with our inner spiritual core so that we can truly bring our psychic powers.

The moment we pass beyond a materialistic plane, it helps us to look at what lies beyond. It becomes easier to delve deep within our core if the flow of energy within our body chakras is fluent. So, when there is ample energy flowing through our third eye chakra, we get opened to a world of new possibilities, filled with new perceptions and awareness. With our third eye-opening, we get initiated to a new light that was so far present and yet was beyond our reach. The corresponding verb that one should technically use while talking about the third eye chakra is "I see."

As mentioned earlier, each of our chakra centers has its respective colors which are defined by what work they do in our body and what subsequent effect that has on us. Going by that, the third eye chakra is associated with the color indigo. The color indigo is said to be in between the color blue and purple. Indigo is recognized to be a color having spiritual power as it enhances self-awareness in us, spiritual powers and at the same time helps us attain peace. This is the very thing that the opening of the third eye chakra does to us. Energy flowing through the third eye chakra helps open those pressure points that release stress which will surely help us find a solution to our problems, thereby finding peace. At the same time, the third eye chakra helps enhance our spiritual capabilities.

As it has already been mentioned, the chakra centers in our body are energy points through which energy flows both upwards and downwards. Now, it might so happen that due to certain reasons, these chakra points can be blocked. And if we don't do anything about it, it will remain blocked, causing serious physical and emotional ailments eventually. It is common sense that if a flow of energy that is otherwise required for our well-being gets blocked, then quite naturally, the all-over balance of all the components of our body will be hampered greatly. As a result, we will start to have many problems. That is the reason it is extremely important to not only take notice as to if any chakra point is blocked, but immediate actions should be taken to open them to maintain proper functioning of the body and the mind.

As far as the third eye chakra is concerned, if you find out that you are getting a lot more confused about various things than you usually get, or when you are having mild to severe headaches, the chances are that your chakra is blocked. You might also experience strain in your eyes along with facing serious cases of mental and emotional stubbornness; if you see that your intuitive qualities are getting hampered and your decision-making skills are impaired, the chances are that your third eye chakra is blocked. Let us then look at ways in which we can awaken this chakra.

Steps to Awaken Your Third Eye

By now, we have already discussed why it is necessary to open your third eye chakra in the first place. Let us look at some of the steps as to how to do that. There are, in fact, many wonderful ways in which our third eye can be opened. We will now discuss in detail two of the main techniques which can come to your aid when you want to open your third eye. The first is known as the portal technique, and the second one is known as the meditation technique. The portal technique can also be learned through astral projection. Both these methods are useful so you can take the help of one or both.

1. **The Portal Technique** – The portal technique is usually a very easy and comfortable technique to use, and with diligent practice, it gets easier. Some prefer trying out the meditation technique first and then gradually progress to the portal technique, but it falls in your discretion what you want to do. But, whatever the technique is, you need to be mentally prepared for the outcome because you are going to experience something new.

   Step 1 – For starting the portal technique, at first, you need to relax both your mind and your body completely. Lay down and try calming yourself completely. Use any technique that suits you best. Breathe deeply and try doing some mindfulness activities. As and when you reach a completely calm state of mind where your body and your mind are relaxed, know that you have reached the Alpha stage. Next, what you need to do is take the pointer finger of either hand and press the bridge of your nose in between your eyes. Next, start circling this area clockwise for some time so that this area is thoroughly massaged. Continue circling this area for at least thirty seconds and then stop your fingers and start pulling away from your hand. If you have done it right by applying the correct amount of pressure, then you will continue noticing the sensation even after you have pulled your fingers away. From you calming yourself and relaxing completely while laying down and then massaging this area for some time in a clockwise motion and then slowly pulling away, this entire stream of events comprises the first step of the portal technique.

Step 2 – After you have done step one, it is now time for step two. Take a pause and try to feel whether you can still feel the tingling sensation in between your eyebrows even when you have removed your fingers. If yes, then you have successfully done what needs to be done. But if, with the removal of your fingers, the tingling sensation is gone, you need to repeat the first step again till it happens. Maybe you are not as calm as you are supposed to be or your mind is still not relaxed. Try doing it again till you get it. When you have done it successfully, you will notice that this tingling sensation has slowly reached your head. It will start resonating in your head area. Tilt your eyes in an upward direction slowly, and you will see that the sensation has intensified, and there will be a swirling feeling inside your head. You should, by now, start feeling a surge of energy in you, and with this stronger sensation, you need to start breathing in through your nose.

The surge of energy should by now slowly reach the soles of your legs. A kind of exchange of energy will start within and without your body. Try to feel that. The energy will slowly rise from the soles of your feet to your groin, then to your hips, your torse, your spine, your shoulders, and finally to your head. Here it will meet with the already existing swirling of energy from earlier. Start inhaling and exhaling this energy with deep breaths as this feeling gets strengthened and makes it pulsate in your body.

Step 3 – Step 3 will need you to repeat this entire procedure eleven times in sets of threes. So, in total, you will need to repeat this thirty-three times. Continue feeling this exchange of energy and of them getting mixed up with one another as they come up through the soles of your legs, travel all the length of your body to finally meet with the energy in your head. You need to do this thirty-three times because only then will it help you stimulate your pineal gland and open up your third eye chakra.

Step 4 – At this time, the swirling sensation in your head should be extremely intense because your third eye has been awakened, and it is located in that area. In case you have lost the sensation that we are talking about, do not worry. It is not uncommon to do that. Try bringing it back by thinking about it with all concentration or start from the beginning once again.

Step 5 - At this point, you need to take some time and repeat all the steps till now for few days. Jumping to the next step at once will not be of any help. Your third eye is awakening, and it will take some time for your body to get used to it completely. It is advisable to do this right after you get up and right before you go to sleep every day. Get used to this sensation. It might take some time, so do not rush with it. In case you see lights at a time, like a green light twisting in a cyclone, remember that it is normal to see this as your third eye is awakening.

Step 6 – As you continue doing the above-mentioned steps, you will become more accustomed to the entire process, and as a result, your conscious awareness will increase a lot. With your conscious awareness intensifying, you will soon be able to go through the tunnel to the astral project. At this point, it is also advisable to mention that all through your journey, it is very helpful for you to keep a journal for all your thoughts, feelings, and all that you are going through. At every point, look back at the journal to get an idea of what's happening and how much you have progressed. If at any point you think that it is becoming too much or getting out of hand, you can always close your third eye and opt for a milder technique.

It is important to understand that the portal technique is really intense, so in case it does not suit you, do not force yourself to do it or put unnecessary pressure on your mind or body. At the same time, even if this process suits you after you have become comfortable with it and you have it in your grasp, you shouldn't do it regularly after two weeks of continuous practice. Do not do it regularly. It is advisable to do it once in a while. Otherwise, there will be a chance for you to fall off the balance completely as there will be no regulation of energy in your body. Do not let it get too hectic for yourself.

2. **The Meditation Technique -** The meditation technique is what most people usually prefer while starting out in this practice as this is not only easy to grasp but also very comfortable for people who are just beginning to open their third eye. If done properly, it should only take ten minutes in total to get it done, but if you are a beginner, the chances are that you will need a bit more time. But once you get into the habit, it won't be a problem at all.

Step 1 – The first step, as usual, is for you to get comfortable and sit in a relaxed position. It is advisable not to wear very tight clothes as that will hamper your concentration. Wear comfortable clothes and avoid wearing any accessories. You can sit in a comfortable way, or if needed, you can also lie down.

Step 2 – After you have relaxed completely, you need to start taking deep breaths. Don't take shallow breaths. Take deep breaths through your nose and exhale them through your mouth. Make sure you can feel the air going deep within your lungs. Start taking deep breaths at the beginning and then go to taking even and regular breaths. Make sure when you are breathing, your stomach should expand.

Step 3 – What you need to do after this is start visualizing the number one. It could be in any size or in any color. What matters is that you take your time to clearly visualize the number one and make sure you are not losing your vision. You should be able to keep seeing it for some time. If you are doing it right, you will find out that you will start feeling a tingling sensation in between your eyebrows. Remember that it is completely normal to feel so, as that means you are successfully opening your third eye because that is the region where our third eye chakra is located. In case you don't get the tingling feeling that we are talking about, do not worry. It just means that you need to do the exercise for some more time.

Step 4 – Step 4 will be all about you taking your time to get comfortable with the previous steps so that visualizing the number should become easy for you. As you start getting better at visualizing, try holding that vision for some time. Increase that time slowly. Once that is done, start visualizing the number two, then three, then four, and go on till you reach ten. You will know that you ready to go to the next step once you successfully visualize all the numbers up to ten and you are able to keep your visions for a certain period of time. Once that is done, you can move to the next step.

Step 5 – Once you have progressed well through the above-mentioned steps, you will find out for yourself that you are starting to get bored with numbers. You will then want to move on to visualizing more complex things like different colors, animals, or flowers. You will see that slowly you are able to visualize all of them eventually. This kind of meditation is known as clairvoyance mediation, and it helps you open your third eye chakra comfortably and successfully.

Step 6 – Once you are absolutely comfortable with visualizing everything and also keeping those visions intact for some time with your eyes closed, it is time for you to now try and do this with your eyes open. This will take some time and regular, diligent practice on your part. You need to keep doing these exercises so that visualizing anything that you want with your eyes open is not a problem anymore. When you see that you have no problem visualizing things with your eyes open, you will know that now you can operate your third eye at your will. You can open it as well as close it whenever you want. All you need to do is set up a doable routine for yourself so that you can be in practice regularly.

3. **Another Meditation Technique** - When it comes to awakening your third eye, there are different types of meditating techniques that could potentially be used as meditation helps us to activate our pineal gland, which in turn is very beneficial for third eye-opening. This one that we are going to be talking about now is also very easy, but it is slightly different from the last one that we talked about.

Step 1 – For this method to work, you need to examine your thoughts properly and see what the things that make you happy and give you real joy are. Try and remember that for any meditating technique to work, your pineal glands need to be activated, and one of the ways to do it is to produce proper vibrations in your body, which will come from things that make you truly happy. Try anything that you want like singing or dancing or taking a walk. Whatever works for you, do that.

Step 2 – After you have invested some time in doing what makes you really happy, sit in a relaxed way and practice breathing steadily. Do not breathe too deeply or too shallowly as that might interrupt your concentration, making you start over all over again. Breathe normally but in a relaxed manner.

Step 3 – After this, what you need to do is face downwards while you face your chin towards your chest. At this point, it might so be that you start feeling a sense of tingling in between your brows and a certain weight pulling your chin down. Remember that this is completely normal. What it means is that your third eye is getting awakened slowly. So you need to continue doing this no matter what sensations you feel.

Step 4 – What you need to do after this is while your chin is still facing towards your chest, you need to try looking up through your inner eye without lifting your head up. Close your eyes at this point while you are looking down, and then focus all your concentration on the point where your third eye chakra lies. It is all right if it is not happening on the first go. It might take some time. So you need to keep on practicing.

Step 5 – You need to maintain this practice for a few minutes every day as you become more comfortable opening your third eye. You might start feeling not only a tingling but also a swirling sensation in between your brows because that is what happens when energy starts passing back and forth through your chakras. With daily practice, you will be able to open your third eye chakra easily at your will. Incorporate this practice with the regular meditation routine that you have, and things will fall in line soon. This type of third eye awakening technique is going to be very beneficial as it is easier to do and will also not overwhelm you at any point.

How Can Third Eye Awakening Benefit Your Psychic Abilities?

- **Astral Projection** – Astral projection, as explained in Chapter 19, is when you can travel both through your physical plane and your spiritual plane simultaneously. This is usually done when your third eye has opened, and you are practicing it through the portal method that we have mentioned earlier.

- **Visions** – Vision can come to you in different forms but mostly when you are asleep. You will rarely get visions when you are awake because in order for you to get visions, your pineal gland needs to be at its best form, which is when you are sleeping, and at the same time visions occur before the pineal gland has been calcified. That is the reason, once you have opened your third eye, getting visions in your sleep is common, which might have deeper meanings.

- **Intuition** – Intuition is one of the most common forms of psychic ability that someone might have, and with the third eye-opening, your intuitions are bound to get stronger and clearer. They are not as descriptive as visions but are usually hunches that guide you in your path and often help you to keep out of danger.

- **Aura** – When you have activated your pineal gland and awakened your third eye, it will become very easy for you to see a person's aura in the form of various bright lights around that concerned person when you meet him\her. When you have opened your third eye, you will get to see what others can't, and it will help you to understand what a person is like in real life rather than having to judge them by their appearance, which can be deceptive. It is not easy to see aura very easily, but with proper practice, it will come under your control easily.

Closing Your Third Eye

So far, we talked about various ways in which we can open our third eye chakra and what help it does to enhance our psychic abilities. Now we shall talk about closing the third eye. Learning to close the third eye is as important as opening it because it can't be open all the time. One must know of the different ways in which they can close their third eye. Let us see different steps in which it could be done.

Step 1 – The first thing you need to do is meditate regularly. Close your eyes and try relaxing. Then focus on each and every part of your body. Maintain regular but steady breathing. Do not rush with your breathing, as that might hamper your concentration. It might so be that once you have opened your third eye, you might want to close it forever. So you should be aware of all the ways you could do that. Once you start concentrating on the third eye region, you will get a tingling sensation, and you can also feel a swirling of energy in that region which is common with the third eye-opening. What you need to do is concentrate on how you are feeling physically and not what your sixth sense is making you feel. Your sixth sense will work according to your third eye. Do not focus on that. Ignore whatever feeling you are getting through your third eye and focus fully on your physical condition.

Step 2 – After you have gotten hold of your physical sensations, focus on the region of your neck that is below your pineal gland, that is where the third eye is stationed. You will feel a host of energy in that area. Slowly try and start releasing this energy that is built up in that region. Visualize that this energy is slowly passing through your entire body as it is traveling downwards, and imagine it passing outside through your feet. It is advised to try this while you are close to nature or in nature itself, maybe in your garden at the least. It helps that way as you get a place to successfully transfer the energy to. If you are in a concrete jungle, it becomes difficult as there is an energy block. Try sitting in a natural environment and transferring the energy in your body outside in nature.

Step 3 – You will feel a physical release of energy from your body once you have successfully released it out in nature. The tingling sensation that you were feeling all this while and at the same time the swirling of energy that you were feeling in between your brows because your third eye was open all this time will automatically lessen down as you slowly start closing your third eye. What you need to do is constantly visualize this energy going outside your body. Eventually, this tingling sensation will subside, and at the same time, the swirling of energy will be gone as your pineal gland will slow down with time. The slowing of your pineal gland will help the third eye to close. It is important to remember that this might take some time, so do not rush yourself. Take your time and continue doing it till the third eye chakra region becomes completely calm, with all the sensations having stopped completely.

Step 4 – Keep in mind that you need to keep your eyes closed at all points when you are closing your third eye. Many thoughts will come to mind during this time. It is natural for that to happen. What you need to do is not give them much importance. Do not disregard them but do not dwell on them as well. Let them come and let them go at their own pace. The moment you start considering them, you will risk opening your third eye once again. So be prompt and dismiss all the thoughts that you might be getting while you are trying to close your third eye. Try not to interact with them. Keep on redirecting all your thoughts when they come until your mind is completely calm and there is absolutely no sensation. It means that you have successfully closed your third eye and your pineal gland is calm completely.

Training to open your third eye by activating your pineal gland is exceptionally beneficial for enhancing your psychic abilities.

Chapter 23: Tips for Raising an Empath Child

In this chapter, we will see what it means to have an empath child and what steps you should follow for their proper upbringing.

Signs That You Have an Empath Child

If you think that your child might be an empath, then look for these signs in him\her which will make you surer of the situation because it is vital to know and understand reality as every child needs care and attention, and there are many ways in which a child who is an empath should be taken care of. Let us look at some of the signs.

- **Sensitivity** - Is your child extremely sensitive than children of his age? It might be because your child is an empath. Empathetic children are usually more sensitive than others and at times to such a degree that they can't tolerate loud noises or can't stand any kind of derogatory language and actions, be it from close ones or strangers. In most cases, children who are empaths have very mature views of the world and people around them, and they easily get affected by things than others would do because they tend to feel everything with great details.

- **Need for Alone Time** – A very potent sign for your child to be an empath is that they require more alone time than others of their age. That is because, at times, things become a bit too much for them. They get overwhelmed easily, and so they need time to replenish themselves in order to get back on their track. It might not seem normal to others because, for others, they don't get affected by things the way an empath does. For an empath, everything becomes personal. And so, it is only natural for them to need time to replenish their thoughts.

- **Feeling Pain** – Is it that your child gets intensely affected by the pain that others feel? That is another sign for him\her to be an empath. Notice that whether your child becomes sad when his friend is scolded or when a bird or an animal gets hurt. Empaths feel and process pain differently than others, and that should be considered.

- **Difficulty Calming Down** – An empathetic child will have a lot of difficulties calming down as they can't control emotions. Be it good or bad. Whether they are happy or sad, they need a lot of time to get back to a calm self and to wind down. That is why they get tired easily because everything for them is personal, and they tend to get emotionally invested in it.

How to Raise an Empath Child?

As a parent, it might be a challenge to raise an empath child if you don't know how to. Things might easily be misunderstood, and there could be created a big communication gap between you and your kid because you can't always feel what they are feeling. Things might also be difficult if you yourself are an empath and don't know the correct way to reach out to your kid. As a result, your kid might stop communicating with you, or it might so happen that your kid traps himself within a shell, fearing to come out to anyone. This will hamper the overall growth of your kid, and you will start feeling helpless as a parent. Also, it becomes very important for you to learn and know how you can help your child become more comfortable with you and with himself and so that he can use his nature to his advantage and not something that brings him pain. Let us look at some of the ways in which you can raise an empath child properly and beautifully.

- **Teach Them to Successfully Manage Their Stress -** Keep this fact in mind constantly that if your kid is an empath, the chances are that they are stressed, and more often than not, they are unable to share it with anyone because they find it very soon that not everyone is an empath and so can't understand them fully. You, as a parent, should ideally be the most approachable person to your kid, whom he\she can go up to, to share what they feel like. So, it is very important to teach your kid strategies that are targeted to help reduce stress. They feel everything with far greater details than you or others around them do. So, most of the time, they feel stressed out from things happening with others around them, and if they are unable to manage that stress properly, it can get really difficult to go on or for them to develop properly. Teach them mindful exercises ad take them to a child therapist if required so that they can get all the healthy opportunities to grow and deal with all kinds of situations.

- **Help Them Set Boundaries –** It is only natural for your child to have a big heart in order for him\her to be an empath in the first place. Only when they have a big heart can they truly feel what the other person is feeling and get affected by it. But the problem here is that not everyone will understand that. Some might feel that they are being extra, some might feel that they are unnecessarily getting involved in other's business, while some might, unfortunately, take advantage of their honesty and true feelings. As a parent, you need to prepare your child for all kinds of situations so that they don't fall prey to the harsh realities and sad truths of this world. Even if they are empaths, they need to learn to protect themselves at all costs. They need to be able to set firm and practical boundaries around them, which will help them to be who they are and at the same time not be taken advantage of. Feeling for others and wanting their well doesn't mean that one has to be in regrettable situations. Setting boundaries is needed and good at the same time. It helps people realize where they stand, it helps people not fall prey to negative situations, and it also helps people protect everyone's feelings at hand. As they learn to set up successful and fruitful boundaries, it becomes easier for them to take part in all events of life, and at the same time, it becomes easier for you as a parent to help them through all situations that they face.

- **Help Them to Keep Their Calendars Light –** You need to keep this in mind at all times that even a normal incident which you and I will not give a second look will come to them as something huge and might become really personal. So, if you think that you can cramp their schedule with everything else that other kids of his age easily do, then you need to think twice. Everything has a much deeper meaning for your child because he is an empath. Once again, this is nothing wrong or unnatural. It is just his way of being. All you need to do is help him through. So, when it comes to your child's schedule, you need to keep it a tad bit lighter. You need to give your child enough time in between all the activities that he is doing so that after each activity, he can get some alone time and replenish his thoughts and collect and compose his emotions. Do not force him into getting involved with a host of different things that he is not yet ready to deal with. At the same time, do not pressurize him to do things or getting himself involved in social gatherings that he might not want to. Getting himself involved with people is not as easy with him as with others. Try and understand him rather than judging him. Draw their schedule in a way where they get to do things that they truly enjoy and at the same time which doesn't emotionally overwhelm them.

- **Help Them to Drown Out the Noise** – Life can become a bit too much for your child at times if he is an empath. He is most likely to be under the emotional pressure of catering to everything that he is feeling all the time. Even a little something that happens to him and happens around him comes to him as something immensely personal and as intensely moving. What might be simple fun and games to us might not be so for them. Empath children cannot tolerate really loud noises or very crowded places. Make sure you have that in mind while you are taking your child to any social event or an outing. Instead of forcing your kid into such situations by telling that he\she will get used to it, try and make things easier for them. Choose such places to visit which are not very crowded or maybe choose a time when you can expect less crowd. Whenever you are organizing any social event, make sure your child will have enough space to breathe literally and metaphorically. Make sure more than enough such people will be there with whom your child is comfortable. Do not let your child alone with people who are unnecessarily loud or impatient. When you are planning to attend an event, keep these things in mind so that it becomes a happy moment for your child rather than another reason to feel overwhelmed.

- **Support Them at All Times of Need** – When you have an empath child, the chances are that they are skeptical of things and people around them, but what is more concerning is that, without proper love and care, they might start doubting themselves because they can see that others around them are not like them and in many cases, people are not welcoming enough or appreciative enough. What you need to do as a parent then is to constantly make them realize

293

that there is nothing wrong with them and that there is nothing wrong with being an empath. You need to sit with them from time to time and have a friendly conversation with them regarding what empathy is and what it means to be an empath. If they are aware of their truth, they will have a better idea as to how to deal with a situation and people. If they know that it is just a way of being, they will stop judging themselves, and they will be able to live a much happier and more stress-free life. Having such conversations with them will also make you closure to them, creating a beautiful and dependable bond where your child will know that they can come to you at all points without having any fear. This assurance that their parents are with them will invariably make them more confident and open to change and growth. No matter how much the world poses a problem, a parent's care and assurance can always make things easier, and that's what will happen with your kid. If they have free access to discussion with you, the chances of them getting overwhelmed will be far less.

- **Help Them Remain Positive** – Your child and you need such people around you who have a positive influence on you, who don't judge you, and who help you in times of need. With such people around, it will be easier for your child to put trust in others without having any worries. It will also be easier for you to trust your child around such people. With a positive atmosphere, your child's emotions will be respected, and he will get ample opportunity to grow with their mental health remaining intact.

Through proper knowledge and education, through ample real-life practices and experience, and through your love and warmth, your child will have a beautiful growing experience where he will have no complaints regarding his being an empath. It might be that at some points, you will get concerned and tired, but then again, that is the same for every parent on earth. But after a long day, when you will see your child growing up to an honest, kind individual, it will be you who will be a winner.

Chapter 24: Famous Psychics You Should Know About

Psychics are probably among the most interesting community of people. They are talented, they are passionate about their practice and art, they are insightful, and at times, they are a bit intimidating. If you are someone who has already been to a psychic for a reading, then you know what I am talking about, but if you haven't been to a psychic for reading before, you might have certain reservations, and you also might be a tad bit scared of how things are going to unfold. Let me assure you from the very beginning that you are not alone in this. And since you have reached this chapter, I am hoping you already have a pretty good idea about how psychic abilities can be honed and how they can be used for so many purposes.

Though things have now turned for the better with more research and knowledge of people in this field, things were not so from the beginning. Psychics have feared for centuries and even persecuted in many places. People were unable to understand their practice and naturally projected them as bad or evil as they deal with spirits. But with changing times and with people's growing interest in this field of learning, society has become more open to this practice and is welcoming it eventually. Psychics, with time, have made their own niche in society, and many of them, with their years of practice and experience, have become extremely famous as well. We shall talk about some of them here.

Psychics are everywhere. Many of us have psychic abilities in us, and no matter where we go, there will be psychics amongst us. Getting your first reading can take a lot of courage as it is usually very intimidating for some. But with time, people get used to it. So much so that many celebrities from all fields of art and entertainment rely completely on such psychic readings to get a prior idea about what might happen and what they can expect.

Edgar Cayce

His years are 18th march, 1877 to 3rd January 1945. He was an American clairvoyant, which means he was a clear seer. He had the ability to get information about any person, location, object, or physical event through his extrasensory perceptions. He got the title of being the "sleeping prophet" because in his sleep, he often used to go in a sort of trance, and it was in this sleeping state that he used to talk and answer questions. His wife, secretary, and his friend Al Layne, once she understood what was happening, started recording his words while he was sleeping as during this time he would answer all kinds of questions posed to him from various fields, be it regarding healing, afterlife, dreams, past-life, reincarnation, nutrition and also future events.

As known by many, Edgar Cayce was a devout catholic, and that is the reason his visions started creating trouble for him because this practice is condemned by the faith in which he belonged. He knew that it was his subconscious mind that was delving into his dream world to get these answers, and so after a point, he had opened a non-profit organization known as Association for Research and Enlightenment in order to help anybody who came to him. He is also known as the "father of holistic medicine."

Rose Ann Schwab

Dr. Rose Ann Schwab is a world-famous clairvoyant psychic medium. She is credited with having almost 98% accuracy in all her sessions. Her predictions are almost perfect every time. She has been instrumental in predicting not only personal and individual questions of healing, afterlife, dreams, past-life, reincarnation, nutrition, and future events but also extremely crucial predictions regarding national security and public health like terrorist attacks on the United States, things as crucial like natural disasters which could save thousands of life and public property. Her 55 years of experience have made her a person who is respected by everyone unanimously. She has been working with national and international organizations in fields of culture, economics, faith, etc. she is one of the most genuine and honest practitioners in this field who keeps her client's privacy and comfort as her top priority. She has had many fatal accidents, and yet, by using her gifts properly, today, she is one of the world's leading psychics.

John Elfreth Watkins Jr.

His dates are from 1st January 1852 to 1st January 1903. John Watkins was a curator of mechanical technology at the national museum of the United States. When in 1900, he wrote for The Ladies Home Journal, everyone was surprised and amazed with all the predictions that he made there. What happens with many people is that despite having psychic abilities, many people don't realize that till a certain point in life. When they do, they either start working on it and enhance their skills, or some people let it go to waste, unfortunately. With John, it was the former. He made some amazing predictions in that journal using his psychic abilities, named "What May Happen in The Next Five Hundred Years."

He said that he had taken the advice of "the most learned and conservative minds in America" for his research, and that is how he came up with his predictions about how life would change before the year 2001. His research had an extremely broad base that took everyone by surprise as so many of them came true, eventually making him one of the most respected and famous psychics of all time.

It was him who came up with so many of the innovations that 20th and 21st century saw from food, to travel to television and life generally. Things that he had predicted and which came true includes "Uber Eats," "Live TV news," "Digital Photography," "Mobile Phones," "Cars," "Modern food and Farming Distribution Practices," "Satellite

Photography," "Modern Medical Imaging," "Nuclear Submarines" among others.

Allison DuBois

Allison DuBois was born on 24th January 1972, and she is well known for being an American author and a world-famous medium. Mediumship is basically the practice of mediating communication between the living beings and the spirits of the dead and departed. People who practice this art are known as "medium" or "spirit mediums." She gained popularity worldwide after using her powers to help the government of the United States law enforcement officials, helping them solve many crucial problems and crimes. It was upon her that the entire base of the famous TV series "Medium" was based. She even appeared in the show called "The Real Housewives of Beverly Hills," where she got to showcase her real-life "mean girl persona."

It was Gary Schwartz of the University of Arizona who first tested her powers as a medium. She has visions concerning the past as well as the future, but they are mainly in the form of dreams. The police have always been greatly indebted to her for her assistance in solving crimes. What is very interesting to know is that she knew of her powers from a very young age, in fact, as little as six years old, and now, she doesn't like to get the word "psychic" being associated with her as she thinks that society has somewhere given it a negative connotation. She uses her powers to contact and communicate with departed souls. During her time at the University of Arizona, she had spent almost four years participating in various tests and studies to improve her skills.

Theresa Caputo

Theresa Caputo was born on the 10th of June 1967. She is a world-famous American psychic medium, and she is best known by everyone for the TLC reality TV series that she did, which was known as "Long Island Medium," and at the same time, she has been an author of two books and done many tours as well. She had literally become an overnight sensation where people started referring to her as someone with her long blonde hair and manicured nails. She got a lot of popularity owing to her show where she talked about her practice and reading sessions. She still continues with her sessions and psychic practices of being a medium.

Tana Hoy

Tana was born with a unique gift of gab with the dead. His birth had been miraculously predicted almost twelve years before he was born by none other than his own aunt Lucille, who, however, dies before he was born. He is famous in the entire world for his prediction of the Oklahoma City bombing that to on a radio show almost 90 minutes before the event actually took place, taking everyone by surprise. He is all the more famous because, throughout his practice career, he has an accuracy rate of almost 94%.

Baba Vanga

Her full name is Vangeliya Pandeva Gushterova. Her dates are from 3rd October 1911 to 11th August 1996. She was not only a psychic but also a mystic, a clairvoyant, and a herbalist from Bulgaria. She had been blind since her childhood, but that didn't stop her from opening her inner eyes to the world of the spirits. Millions of people used to believe, and some still do, that she used to possess paranormal abilities and could establish a strong connection between the world of the living and the world of the dead. She lost her mother at a very young age, and while she was being brought up by helpful neighbors, she used to be regarded as a truly intelligent child all her life. Her powers were always present in her, and she started getting inclined towards her inner calling when during her childhood, she started inventing games that she used to call "healing," where she used to prescribe certain herbs to her friends who used to pretend to be ill.

In her own testimony, she truly came face-to-face with her powers when once a tornado had lifted her up, throwing her into a field. It was during this incident that she lost her eyesight. During the second world war, she started attracting a lot of people towards her powers as she could soothsay and also had healing powers. People used to come to visit her wanting to know whether their relatives were alive or not. She went on to become extremely famous, and since the war, dignitaries started visiting her often in want of answers. She died a happy death eventually, after having helped a lot of people, and her funeral attracted a lot of people.

Nostradamus

A French astrologer, his dates are from 21st December 1503 to 1st or 2nd July 1566. He was reputed as not only an astrologer but also a seer and a physician. His book "Les Propheties" was first published in 1555, which had predictions regarding future events. Since the time his book came out, he has attracted many loyal followers over the years who have been surprised and amazed by what he had predicted all those years ago. He used to practice occultism which eventually led to him enhancing his psychic abilities as well.

He used to accept his clients to provide him with their individual correct birth charts through which he used to find out accurate answers to all their questions. But with time, he couldn't keep up with his client's pace, and so he started writing a book of predictions rather than doing astrology to individual people. After reading his predictions in which he had written about some impending threats to the royal family, the queen had called him to her palace and asked him to draw her a proper chart of horoscope for all the royal members. He then became a trusted counsel of the royal throne. It is known that at the time of his death in 1555, he was, in fact, the chief counselor and also the physician-in-ordinary to the queen's son, who was Charles IX of France.

I hope this chapter was able to inspire you into the world of psychics seeing how these famous psychics have left their mark in the world.